Russian

phrase book
&
dictionary

Berlitz Publishing Company, Inc.

Moscow
Living Language Ltd.
2002

УДК 811.161.1'374.822
ББК 81.2Рус-4
   Р89

Р89 Russian phrase book & dictionary. – Moscow: Living Language Ltd.,
2002. – 224 p.

   ISBN 5-8033-0120-5

The phrase book can be used both by people who do not know Russian at
all and the ones who can read and write in Russian but have no communi-
cating skills. The phrase book may also be helpful while learning Russian. For
getting the best results a pack with an audiocassette is also available.

Living Language, Ltd.
13/1, 5-th Kozhukhovskaya st., Moscow, 109193 Russia
License ЛР № 065389 of 09.08.97
Mail adress: P.O. box 14, Moscow, 113162 Russia
www.lll.ru
e-mail: lll@lll.ru

Circulation 10 000. The order № 1185
Printed by printing-house "Molodaya gvardia":
Moscow, 101503, Sushchevskaya street, 21
ООО «Криспин Инк»

   ISBN 5-8033-0120-5   © 1998 by Berlitz Publishing Company, Inc.

This book is for sale only on the territory of the former Soviet Union.
Данное издание предназначено для продажи только на территории
бывшего СССР.

Published in Russia, by LIVING LANGUAGE LTD. PUBLISHERS
under Berlitz Publishing Company, Inc. licence
400 Alexander Park, Princeton, NJ 08540 USA
9-13 Grosvenor St., London WIX 9FB UK

Contents

Pronunciation

This section is designed to make you familiar with the sounds of Russian using our simplified phonetic transcription. You'll find the pronunciation of the Cyrillic (Russian) letters and sounds explained below, together with their "imitated" equivalents. To use this system, found throughout the phrase book, simply read the pronunciation as if it were English, noting any special rules below.

The Russian language

Russian is a language with a long history. Like most other European languages it has its origin in Sanskrit and is part of the Indo-European group. The Cyrillic alphabet is named after St. Cyril, the apostle of the Slavs, who devised it for the translation of the Bible and the liturgy in the ninth century.

Russian is a phonetic language, and its pronunciation is much more systematic than that of English. It conforms fairly closely to consistent rules so that the different pronunciations of the English "ough," as in "ought," "though," "cough," and "bough," do not occur. But the rules are complicated. The following information gives details about some of the more significant rules of pronunciation.

Pronunciation of Russian consonants

The pronunciation of Russian consonants can be either "hard" or "soft." Consonants are "soft" when followed by the vowels я, е, и, ё, ю, and the "soft sign," ь. When a letter is soft it is generally followed by a "y" before the vowel in our phonetic transcription. This "y" is pronounced like the "y" in "yet."

The letter ъ, known as the "hard sign," is rarely used in modern Russian. However, when it is used it always precedes a vowel and is also pronounced like the "y" in "yet." It also indicates that the preceding consonant is pronounced "hard."

As in English, certain consonants are termed "voiced" because their pronunciation is accompanied by a resonance of the voice. In Russian these "voiced" consonants are б, в, г, д, ж, and з (**b**, **v**, **g**, **d**, **zh**, and **z**, respectively). Each of them has an "unvoiced" equivalent, that is a consonant which is pronounced in exactly the same way, but without any resonance, almost as though whispered. These are п, ф, к, т, ш, and с (**p**, **f**, **k**, **t**, **sh**, and **s**, respectively).

This change from "voiced" to "unvoiced" consonant occurs at the end of a word, e.g., the word for "bread" – хлеб – is pronounced **khlyep**, and when immediately followed by an "unvoiced" consonant. Hence the preposition for "in/to" – в – is pronounced **f** when it precedes п, ф, к, т, ш, с, х, ц, ч, and щ, (**p**, **f**, **k**, **t**, **sh**, **s**, **kh**, **ts**, **ch**, and **shch**, respectively). For example, "in the park" – в парке – is pronounced **f parkye**.

Conversely, "unvoiced" consonants become "voiced" when they occur before another "voiced" consonant, except before в. Thus the verb for "to do" – сделать – is pronounced **zdyelat'**, but свидание is pronounced **sveedaneeya**.

Consonants

Letter	Approximate pronunciation	Symbol	Example	Pron.
б	like *b* in *b*it	b	был	*bill*
в	like *v* in *v*ine	v	ваш	*vash*
г	like *g* in *g*o	g	город	*gorat*
д	like *d* in *d*o	d	да	*da*
ж	like *s* in plea*s*ure	zh	жаркий	*zharkeey*
з	like *z* in *z*oo	z	завтра	*zaftra*
к	like *k* in *k*itten	k	карта	*karta*
л	like *l* in *l*ily	l	лампа	*lampa*
м	like *m* in *m*y	m	масло	*masla*
н	like *n* in *n*ot	n	нет	*nyet*
п	like *p* in *p*ot	p	парк	*park*
р	trilled (like a Scottish *r*)	r	русский	*rooskeey*
с	like *s* in *s*ee	s	слово	*slova*
т	like *t* in *t*ip	t	там	*tam*
ф	like *f* in *f*ace	f	ферма	*fyerma*
х	like *ch* in Scottish lo*ch*	kh	хлеб	*khlyep*
ц	like *ts* in si*ts*	ts	цена	*tseena*
ч	like *ch* in *ch*ip	chy	час	*chyas*
ш	like *sh* in *sh*ut	sh	ваша	*vasha*
щ	like *sh* followed by *ch*, as in fre*sh ch*eese	shch	щи	*shchee*

Vowels

Vowels can be "stressed" and "unstressed". The vowels o, e, a, and я change their pronunciation when they are unstressed. This is reflected in the phonetic transcription.

Letter	Approximate pronunciation	Symbol	Example	Pron.
а	between *a* in c*a*t and *u* in c*u*t	**a**	как	*kak*
е	like *ye* in *ye*t	**ye**	где	*gdye*
ё	like *yo* in *yo*nder	**yo**	мёд	*myot*
и	like *ee* in s*ee*	**ee**	синий	*__seen__yeey*
й*	like *y* in bo*y*	**y**	бой	*boy*
о**	like *o* in h*o*t	**o**	стол	*stol*
у	like *oo* in b*oo*t	**oo**	улица	*__oo__leetsa*
ы	like *i* in *i*ll	**i**	вы	*vi*
э	like *e* in m*e*t	**e**	эта	*__e__ta*
ю	like *you* in *you*th	**yoo**	юг	*yook*
я	like *ya* in *ya*rd	**ya**	мясо	*__mya__sa*

* й is a semi-vowel and occurs with other full vowels. It is mainly used to form diphthongs.

** When о is unstressed it is pronounced like the Russian a.

Diphthongs

Letter	Approximate pronunciation	Symbol	Example	Pron.
ай	like *y* in m*y*	**ay**	май	*may*
яй	like *y* in m*y*, preceded by *y* in *y*es	**yay**	негодяй	*neega__dyay__*
ой	like *oy* in b*oy*	**oy**	вой	*voy*
ей	like *ey* in ob*ey*, preceded by *y* in *y*es	**yey**	соловей	*sala__vyey__*
ий	like *ee* in s*ee*, followed by *y* in *y*es	**eey**	ранний	*__ran__neey*
ый	like *i* in *i*ll, followed by *y* in *y*es	**iy**	красивый	*kra__see__viy*
уй	like *oo* in g*oo*d, followed by *y* in *y*es	**ooy**	дуй	*dooy*
юй	as уй above, preceded by *y* in *y*es	**yooy**	плюй	*plyooy*

8

Stress

Stress in Russian is irregular and must simply be learned. If a vowel or diphthong is not stressed, it often changes its pronunciation. However, for the purposes of the phrase book, the stress has been marked, the stressed syllable being underlined, and any pronunciation changes are reflected in the phonetic transcription.

The Russian alphabet

А а	*a*		Р р	*er*
Б б	*be*		С с	*es*
В в	*ve*		Т т	*te*
Г г	*ge*		У у	*oo*
Д д	*de*		Ф ф	*ef*
Е е	*ye*		Х х	*kha*
Ё ё	*yo*		Ц ц	*tse*
Ж ж	*zhe*		Ч ч	*chya*
З з	*ze*		Ш ш	*sha*
И и	*ee*		Щ щ	*shchya*
Й й	*ee kratkaye*		Ъ ъ	*tvyordiy znak*
К к	*ka*		Ы ы	*i*
Л л	*el'*		Ь ь	*myakhkeey znak*
М м	*em*		Э э	*ee abarotnaye*
Н н	*en*		Ю ю	*yoo*
О о	*o*		Я я	*ya*
П п	*pe*			

Basic Expressions

ESSENTIAL

Yes./No.	Да./Нет.	*da/nyet*
Okay.	Хорошо./О'кей.	*kharasho/o ke*
Please.	Пожалуйста.	*pazhalsta*
Thank you (very much).	Спасибо (большое).	*spaseeba (bal'shoye)*

Greetings/Apologies
Приветствия/Извинения

Hello./Hi!	Здравствуй(те)./Привет!	*zdrastvooy(tye)/preevyet*
Good morning.	Доброе утро.	*dobraye ootra*
Good afternoon/evening.	Добрый день/вечер.	*dobriy dyen'/vyechyeer*
Good night.	Спокойной ночи.	*spakoyniy nochyee*
Good-bye.	До свидания.	*da sveedaneeya*
Excuse me. (getting attention)	Извините./Простите.	*eezveeneetye/ prasteetye*
Excuse me. (May I get past?)	Разрешите. (Разрешите пройти.)	*razreeshitye (razreeshitye praytee)*
Excuse me!/Sorry!	Извините!/Простите!	*eezveeneetye/prasteetye*
Don't mention it.	Не за что.	*nye za shta*
Never mind.	Ничего.	*neechyeevo*

Communication difficulties
Трудности при разговоре

Do you speak English?	Вы говорите по-английски? *vi gavareetye pa-angleeyskee*
Does anyone here speak English?	Здесь кто-нибудь говорит по-английски? *zdyes' ktoneebood' gavareet pa-angleeyskee*
I don't speak (much) Russian.	Я плохо говорю по-русски. *ya plokha gavaryoo pa-rooskee*
Could you speak more slowly?	Говорите медленнее, пожалуйста. *gavareetye myedlennee pazhalsta*
Could you repeat that?	Повторите, пожалуйста. *paftareetye pazhalsta*
Excuse me? [Pardon?]	Извините. *eezveeneetye*
What was that?	Что такое? *shto takoye*
Could you spell it?	Назовите по буквам, пожалуйста. *nazaveetye pa bookvam pazhalsta*
Please write it down.	Напишите, пожалуйста. *napeeshitye pazhalsta*
Can you translate this for me?	Переведите мне это, пожалуйста. *peereeveedeetye mnye eta pazhalsta*
What does this/that mean?	Что это/то значит? *shto eta/to znachyeet*
Please point to the phrase in the book.	Пожалуйста, покажите эту фразу в книге. *pazhalsta pakazhitye etoo frazoo f kneegye*
I understand.	Я понимаю. *ya paneemayoo*
I don't understand.	Я не понимаю. *ya nee paneemayoo*
Do you understand?	Вы понимаете? *vi paneemayetye*

– *sto treetsat' pyat' rooblyey.*
– *ya nee paneemayoo.*
– *sto treetsat' pyat' rooblyey.*
– *napeesheetyee pazhalsta.* ... aa, "135 rubles"!
– *vot pazhalsta.*

Questions   Вопросы

You can form a simple question in Russian by repeating the same words of the positive statement, without altering the word order, but adding interrogatory intonation (letting the voice rise at the end of the sentence).

Здесь есть факс.   There is a fax machine here.
zdyes' yest' faks

Здесь есть факс?   Is there a fax machine here?
zdyes' yest' faks

Where?   Где?/Куда?*

Where is it?	Где это? gdye eta
Where are you going?	Куда Вы идёте? kooda vi eedyotye
across the road	через дорогу chyeereez darogoo
around the town	по городу pa goradoo
at the meeting place [point]	на месте встречи na myestye fstryechyee
far from here	далеко отсюда daleeko atsyooda
from the U.S.	из Америки eez amyereekee
here (to here)	здесь (сюда) zdyes' (syooda)
in Russia	в России v raseeyee
in the car	в машине v mashinye
inside	внутри (position)/внутрь (motion) vnootree/vnootr'
near the bank	около банка okala banka
next to the post office	рядом с почтой ryadam s pochtay
opposite the market	напротив рынка naproteef rinka
on the left/right	направо/налево naprava/nalyeva
on the sidewalk [pavement]	на тротуаре na tratooarye
there (to there)	там (туда) tam (tooda)
to the hotel	в гостиницу/отель v gasteeneetsoo/atyel
up to the traffic lights	до светофора da sveetafora

* Где is used to ask a question about where something is positioned; куда is used to ask a question about where something/someone is going.

When? Когда?/Во сколько?

When does the museum open?	Когда открыт музей? *kagda atkrit moozyay*
When does the train arrive?	Во сколько приходит поезд? *va skol'ka preekhodeet poeest*
10 minutes ago	10 минут назад *dyeseet' meenoot nazat*
after lunch	после обеда *poslee abyeda*
always	всегда *fseegda*
around midnight	около полуночи *okala paloonachyee*
at 7 o'clock	в 7 часов *f syem' chyasof*
before Friday	до пятницы *da pyatneetsi*
by tomorrow	к завтрашнему дню *k zaftreeshneemoo dnyoo*
every week	каждую неделю *kazhdooyoo needyelyoo*
for 2 hours	2 часа *dva chyasa*
from 9 a.m. to 6 p.m.	с 9-ти утра до 6-ти вечера *z deeveetee ootra da sheestee vyechyeera*
in 20 minutes	через 20 минут *chyeereez dvatsat' meenoot*
never	никогда *neekagda*
not yet	нет ещё *nyet eeshchyo*
now	сейчас/теперь *seechyas/teepyer'*
often	часто *chyasta*
on March 8	8-го марта *vas'mova marta*
on weekdays	в будние (дни) *v boodneeye (dnee)*
sometimes	иногда *eenagda*
soon	скоро *skora*
then	затем/потом *zatyem/patom*
within 2 days	за 2 дня *za dva dnya*

What sort of …?   Какой ...?

I'd like something …
Я хотел(а) бы что-нибудь …
ya khatyel(a) bi shtoneebood' ...

It's …
Это ... *eta ...*

beautiful/ugly	красивый/некрасивый *kraseeviy/neekraseeviy*
better/worse	лучше/хуже *loochshe/khoozhe*
big/small	большой/маленький *bal'shoy/maleen'keey*
cheap/expensive	дешёвый/дорогой *deeshoviy/daragoy*
clean/dirty	чистый/грязный *chyeestiy/gryazniy*
dark/light	тёмный/светлый *tyomniy/svetliy*
delicious/revolting	вкусный/невкусный *fkoosniy/neefkoosniy*
early/late	ранний/поздний *ranneey/pozneey*
easy/difficult	лёгкий/трудный *lyokhkeey/troodniy*
empty/full	пустой/полный *poostoy/polniy*
good/bad	хороший/плохой *kharosheey/plakhoy*
heavy/light	тяжёлый/лёгкий *teezholiy/lyokhkeey*
hot/warm/cold	горячий/тёплый/холодный *garyachyeey/tyopliy/khalodniy*
narrow/wide	узкий/широкий *ooskeey/shirokeey*
next/last	следующий/последний *slyedooyooshchyeey/paslyedneey*
old/new	старый/новый *stariy/noviy*
open/shut	открытый/закрытый *atkritiy/zakritiy*
pleasant/nice/unpleasant	приятный/хороший/неприятный *preeyatniy/kharosheey/neepreeyatniy*
quick/slow	быстрый/медленный *bistriy/myedleenniy*
quiet/noisy	тихий/шумный *teekheey/shoomniy*
right/wrong	правильный/неправильный *praveel'niy/neepraveel'niy*
tall/short	высокий/низкий *visokeey/neezkeey*
thick/thin	толстый/тонкий *tolstiy/tonkeey*
vacant/occupied	свободный/занятый *svabodniy/zaneetiy*
young/old	молодой/старый *maladoy/stariy*

Russian nouns are either masculine, feminine, or neuter.
Unless they are indeclinable (these are mostly foreign "loan" words) they change their endings, and often their appearance, according to the case they are in, and according to whether they are singular or plural ➤ 169.

Masculine nouns:	usually end in a hard consonant, e.g., автобу<u>с</u>
Feminine nouns:	usually end in -a or -я, e.g., газет<u>а</u>, недел<u>я</u>
Neuter nouns:	usually end in -o or -e, e.g., мест<u>о</u>, здани<u>е</u>

How much/many?   Сколько?

How much is that?	Сколько стоит? <u>skol</u>'ka <u>sto</u>eet
How many are there?	Сколько здесь? <u>skol</u>'ka zdyes'
1	один/одна a<u>deen</u>/ad<u>na</u>
2	два/две dva/dvye
3/4/5	три/четыре/пять tree/chyee<u>ti</u>ree/pyat
none	нисколько nee<u>skol</u>'ka
about 100 rubles [roubles]	около 100 рублей <u>okala</u> sta roo<u>blyey</u>
a little	немного nee<u>mno</u>ga
a lot of traffic	много машин <u>mnoga</u> ma<u>shin</u>
enough	достаточно da<u>sta</u>tachna
few/a few of them	несколько <u>nye</u>skal'ka
many people	много людей <u>mnoga</u> lyoo<u>dyey</u>
more than that	больше, чем <u>bol</u>'she chyem
less than that	меньше, чем <u>myen</u>'she chyem
much more	намного больше na<u>mnoga</u> <u>bol</u>'she
nothing else	ничего больше neechyee<u>vo</u> <u>bol</u>'she
too much	слишком много <u>sleeshkam</u> <u>mnoga</u>

Why?   Почему?

Why is that?	Почему это так? pachyee<u>moo</u> eta tak
Why not?	Почему нет? pachyee<u>moo</u> nyet
It's because of the weather.	Из-за погоды. eez-za pa<u>go</u>di
It's because I'm in a hurry.	Потому что я спешу. pata<u>moosh</u>to ya spee<u>shoo</u>
I don't know why.	Я не знаю почему. ya nee <u>znay</u>oo pachyee<u>moo</u>

Who?/Which? Кто?/Какой?

Who is it for?	Кому это?	*kamoo eta*
(for) her/him	ей/ему	*yey/eemoo*
(for) me	мне	*mnye*
(for) you	Вам/тебе	*vam/teebye*
(for) them	им	*eem*
no one	никому	*neekamoo*
Which one do you want?	Какой Вы хотите?	*kakoy vi khateetye*
that one/this one	вон тот (та)/вот этот (эта)	*von tot (ta)/vot etat (eta)*
one like that	такой как тот (та)	*takoy kak tot (ta)*
not that one	не тот (та)	*nye tot (ta)*
something	что-то	*shtoto*
nothing	ничего	*neecheevo*

Whose? Чей?

Whose is that?	Чьё это?*	*chyo eta*
It's ...	Это	*eta*
mine (masculine/feminine)	мой/моя	*moy/maya*
ours (masculine/feminine)	наш/наша	*nash/nasha*
yours (masculine/feminine)	ваш/ваша	*vash/vasha*
his/hers/theirs	его/её/их	*eevo/eeyo/eekh*
It's ... turn.	Это ... очередь.‡	*eta ... ochyeereed'*
my/our/your	моя/наша/ваша	*maya/nasha/vasha*
his/her/their	его/её/их	*eevo/eeyo/eekh*

* чей = *whose* (masculine singular), чья = *whose* (feminine singular),
чьё = *whose* (neuter singular)

‡ The word for "turn" – очередь – is feminine and takes the feminine form of the possessive adjective. The words for "his," "her," and "their" are indeclinable and are identical with the possessive pronouns "his," "hers," and "theirs."

GRAMMAR

As nouns in Russian decline according to gender, plurality, and case, so do pronouns. Personal pronouns can look very different from their base forms according to what "role" they play in the sentence. Possessive pronouns behave like adjectives, and vary according to the gender, plurality, and case of the noun they modify ► 169.

How? Как?

How would you like to pay?	Как будете платить? **kak _boo_deetye pla_teet'_**
by cash	наличными **na_leech_nimy**
by credit card	кредитной карточкой **kree_deet_noy _kar_tachkoy**
How are you getting here?	Как Вы добираетесь сюда? **kak vi dabee_rae_etyes' syoo_da_**
by car/bus/train	машиной/автобусом/поездом **ma_shee_nay/af_to_boosam/_poo_ezdam**
on foot	пешком **peesh_kom_**
quickly	быстро **_bis_tra**
slowly	медленно **_my_edleena**
too fast	слишком быстро **_sleesh_kam _bis_tra**
totally	полностью **_pol_nastyoo**
very	очень **_o_chyeen'**
with a friend	с другом **z _droo_gam**
without a passport	без паспорта **byes _pas_parta**

Is it …?/Are there …? Есть …?

Is it free of charge?	Бесплатно? **Bees_plat_na**
It isn't ready.	Не готово. **nee ga_to_va**
Is there a shower in the room?	В комнате есть душ? **f _kom_natye yest' doosh**
Is there a bus into town?	Есть автобус в город? **yest' af_to_boos v _go_rad**
There it is/they are.	Вон там./Вон они. **von tam/vot a_nee_**
There is a good restaurant near here.	Здесь рядом есть хороший ресторан. **zdyes' _rya_dam yest' kha_ro_sheey reesto_ran_**
Here it is.	Вот, пожалуйста. **vot pa_zhal_sta**
Here they are.	Вот они. **vot a_nee_**

GRAMMAR

The verb *to be* is not used in the present tense. Therefore the words *am*, *is*, and *are* are omitted. However, the word есть is sometimes used to translate *is* and *are*. Besides meaning *no*, the word нет also means *there is not* and *there are not*.

17

Can/May?   Можно?

Can I ...?	Можно мне ...? *mozhna mnye ...*
Can we ...?	Можно нам ...? *mozhna nam ...*
Can you show me ...?	Покажите мне ... *paka**zhee**tye mnye ...*
Can you tell me?	Скажите, пожалуйста. *ska**zhi**tye pa**zhal**sta*
Can you help me?	Помогите мне. *pama**gee**tye mnye*
May I help you?	Вам помочь? *vam pa**moch'***
Can you direct me to ...?	Покажите мне дорогу к ... *paka**zhi**tye mnye da**ro**goo k ...*
I can't.	Я не могу. *ya nee ma**goo***

What do you want?   Что Вы хотите?

I'd like ...	Я хотел(а) бы ... *ya khat**yel**(a) bi ...*
Could I have ...?	Можно мне ...? *mozhna mnye ...*
We'd like ...	Мы хотели бы ... *mi khat**ye**lee bi ...*
Give me ...	Дайте мне ... *day**tye mnye ...*
I'm looking for ...	Я ищу ... *ya ee**shch**yoo ...*
I need to ...	Мне нужно ... *mnye noozhna ...*
go	пойти *pay**tee***
find	найти *nay**tee***
see	посмотреть *pasma**tryet'***
speak to ...	поговорить с ... *pagava**reet' s ...***

– eezvee**ni**tyee pa**zhal**sta.
– da? vam pa**moch'**?
– *mozhna mnye pagava**reet'** s gaspa**dee**nom Eeva**no**vim.*
– da ka**nye**shna.

18

Other useful words
Другие полезные слова

fortunately	к счастью *k shchyastyoo*
hopefully (*lit.* I hope)	я надеюсь *ya adyeyoos'*
of course	конечно *kanyeshna*
perhaps	может быть *mozhet' bit'*
unfortunately	к сожалению *k sazhalyeneeyoo*
also/but	также/но *tagzhe/no*
and/or	и/или *ee/eelee*

Exclamations   Восклицания

At last!	Наконец! *nakanyets*
Go on.	Дальше. *dal'she*
Nonsense!	Ерунда! *eeroonda*
That's true!	Совершенно верно! *saveershenna praveel'na*
No way!	Вы шутите! *vi shooteetye*
How are things?	Как дела? *kag deela*
great/terrific	замечательно *zamyechateel'niy*
very good	отлично *atleechna*
fine	прекрасно *preekrasna*
not bad	неплохо *neeplokha*
okay	хорошо *kharasho*
not good	не очень хорошо *nee ocheen' kharasho*
fairly bad	довольно плохо *davol'na plokha*
terrible	ужасно *oozhasna*

GRAMMAR

Russian has no articles, i.e., no words for *a/an* or *the*. Thus *a telephone* or *the telephone* are simply conveyed as:

(a/the) telephone   телефон **teeleefon**

However, remember that this noun (masculine) will change according to number and case ➤ 169

Accommodations

Arrangements. You must make hotel reservations before leaving your own country. Russian visas are only issued after reservations have been confirmed. If at all possible, arrange to be met at the airport by a representative from your hotel. Travelers with Intourist will be met by a representative upon exiting customs. If no one is meeting you, try to use public transportation to get to your hotel. Avoid using a "taxi" offered by a taxi-tout. Many travelers have been robbed when using these "taxis," especially in Moscow after dark.

The travel bureau. Intourist no longer holds a monopoly on accommodations in Russia, and in major cities an increasing number of new or newly renovated hotels are now jointly run with Western companies. These first-class ventures offer a new, if pricey, degree of choice accommodation to the traveler. If you are on an Intourist package tour, you can state your preference of hotel, but the final arrangements rest with Intourist, which will let you know where you are staying upon arrival at the airport.

Arrival. Upon arrival at the hotel, check in at reception and hand over all your documents and vouchers. The desk clerk won't give you a key to your room but a hotel pass (пропуск **propoosk**) that gives your name, length of stay, and room number. You have to present this to the doorman every time you enter the hotel and hand it to the "floor manager" (дежурная **deezhoornaya**), who not only keeps the keys but an eye on the guests, too. These are mostly middle-aged women who will also make tea, call a taxi for you, and solve any other problem.

Intourist hotels. These hotels have service bureaus (бюро обслуживания **byooro apsloozheevanya**) manned by multilingual staff who provide information, arrange outings and excursions, make reservations, and give general assistance.

Other accommodation. Apart from big hotels, no other form of accommodation is available. However, foreigners are now allowed to stay in the home of a Russian friend or contact, but a letter of invitation must accompany your visa application.

Reservations   Заказ

In advance   Предварительно

Travelers with Intourist will be met by a representative upon exiting customs.

Can you recommend a hotel in …?	Какой отель Вы рекомендуете в ...? *kakoy atyel' vi reekameendooeetye v ...*
Is it near the center of town?	Это близко от центра города? *eta bleeska at tsentra gorada*
How much is it per night?	Сколько стоит номер в сутки? *skol'ka stoeet nomeer f sootkee*
Do you have a cheaper room?	Дешевле нет? *deeshevlye nyet*
Could you reserve me a room there, please?	Можно мне заказать номер? *mozhna mnye zakazat' nomeer*
How do I get there?	Как туда добраться? *kak tooda dabrat'sa*

At the hotel   В гостинице

Do you have a room?	Есть свободные места? *yest' sfabodniye meesta*
I'm sorry, we're full.	Извините, мест нет. *eezveeneetye myest nyet*
Is there another hotel nearby?	Здесь рядом есть другая гостиница? *zdyes' ryadam yest' droogaya gasteeneetsa*
I'd like a single/double room.	Я хотел(а) бы одноместный/ двухместный номер. *ya khatyel(a) bi adnamyestniy/dvookhmyestniy nomeer*
Can I see the room, please?	Можно посмотреть комнату? *mozhna pasmatryet' komnatoo*
I'd like a room with …	Я хотел(а) бы номер с ... *ya khatyel (a) bi nomeer s ...*
twin beds	двумя кроватями *dvoomya kravatyamee*
a double bed	двуспальной кроватью *dvoospal'ni kravatyoo*
a bath/shower	ванной/душем *vanni/dooshem*

– yest' sfabodniye meesta?
  – eezveeneetye myest nyet.
– zdyes' ryadam yest' droogaya gasteeneetsa?
  – da yest'. paprobooyeetye v Ambasadorye chyeryez darogoo.

Reception   Приём

I have a reservation.	У меня заказ. *Oo meenya zakas*
My name is …	Моя фамилия … *maya fameeleeya …*
We've reserved a double and a single room.	Мы заказали двухместный и одноместный номера. *Mi zakazalee dvookhmyestniy ee adnamyestniy nameera*
I've reserved a room for two nights.	Я заказал номер на двое суток. *ya zakazal nomeer na dvoye sootok*
I confirmed my reservation by mail.	Я послал(а) подтверждение письмом. *ya paslal(a) pattveerzhdyeneeye pees'mom*
Could we have adjoining rooms?	Можно нам номера рядом? *Mozhna nam nameera ryadam*

Amenities and facilities   Удобства и комфорт

Is there (a/an) … in the room?	В номере есть …? *v nomeerye yest' …*
air conditioning	кондиционер *kandeetseeonyer*
TV/telephone	телевизор/телефон *teeleeveezar/teeleefon*
Does the hotel have a(n) …?	В гостинице есть …? *v gasteeneetse yest' …*
fax	факс *faks*
laundry service	прачечная *prachyeechnaya*
satellite TV	спутниковое телевидение *spootneekavaye tyelyeveedyeneeye*
sauna	сауна *saoona*
swimming pool	бассейн *bassyeyn*
Could you put … in the room?	Можно поставить … в комнату? *mozhna pastaveet' … f komnatoo*
an extra bed	ещё одну кровать *eeshcho adnoo kravat'*
a crib [a child's cot]	детскую кроватку *dyetskooyoo kravatkoo*
Do you have facilities for children/the disabled?	Здесь есть удобства для детей/инвалидов? *zdyes' yest' oodobstva dlya deetyey/eenvaleedaf*

How long ...?   Как долго ...?

We'll be staying ...	Мы пробудем ... *mi pra**boo**deem ...*
overnight only	только одну ночь *tol'koo adnoo noch'*
a few days	несколько дней *nyeskal'ka dnyey*
a week (at least)	неделю (по крайней мере) *needyelyoo (pa kraynyee myerye)*
I'd like to stay an extra night.	Я хотел(а) бы остаться ещё на одну ночь. *ya khatyel(a) bi astat'sa eeshchyo na adnoo noch'*

– *oo meenya zakas. maya fameeleeya nyooton.*
– *zdrastvooytye gaspadeen nyooton.*
– *mi praboodeem nyeskal'ka dneyey.*
– *kharasho. pazhalsta raspisheetyes' zdyes'.*

May I see your passport, please?	Ваш паспорт, пожалуйста.

Please fill out this form/
  sign here.
	Заполните бланк/распишитесь
	  здесь.

What is your car license number?	Какой номер Вашей машины?

КОМНАТА ТОЛЬКО ... РУБЛЕЙ	ROOM ONLY ... RUBLES
ЗАВТРАК ВХОДИТ В ЦЕНУ	BREAKFAST INCLUDED
РЕСТОРАН К ВАШИМ УСЛУГАМ	MEALS AVAILABLE
ФАМИЛИЯ/ИМЯ	LAST/FIRST NAME
АДРЕС	HOME ADDRESS
НАЦИОНАЛЬНОСТЬ/ ПРОФЕССИЯ	NATIONALITY/PROFESSION
ДАТА/МЕСТО РОЖДЕНИЯ	DATE/PLACE OF BIRTH
НОМЕР ПАСПОРТА	PASSPORT NUMBER
НОМЕР МАШИНЫ	CAR LICENSE NUMBER
МЕСТО/ДАТА	PLACE/DATE
ПОДПИСЬ	SIGNATURE

Price   Цена

All accommodation must be paid for in advance. The price usually includes full board. When checking out you get a pass proving that you have paid your bill.

How much is it …?	Сколько стоит …? _skol'ka stoeet …_
per night/week	в сутки/в неделю f _sootkee_/v _needyelyoo_
for bed and breakfast	с завтраком z _zaftrakam_
excluding meals	без питания _byes peetaneeya_
for full board (American Plan [A.P.])	с полным питанием s _peetaneeyem_ s _polneem peetaneeyem_
for half board (Modified American Plan [M.A.P.])	с завтраком и ужином z _zaftrakam_ ee _oozhinam_
Does the price include …?	Цена включает …? _fkhodeet_ v _stoeemast'_ …
breakfast	завтрак _zaftrak_
service	услуги _oosloogee_
sales tax [VAT]	НДС _en de es_
Do I have to pay a deposit?	Нужно платить аванс? _noozhna plateet' avans_
Is there a discount for children?	Есть скидка для детей? _yest' skeetka dlya deetyey_

Decision   Выбор номера

May I see the room?	Можно мне посмотреть комнату? _mozhna mnye pasmatryet' komnatoo_
That's fine. I'll take it.	Хорошо. Подойдёт. _kharasho padaydyot_
It's too …	Слишком … _sleeshkam_ …
dark/small	темно/тесно _teemno_/_tyesno_
noisy	шумно _shoomna_
Do you have anything …?	Есть что-нибудь …? _yest' shtoneebood'_ …
bigger/cheaper	побольше/подешевле _pabol'she_/_padeeshevlye_
quieter/warmer	потише/потеплее _pateeshe_/_pateeplyeye_
No, I won't take it.	Нет, это не подойдёт. _nyet eta nee padaydyot_

24

Problems Проблемы

The … doesn't work.	… не работает. *… nee ra<u>bo</u>tayet*
air conditioning	кондиционер *kandeetsee<u>on</u>yer*
fan	вентилятор *veentee<u>lya</u>tar*
heating	отопление *ata<u>plye</u>neeye*
light	свет *svyet*
I can't turn the heat [heating] on/off.	Я не могу включить/выключить отопление. *ya nee ma<u>goo</u> fklyoo<u>chyeet'</u>/<u>vik</u>lyoochyeet'*
There is no hot water/ toilet paper.	Нет горячей воды/туалетной бумаги. *nyet gar<u>ya</u>chyee va<u>di</u>/tooal'<u>et</u>ni boo<u>ma</u>gee*
The faucet [tap] is dripping.	Кран течёт. *kran tee<u>chyot</u>*
The sink/toilet is blocked.	Раковина/туалет засорен(а). *<u>ra</u>kaveena/tooa<u>lyet</u> za<u>so</u>reena*
The window/door is jammed.	Окно/дверь не закрывается. *ak<u>no</u>/dvyer' nee zakriv<u>a</u>eetsa*
My room has not been made up.	Мой номер не убран. *moy <u>no</u>meer nee <u>oo</u>bran*
The … is/are broken.	… сломан(а)/(ы). *… <u>slo</u>man(a)/(i)*
blinds/shutters	жалюзи/ставни *zha<u>lyoo</u>zee/<u>stav</u>ni*
lamp	лампа *<u>lam</u>pa*
lock	замок *za<u>mok</u>*
There are insects in our room.	У нас в комнате насекомые. *oo nas f <u>kom</u>natye nase<u>ko</u>miye*

Action Просьбы

Could you have that seen to?	Не могли бы Вы посмотреть? *nee mag<u>lee</u> bi vi pasmat<u>ryet'</u>*
I'd like to move to another room.	Я хотел(а) бы другую комнату. *ya kha<u>tyel</u>(a) bi droo<u>goo</u>yoo <u>kom</u>natoo*
I'd like to speak to the manager.	Я хотел(а) бы поговорить с директором. *ya kha<u>tyel</u>(a) bi pagava<u>reet'</u> z dee<u>rek</u>taram*

Requirements   Общие требования

While 220 volts AC tends to be standard, you'll still find 110–120 volts AC in some places. Western plugs aren't the same as Russian ones, but large hotels often have sockets suited to Western plugs. However, suitable adapters are sometimes still hard to find in Russia, especially outside the big urban centers, so it is wise to take one with you.

About the hotel   О гостинице

Where's the …?	Где ...? *gdye ...*
bar	бар *bar*
bathroom	ванная *v**a**naya*
bathroom [toilet]	туалет *too**a**l**yet***
dining room	ресторан *rest**a**ran*
elevator [lift]	лифт *leeft*
parking lot [car park]	автостоянка *aftasta**ya**nka*
shower room	душ *doosh*
swimming pool	бассейн *b**a**seyn*
tour operator's bulletin board	доска объявлений *d**a**s**ka abyeevl**yen**eeye*
Does the hotel have a garage?	В отеле есть гараж? *v at**yel**ye yest' g**a**rash*
Can I use this adapter here?	Здесь можно использовать этот адаптер? *zdyes' m**ozh**na eespol'zavat et**a**t **a**dapteer*

ТОЛЬКО ДЛЯ БРИТВ	RAZORS [SHAVERS] ONLY
ПОЖАРНЫЙ ВЫХОД	EMERGENCY EXIT / FIRE EXIT
НЕ БЕСПОКОИТЬ	DO NOT DISTURB.
НАБЕРИТЕ ... В ГОРОД	DIAL ... FOR AN OUTSIDE LINE
НАБЕРИТЕ ... В БЮРО ОБСЛУЖИВАНИЯ	DIAL ... FOR RECEPTION
НЕ УНОСИТЕ ПОЛОТЕНЦА ИЗ НОМЕРА	DON'T REMOVE TOWELS FROM ROOM.

Personal needs Личные нужды

The key to room …, please.
Ключ от номера …, пожалуйста. *klyooch at nomeera … pazhalsta*

I've lost my key.
Я потерял(а) ключ. *ya pateeryal(a) klyooch*

I've locked myself out of my room.
Я случайно захлопнул(а) дверь. *ya sloochyayna zakhlopnool(a) dvyer'*

Could you wake me at …?
Разбудите меня в … *razboodeetye meenya v …*

I'd like breakfast in my room.
Я хотел(а) бы завтрак в номер. *ya khatyel(a) bi zaftrak v nomeer*

Can I leave this in the safe?
Можно оставить это в сейфе? *mozhna astaveet' eta v syeyfye*

Could I have my things from the safe?
Можно взять вещи из сейфа? *mozhno vzyat' vyeshchyee eez syeyfa*

Where can I find (a) …?
Где я могу найти …? *gdye ya magoo naytee …*

maid
горничную *gorneechnayoo*

our tour guide
экскурсовода *ekskoorsavoda*

May I have (an) extra …?
Можно (ещё одно) …? *mozhna (eeshchyo adno) …*

bath towel
большое полотенце *bal'shoye palatyentse*

blanket
одеяло *adeeyala*

hanger
(ещё одну) вешалку *(eeshchyo adnoo) veeshalkoo*

pillow
(ещё одну) подушку *(eeshchyo adnoo) padooshkoo*

soap
мыло *mila*

Is there any mail for me?
Есть почта для меня? *yest' pochta dlya meenya*

Are there any messages for me?
Мне что-нибудь передавали? *mnye shtoneebood' peereedavalee*

Could you mail this for me, please?
Вы могли бы отправить вот это, пожалуйста? *vi maglee bi atpraveet' vot eta pazhalsta*

BREAKFAST ➤ 43; CHANGING MONEY ➤ 138

Renting   Аренда квартиры/дачи

We reserved an apartment/cottage …	Мы сняли квартиру/дачу … *mi snyalee kvarteeroo/dachyoo …*
in the name of …	на имя … *na eemya …*
Where do we pick up the keys?	Где взять ключи? *gdye vzyat' klyoochyee'*
Where is the…?	Где …? *gdye …*
electricity meter	счётчик *shchyotchyeek*
fuse box	распределительный щит *raspreedeeleeteel'niy shchyeet*
valve [stopcock]	запорный кран *zaporniy kran*
water heater	водонагреватель *vadanagreevateel'*
Are there any spare …?	Есть запасные …? *yest' zapasniye …*
fuses	пробки *propkee*
gas bottles	газовые баллоны *gazaviye baloni*
sheets	простыни *prostinyee*
Which day does the maid come?	В какой день приходит уборщица? *f kakoy dyen' preekhodeet ooborshchyeetsa*
When do I put out the trash [rubbish]?	Когда выносить мусор? *kagda vinaseet' moosar*

Problems   Проблемы

Where can I contact you?	Где я могу Вас найти? *gdye ya magoo vas naytee*
How does the stove [cooker]/ water heater work?	Как работает плита/водонагреватель? *kak rabotayet pleeta/vadanagreevateel'*
The … is/are dirty.	… грязно. *… gryazna*
The … has broken down.	… не работает. *… nee rabotayet*
We accidentally broke/lost …	Мы случайно сломали/потеряли … *mi sloochyayna slamalee/pateeryalee …*
That was already damaged when we arrived.	Это было уже сломано, когда мы приехали. *eta bila oozhe slomana kagda mi preeyekhalee*

Useful terms Полезные слова

boiler	бойлер **_boyleer_**
crockery	посуда **_pasooda_**
cutlery	прибор **_preebor_**
freezer	морозильная камера **_marazeel'naya kameera_**
frying pan	сковорода **_skavarada_**
kettle	чайник **_chyayneek_**
lamp	лампа **_lampa_**
refrigerator	холодильник **_khaladeel'neek_**
saucepan	кастрюля **_kastryoolya_**
stove [cooker]	плита **_pleeta_**
washing machine	стиральная машина **_steeral'naya mashina_**

Rooms Комнаты

balcony	балкон **_balkon_**
bathroom	ванная **_vannaya_**
bedroom	спальня **_spal'nya_**
dining room	столовая **_stalovaya_**
kitchen	кухня **_kookhnya_**
living room	гостиная **_gasteenaya_**
toilet	туалет **_tooalyet_**

Youth hostel Общежитие

Sputnik, the Russian youth travel association, organizes group tours for
students with accommodation in youth hostels (молодёжная турбаза
maladyozhnaya toorbaza).

Do you have any places left for tonight?	Есть свободные места сегодня? **_yest' svabodniye meesta seevodnya_**
Do you rent [hire] out bedding?	Вы даёте напрокат постельное бельё? **_vi dayotye naprakat pastyel'naye beelyo_**
What time are the doors locked?	Во сколько закрывается вход? **_va skol'ka zakrivaeetsa fkhot_**
I have an International Student Card.	У меня студенческий билет. **_oo meenya stoodyenchyeeskyee beelyet_**

REQUIREMENTS ➤ 26; CAMPING ➤ 30

Camping Кемпинг

During the summer season – June to August and, in some areas, part of September – authorized campsites are operated near many cities. Campers may park a car and pitch a tent for a fixed rate that includes such amenities as showers and cooking facilities, plus a guided tour of nearby attractions. Arrangements must be made in advance through travel agents outside Russia. Note: Ask your travel agent to check on the security at your chosen campsite before you go.

Reservations Приезд

Is there a camp site near here?	Здесь есть кемпинг поблизости? *zdyes' yest' kyempeeng pableezastee*
Do you have space for a tent/ trailer [caravan]?	Есть место для палатки/трейлера? *yest' myesta dlya palatkee/tryeyleera*
What is the charge …?	Сколько стоит …? *skol'ka stoeet …*
per day/week	в день/неделю *v dyen'/needyelyoo*
for a tent/car	за палатку/машину *za palatkoo/mashinoo*
for a trailer [caravan]	за трейлер *za tryeyleer*

Facilities Удобства

Are there cooking facilities on site?	Здесь можно готовить? *zdyes' mozhna gatoveet'*
Are there any electrical outlets [power points]?	Здесь есть розетки? *zdyes' yest' razyetkee*
Where is/are the …?	Где …? *gdye …*
drinking water	питьевая вода *peeteevaya vada*
trash cans [dustbins]	мусорные баки *moosarniye bakee*
laundry facilities	прачечная *prachyeechnaya*
showers	душ *doosh*
Where can I get some butane gas?	Где можно достать газовые баллоны? *gdye mozhna dastat' gazaviye baloni*

СТОЯНКА ТУРИСТОВ ЗАПРЕЩЕНА	NO CAMPING
ПИТЬЕВАЯ ВОДА	DRINKING WATER
РАЗЖИГАТЬ КОСТРЫ ЗАПРЕЩАЕТСЯ	NO FIRES

Complaints   Жалобы

It's too sunny here.	Здесь слишком на солнце. *zdyes sleeshkam na-sontse.*
It's too shady/crowded here.	Здесь слишком в тени/ тесно. *zdyes sleeshkam f tyenee/tyesno*
The ground's too hard/uneven.	Почва слишком твердая/неровная. *pochva sleeshkam tvyordaya/neerovnaya*
Is there a more level spot?	Есть место поровнее? *yest' myesta paravnyeye*
You can't camp here.	Здесь нельзя ставить палатки. *zdyes' neel'zya staveet' palatkoo*

Camping equipment   Снаряжение

butane gas	газовый баллон *gazaviy ballon*
campbed	раскладушка *raskladooshka*
charcoal	уголь *oogal'*
flashlight [torch]	фонарь *fanar'*
groundcloth [groundsheet]	полотнище *palotneeshchye*
guy rope	оттяжка *atyashka*
hammer	молоток *malatok*
kerosene [primus] stove	примус *preemoos*
knapsack	рюкзак *ryoogzak*
mallet	деревянный молоток *deereevyanniy malatok*
matches	спички *speechkee*
(air) mattress	(надувной) матрас *(nadoovnoy) matras*
paraffin	керосин *keeraseen*
sleeping bag	спальный мешок *spal'niy meeshok*
tent	палатка *palatka*
tent pegs	колышки *kolishkee*
tent pole	шест *shest*

Checking out   Отъезд

When checking out, you'll get a pass proving that you have paid your bill.

What time do we have to check out by?	Во сколько надо освободить комнату? *va skol'ka nada asvabadeet' komnatoo*
Could we leave our baggage [luggage] here until … p.m.?	Здесь можно оставить багаж до ...? *zdyes' mozhna astaveet' bagash da ...*
I'm leaving now.	Я уезжаю сейчас. *ya ooyeezhzhayoo seechyas*
Could you order me a taxi, please?	Вы могли бы заказать мне такси? *vi maglee bi zakazat' mnye taksee*
It's been a very enjoyable stay.	Мне (нам) очень понравилось здесь. *mnye (nam) ochyeen' panraveelas' zdyes'*

Paying   Оплата

In Russia it is customary to tip taxi drivers and restaurant waiters. The size of the tip is optional but usually does not exceed 15%. Service is never included in any bill.

May I have my bill, please?	Можно счёт, пожалуйста? *mozhna shchyot pazhalsta*
How much is my telephone bill?	Сколько за телефон? *skol'ka za teeleefon*
I think there's a mistake in this bill.	Мне кажется, Вы ошиблись. *mnye kazhetsa vi ashiblees'*
I've made … telephone calls.	Я звонил(а) ... раз(а). *ya zvaneel(a) ... raz(a)*
I've taken … from the mini-bar.	Я брал(а) ... из мини-бара. *ya bral(a) ... eez meeneebara*
Can I have an itemized bill?	Можно счёт по пунктам? *mozhna shchyot pa poonktam*
Could I have a receipt, please?	Можно чек, пожалуйста? *mozhna chyek pazhalsta*

TIME ➤ 220

Eating Out

Restaurants   Рестораны

Бар *bar*
Bar. These are usually found in hotels and only accept foreign currency.

Блинная *bleenaya*
Blini bar. Serves блины (**bleeni**), Russian pancakes, with various toppings, sweet and savory.

Буфет *boofyet*
Snack bar. These are found in hotels, theaters, at stations, etc., and are good for light meals. You can buy food and drink and eat at one of the tables or take your food away with you.

Закусочная *zakoosachnaya*
A kind of snack bar.

Кафе *kafye*
Café. Despite its name, a Russian "café" is the equivalent of a Western restaurant. Many close by 9 p.m., 11 p.m. at the latest.

Кафе-кондитерская *kafye-kandeetyerskaya*
Also called simply кондитерская; these cafés serve coffee and cakes.

Кафе-мороженое *kafye-marozhenaya*
Ice-cream parlor. These establishments serve ice cream, drinks, and cocktails.

Кафетерий *kafeetyereey*
Cafeteria. Usually with no seats, serving small dishes, snacks, and salads.

Пельменная *peelmyenaya*
Small restaurants serving mainly пельмени (**peelmyenee**), a kind of meat dumpling.

Пивной бар *peevnoy bar*
Beer bar. Serves beer and appetizers, always crowded.

Пирожковая *peerashkovaya*
Snack bar. Sells only пирожки (**peerashkee**), savory pastries with various fillings (meat, cabbage, rice, jam, etc.).

Ресторан *reestaran*
Restaurant. In most cases it's a place where you go not just for a meal but for a whole evening's entertainment, with music and dancing. It is advisable to reserve a table in advance.

If you have a chance, don't restrict yourself to Russian food, but try restaurants where they serve Georgian, Armenian, Azerbaijani, or Uzbek specialities.

All restaurants close by midnight. Many close at 5 p.m. and re-open at 7 p.m.

Столовая *stalovaya*
Cafeteria or canteen (public establishment). Self-service, low prices, no alcohol.

Чайная *chaynaya*
Tearoom or small café.

Шашлычная *shashlichnaya*
An establishment serving шашлык (**shashlik**), pieces of lamb grilled on skewers, as well as other typical dishes from the Caucasus and Central Asia.

Meal times   Часы работы

Breakfast (завтрак **zaftrak**): served from 7 a.m. to 10 a.m.

Lunch (обед **abyet**): served from about 11 a.m. to 4 p.m.

Dinner (ужин **oozhin**): served from about 6 p.m. to 10 or 10:30 p.m.
As restaurants close at 11 p.m. (midnight at the latest), Russians usually arrive early.

Russian cuisine   Русская кухня

The country's geographical, climatic, and ethnic variety is reflected in a rich and varied cuisine. The Russians have a "sweet tooth" and are very fond of desserts and pastries, as well as their excellent ice cream.

Eating plays an important part in Russian social life, and it is while dining that you'll find Russians at their most hospitable. Don't forget to wish your table companions a hearty appetite – Приятного аппетита! (**preeyatnava apeeteeta**).

A table for…	Столик на … *stoleek na …*
1/2/3/4	одного/двоих/троих/четверых *adnavo/dvaeekh/traeekh/cheetveerikh*
Thank you.	Спасибо. *spaseeba*
The bill, please.	Пожалуйста, счёт. *pazhalsta shchyot*

Finding a place to eat
Где можно поесть?

Can you recommend a good restaurant?	Какой ресторан Вы рекомендуете? *kakoy reestaran vi reekameendooeetye*
Is there a(n) … near here?	Здесь есть … поблизости? *zdyes' yest' … pableezastee*
traditional local restaurant	национальный ресторан *natsianal'niy reestaran*
Chinese restaurant	китайский ресторан *keetayskeey reestaran*
fish restaurant	рыбный ресторан *ribniy reestaran*
Russian/Georgian restaurant	русский/грузинский ресторан *roosskeey/groozeenskeey reestaran*
Italian restaurant	итальянский ресторан *eetalyanskeey reestaran*
inexpensive restaurant	недорогой ресторан *needaragoy reestaran*
vegetarian restaurant	вегетарианский ресторан *veegeetaryanskiy reestaran*
Where can I find a(n) …?	Где находится …? *gdye nakhodeetsa …*
burger stand	кафе-гамбургер *kafe gamboorgeer*
café	кафе *kafe*
ice-cream parlor	кафе-мороженое *kafe marozheenaye*
pizzeria	пиццерия *peetseereeya*

DIRECTIONS ➤ 94

Reserving a table Заказ столика

I'd like to reserve a table for two.	Я хотел(а) бы заказать столик на 2. *ya kha<u>tyel</u>(a) bi zaka<u>zat'</u> <u>sto</u>leek na dva<u>eekh</u>*
For this evening/tomorrow at …	на сегодня вечером/завтра на … *na see<u>vod</u>nya <u>vye</u>cheeram/<u>zaf</u>tra na …*
We'll come at 8:00.	Мы будем в 8 часов. *mi <u>boo</u>dem v <u>vo</u>seem' chya<u>sof</u>*
A table for two, please.	Столик на двоих, пожалуйста. *<u>sto</u>leek na dva<u>eekh</u> pazhalsta*
We have a reservation.	У нас заказ. *oo nas za<u>kas</u>*

Ваша фамилия?	What's the name, please?
Во сколько Вы будете?	What time will you be arriving?
Извините, мест нет.	I'm sorry. We're very busy/full up.
Столик освободится через … минут.	We'll have a free table in … minutes.
Вам придётся прийти через … минут.	You'll have to come back in … minutes.

Where to sit Где можно сесть?

Could we sit …?	Можно нам сесть …? *<u>mozh</u>na nam syest' …*
over there/outside	вон там/на улице *von tam/na <u>oo</u>leetse*
in a non-smoking area	где не курят *gdye nyee <u>koo</u>ryat*
by the window	у окна *oo ak<u>na</u>*
Smoking or non-smoking?	Курящий или некурящий? *koo<u>ryash</u>chyeey <u>ee</u>lee neekoo<u>ryash</u>chyeey*

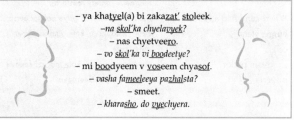

– ya kha<u>tyel</u>(a) bi zaka<u>zat'</u> <u>sto</u>leek.
–na <u>skol'</u>ka chyela<u>vyek</u>?
– nas chyetvee<u>ro</u>.
– vo <u>skol'</u>ka vi <u>boo</u>deetye?
– mi <u>boo</u>dyeem v <u>vo</u>seem chya<u>sof</u>.
– vasha fa<u>mee</u>leeya pazha<u>lsta</u>?
– smeet.
– khara<u>sho</u>, do <u>vye</u>chyera.

Ordering Заказ

Always check prices carefully before ordering, to avoid an
unpleasant surprise.

Waiter!/Waitress!	Официант!/Официантка! *ofeetsiant/ofeetsiantka*
May I see the wine list, please?	Можно посмотреть карту вин? *mozhna pasmatryet' kartoo veen*
Do you have a set menu?	У Вас есть меню? *oo vas yest' meenyoo*
Can you recommend some typical local dishes?	Что Вы рекомендуете типично местное? *shto vi reekameendooeetye teepeechna meestnaye*
Could you tell me what … is?	Скажите, что такое …? *skazhityе shto takoye …*
What's in it?	Что туда входит? *shto tooda fkhodeet*
What kind of … do you have?	Какой … у вас есть? *kakoy … oo vas yest'*
I'll have …	Я возьму … *ya vaz'moo …*
a bottle/glass/carafe of …	бутылку/стакан/графин … *booteelkoo/stakan/grafeen …*

Будете заказывать?	Are you ready to order?
Что Вы хотите?	What would you like?
Что будете пить?	Would you like to order drinks first?
Я бы рекомендовал(а) …	I recommend …
У нас нет …	We don't have …
Будет готово через … минут.	That will take … minutes.
Приятного аппетита!	Enjoy your meal.

– *boodeetye zakazivat'?*
– *shto vi rekamyendooeetye teepeechna meestnaye?*
– *ya bi rekamandaval(a) ….*
– *kharasho ya vaz'moo eta.*
– *pazhalsta a shto vi boodeetye peet'?*
– *grafeen krasnava veena pazhalsta.*
– *kharasho.*

DRINKS ➤ 50; MENU READER ➤ 52

Side dishes/Accompaniments
Салаты/Гарниры

Could I have … without …?	Можно мне … без …? *mozhna mnye … byez …*
With a side order of …	С гарниром из … *z garneeram eez …*
Could I have salad instead of vegetables, please?	Можно мне салат вместо овощей? *mozhna mnye salat vmyesta avashchyey*
Does the meal come with vegetables/potatoes?	Это блюдо с овощами/с картошкой? *eta blyooda s avashchyamee/ s kartoshkoy*
Do you have any sauces?	У вас есть соусы? *oo vas yest' so-oosi*
Would you like … with that?	Вам с …? *vam s …*
vegetables/salad	овощами/салатом *avashchyamee/salatam*
potatoes/fries	картофелем/жареным картофелем *kartofeeleem/zhareenim kartofeeleem*
rice	рисом *reesam*
sauce	соусом *so-oosam*
ice	льдом *l'dom*
May I have some …?	Можно мне …? *mozhna mnye …*
bread	хлеба *khlyeba*
butter	масла *masla*
lemon	лимон *leemon*
mustard	горчицу *garchyeetsa*
pepper	перец *pyereets*
salt	соль *sol'*
seasoning	приправы *preepravi*
sugar	сахар *sakhar*
artificial sweetener	сахарин *sakhareen*
blue cheese dressing	сырная заправка *sirnaya zaprafka*
vinaigrette [French dressing]	уксусная заправка *ooksoosnaya zaprafka*

General questions Общие вопросы

Could I/we have a(n) (clean) …, please?	Можно (чистый) …, пожалуйста? *mozhna (chyeestiy) … pazhalsta*
ashtray	пепельницу *pyepeel'neetsoo*
cup/glass	чашку/стакан *chyashkoo/stakan*
fork/knife/spoon	вилку/нож/ложку *veelkoo/nosh/loshkoo*
serviette [napkin]	салфетку *salfyetkoo*
plate/spoon	тарелку *taryelkoo*
I'd like some more …, please.	Можно ещё …, пожалуйста. *mozhna eeshchyo… pazhalsta*
Nothing more, thanks.	Ничего больше, спасибо. *neechyeevo bol'she spaseeba*
Where are the bathrooms [toilets]?	Где туалет? *gdye tooalyet*

Special requirements Особые требования

I can't eat food containing …	Мне нельзя есть … *mnye neel'zya yest'* …
flour/fat	мучное/жирное *moochnoye/zheernaya*
salt/sugar	солёное/сладкое *salyonaye/slatkaye*
Do you have meals/drinks for diabetics?	Есть что-нибудь для диабетиков? *yest' shtoneebood' dlya deeabyeteekaf*
Do you have vegetarian dishes?	Есть что-нибудь для вегетарианцев? *yest' shtoneebood' dlya veegeetareeantsef*

For the children Для детей

Do you have children's portions?	У вас есть детские порции? *oo vas yest' dyetskeeye portsiyee*
Could we have a child's seat, please?	Можно детский стульчик, пожалуйста. *mozhna dyetskeey stool'chyeek pazhalsta*
Where can I feed the baby?	Где можно покормить ребёнка? *gdye mozhna pakarmeet' reebyonka*
Where can I change the baby?	Где можно перепеленать ребёнка? *gdye mozhna peereepeeleenat' reebyonka*

CHILDREN ➤ 113

Fast food/Café Кафе

Something to drink Что-нибудь попить

I'd like …	Я хотел(а) бы … *ya khatyel(a) bi …*
beer	пиво *peeva*
(hot) chocolate	(горячий) шоколад *(garyacheey) shakalat*
tea/coffee	чай/кофе *chyay/kofye*
black/with milk	чёрный/с молоком *chyorniy/s malakom*
fruit juice	сок *sok*
mineral water	минеральную воду *meeneeral'nooyoo vodoo*
red/white wine	красное/белое вино *krasnaye/byelaye veeno*

And to eat … И поесть …

A piece of …, please.	Кусочек …, пожалуйста. *koosocheek … pazhalsta*
I'd like two of those.	Два кусочка вон того. *dva koosochka von tavo*
burger	гамбургер *gamboorgeer*
cake (small/large)	пирожное /торт *peerozhnaye/ tort*
fries/omelet	чипсы/омлет *cheepsi/amlyet*
sandwich	бутерброд *bootirbrot*
A … ice cream, please.	… мороженое, пожалуйста. *… marozheenaye, pazhalsta*
vanilla/chocolate/strawberry	ванильное/шоколадное/клубничное *vaneel'naye/shakalatnaye/ kloobneechnaye*
A … portion, please.	Порцию …, пожалуйста. *portsiyoo … pazhalsta*
small/medium/large	маленькую/среднюю/большую *aleen'kooyoo/sryednyooyoo/bal'shooyoo*
It's to go [take away].	Это с собой. *eta s saboy*
That's all, thanks.	Это всё, спасибо. *eta fsyo spaseeba*

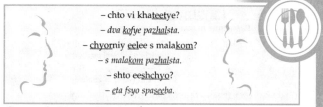

– chto vi kha<u>tee</u>tye?

– dva <u>ko</u>fye pa<u>zhal</u>sta.

– <u>chyor</u>niy <u>ee</u>lee s mala<u>kom</u>?

– s mala<u>kom</u> pa<u>zhal</u>sta.

– shto <u>eesh</u>chyo?

– <u>e</u>ta fsyo spa<u>see</u>ba.

Complaints Жалобы

I don't have a knife/fork/spoon.	У меня нет ножа/вилки/ложки. *oo mee<u>nya</u> nyet na<u>zha</u>/<u>veel</u>kee/<u>losh</u>kee*
There must be some mistake.	Вы должно быть ошиблись. *vi dalzh<u>no</u> bit' a<u>shib</u>lees'*
That's not what I ordered.	Это не то, что я заказывал(а). *<u>e</u>ta nee to shto ya za<u>ka</u>zival(a)*
I asked for …	Я просил(а)… *ya pra<u>seel</u>(a) …*
I can't eat this.	Это невозможно есть. *<u>e</u>ta neeva<u>mozh</u>na yest'*
The meat is …	Мясо … *<u>mya</u>sa …*
overdone	пережарено *peeree<u>zha</u>reena*
underdone	недожарено *needa<u>zha</u>reena*
too tough	очень жёсткое *<u>ochyeen</u>' <u>zhost</u>kaye*
This is too …	Это очень … *<u>e</u>ta <u>ochyeen</u>'…*
bitter/sour	горькое/кислое *<u>gor'</u>kaye/<u>kees</u>laye*
The food is cold.	Это холодное. *<u>e</u>ta kha<u>lod</u>naye*
This isn't fresh.	Это несвежее. *<u>e</u>ta nee<u>svye</u>zheeye*
How much longer will our food be?	Сколько ещё ждать? *<u>skol'</u>ka ee<u>sh</u>chyo zhdat'*
We can't wait any longer. We're leaving.	Мы не можем больше ждать. Мы уходим. *mi nee <u>mo</u>zhem <u>bol'</u>she zhdat'. mi oo<u>kho</u>deem*
Have you forgotten our drinks?	Вы не забыли про наши напитки? *vi nee za<u>bi</u>lee pra <u>na</u>shi na<u>peet</u>kee*
This isn't clean.	Это грязное. *<u>e</u>ta <u>gryaz</u>naye*
I'd like to speak to the head waiter/manager.	Я хочу поговорить с метрдотелем/ директором. *ya kha<u>chyoo</u> pagava<u>reet</u>' s myetrdat<u>ye</u>leem/dee<u>rek</u>taram*

Paying Оплата

Remember to add 15% for service ➤ 32.

The bill, please.	Можно счёт, пожалуйста? _mozhna shchyot pazhalsta_
I'd like to pay.	Я хотел(а) бы заплатить. _ya khatyel(a) bi zaplateet'_
We'd like to pay separately.	Мы будем платить отдельно. _mi boodeem plateet' addyel'na_
It's all together, please.	Всё вместе, пожалуйста. _fsyo vmyestye pazhalsta_
I think there's a mistake.	Мне кажется, Вы ошиблись. _mnye kazheetsa vi asheeblees'_
What is this amount for?	А это за что? _a eta za shto_
I didn't have that. I had …	Я это не заказывал(а). У меня было … _ya eta nee zakazival(a) oo meenya bila …_
Is service included?	Счёт включает обслуживание? _schyot fklyoochayeet apsloozhevaneeye_
Can I pay with this credit card?	Можно платить кредитной карточкой? _mozhna plateet' kreedeetnigh kartachkoy_
I forgot my wallet.	Я забыл(а) кошелёк. _ya zabil(a) kasheelyok_
I don't have enough money.	У меня не хватает денег. _oo meenya nee khvataeet dyeneek_
Could I have a receipt, please?	Можно отдельный чек? _mozhna addyel'niy chyek_
Can I have an itemized bill, please?	Можно счёт по пунктам? _mozhna shchyot pa poonktam_
That was a very good meal.	Всё было очень вкусно. _fsyo bila ochyeen' fkoosna_

– afitsyant schyot pazhalsta.
   – _pazhalsta. vot._
– schyot fklyoochayeet apsloozhevaneeye?
   – _da._
– _mozhna plateet' kreedeetniy kartachkoy?_
   – _kanyeshna._
– spaseeba. fsyo bila ochyeen' fkoosna.

Course by course
Блюдо за блюдом

Breakfast   Завтрак

A Russian breakfast can be quite hearty. You can either have tea or coffee with bread, butter, and jam or, if you are feeling hungry, try hot cereals, ham, eggs, sausages, and cheese.

I'd like to have breakfast.	Я хотел(а) бы позавтракать. *ya khatyel(a) bi pazaftrakat'*
I'd like …	Я бы хотел(а) … *ya bi khatyel(a) …*
a boiled egg	варёное яйцо *varyonaye yaytso*
fried eggs	яичницу *yaychneetsoo*
scrambled eggs	яичницу-болтунью *yaychneetsoo-baltoonyoo*
ham and eggs	яичницу с ветчиной *yaeechneetsoo c veechyeenoy*
oatmeal porridge/yogurt	овсянку/йогурт *avsyankoo/yagoort*
fruit juice	фруктовый сок *frooktoviy sok*
orange/grapefruit juice	апельсиновый/грейпфрутовый сок *apeel'seenoviy/greypfrootaviy sok*
jam/honey	джем/мёд *dzhem/myot*
bread/toast	хлеб/тост *khlyep/tost/*

Appetizers/Starters   Закуски

These are often divided into "hot" and "cold." When ordering a starter, just say На закуску … (**na zakooskoo**) and the name of the dish(es).

assorted meats/fish	ассорти мясное/рыбное *asartee myasnoye/ribnaye*
caviar	икра *eekra*
ham	ветчина *veetchyeena*
mushrooms	грибы *greebi*
spiced herring (sprats)	кильки *keel'kee*
sausage (mortadella)	колбаса *kalbasa*
shrimp [prawns]	креветки *kreevyetkee*
sturgeon	осетрина *asyertreena*
paté (mostly liver)	паштет *pashtyet*
herring	селёдка, сельдь *seelyotka, syel'd'*

Soups   Супы

broth/consommé	бульон **boolyon**
chicken soup	суп из курицы **eez kooreetsi**
fish soup	уха **ookha**
mushroom soup	грибной суп **greebnoy soop**
pea soup	гороховый суп **garokhaviy soop**
potato soup	картофельный **kartofeel'niy soop**
… with noodles/savory pastries/croutons	… с лапшой/пирожками/гренками **s lapshoy/peerozhkamee/gryenkamee**

Борщ **borshch**
Borscht is a substantial dish made from beef, vegetables (chiefly beets), and sour cream. There are a number of regional varieties, including московский **maskofskee** (Moscow borscht with extra bacon); украинский **ookrayeenskee** (Ukrainian borscht with garlic); and холодный **khalodniy** (cold borscht).

Окрошка **akroshka**
A cold summer soup made from kvass (a Russian soft drink), cucumber, egg, onion, and sour cream.

Солянка **salyanka**
A soup made with salted cucumbers and olives, with either meat or fish.

Харчо **kharcho**
A spicy Georgian soup made with mutton and rice.

Шурпа **shoorpa**
Uzbek mutton soup with bacon and tomatoes.

Щи **shchyee**
Shchee is a thick Russian speciality soup made with cabbage or sauerkraut. There are a number of regional varieties, including зелёные с яйцом **zeelyonye s yeetsom** (flavored with sorrel and thickened with beaten egg); кислые **keesliye** (made with sauerkraut); and свежие **svyezhiye** (made with fresh cabbage).

Salads   Салаты

зелёный салат	**zeelyoniy salat**	green salad
картофельный салат	**kartofeelniy salat**	potato salad
салат из крабов	**salat eez krabaf**	crabmeat salad
салат из редиски	**salat eez reedeeskee**	radish salad
салат из свежей капусты	**salat eez svyezhey kapoostee**	raw cabbage salad
салат с сельдью	**salat s syel'dyoo**	herring salad

Fish and seafood Рыба и дары моря

треска	*treeska*	cod
карп	*karp*	carp
краб	*krap*	crab
палтус	*paltoos*	halibut
сельдь, селёдка	*syel'd', seelyotka*	herring
омар	*amar*	lobster
макрель	*makryel'*	mackerel
устрицы	*oostreetsi*	oysters
креветки	*kreevyetkee*	shrimp [prawns]
сёмга	*syomga*	salmon
лососина	*lasaseena*	salmon
шпроты	*shproti*	sprats (herring)
форель	*faryel'*	trout
тунец	*toonyets*	tuna

Осетрина под белым соусом *aseetreena pad byelim sooosam*
Sturgeon served with a white sauce.

Осетрина паровая *aseetreena paravaya*
Steamed sturgeon served with a light sauce.

Осетрина по-русски *aseetreena parooskee*
Poached sturgeon served with a tomato sauce and vegetables.

Судак жареный в тесте *soodak zharyeniy v tyestee*
Pike perch fried in batter.

Судак отварной с яичным соусом
soodak atvarnoy s yaeechnim sooosam
Pike perch poached and served with an egg sauce.

Meat/Poultry   Мясо/Птица

говядина	*gavyadeena*	beef
молодая баранина	*maladaya baraneena*	lamb
печёнка	*peechyonka*	liver
свинина	*sveeneena*	pork
телятина	*teelyateena*	veal
кура	*koora*	chicken
утка	*ootka*	duck
гусь	*goos'*	goose
кролик	*kroleek*	rabbit
индейка	*eendyeyka*	turkey

Meat cuts   Сорта мяса

грудинка/нога/крыло	*groodeenka/naga/krilo*	breast/leg/wing
антрекот/ромштекс/филе	*antreekot/ramshteks/feele*	entrecote/rump/fillet
биточки	*beetochbki*	rissoles
котлета	*katlyeta*	cutlet/chop
ростбиф	*rostbeef*	roast beef

Азу *azoo*
Chopped meat in a savory sauce.

Бефстроганов *beefstroganaf*
The famous Russian dish Beef Stroganoff. Fine strips of steak cooked in a cream and brandy sauce.

Говядина тушёная *gavyadeena tooshonaya*
Braised beef with aromatic vegetables.

Голубцы *galloopsi*
Cabbage stuffed with meat and rice.

Шашлык *shashlik*
Caucasian shashlik – pieces of lamb grilled on skewers.

Утка тушёная с яблоками *ootka tooshyonaya s yablakamee*
Duck roasted with apples.

Котлеты по-киевски *katlyeti pa keeyefskee*
Chicken Kiev – breast of chicken stuffed with butter and garlic.

Чахохбили из кур *chakhakhbeelee ees koor*
Caucasian chicken casserole, served with tomatoes and lots of onions.

Vegetables Овощи

фасоль	*fasol'*	beans
свёкла	*svyokla*	beetroot
капуста	*kapoosta*	cabbage
морковь	*markof'*	carrots
цветная капуста	*tsvyeetnaya kapoosta*	cauliflower
огурец	*agooryets*	cucumber
баклажан	*baklazhan*	eggplant [aubergine]
грибы	*greebi*	mushrooms
лук	*look*	onions
горох	*garokh*	peas
перец	*pyereets*	pepper
картофель	*kartofeel'*	potato
сладкая кукуруза	*slatkaya kookoorooza*	sweetcorn
помидоры	*pomeedori*	tomatoes
молодые кабачки	*maladiye kabachkee*	zucchini [courgettes]

Fruit Фрукты

яблоки	*yablaki*	apples
абрикосы	*abreekosi*	apricots
бананы	*banani*	bananas
черешня	*chyeeryeshnya*	cherries
виноград	*veenagrad*	grapes
лимоны	*leemoni*	lemons
дыня	*dinya*	melon
апельсины	*apeel'seeni*	oranges
персики	*pyerseeki*	peaches
груши	*grooshi*	pears
ананас	*ananas*	pineapple
сливы	*sleevi*	plums
клубника	*kloobneeka*	strawberries
арбуз	*arboos*	watermelon

Cheese and dairy products
Сыр и молочные продукты

брынза	**brinza**	ewe's milk cheese (salty)
кефир	**keefeer**	kefir (butter milk)
ряженка	**ryazhinka**	baked sour milk, often served chilled
сливки	**sleefkee**	cream

сметана **smeetana**
Sour cream, an integral part of Russian cuisine, used in soups, salads, vegetable and meat dishes as well as in desserts.

сыр ... **sir ...** Cheeses come in many regional varieties:

латвийский	**latveeskeey**	Latvian
пошехонский	**pashyekhonskeey**	Poshekhonsky
российский	**rasseeyskee**	Russian

сырок **sirok**
Fresh white cheese (or spread).

творог **tvarok**
White unsalted cheese similar to cottage cheese – extremely popular and used in many dishes.

топлёное молоко **taplyonoye malako**
Baked milk, served chilled.

ватрушка **vatrooshka**
Cheese pastry (made from white cheese) often served as a savory with soups or as a sweet with tea, milk, etc.

Pies and dumplings   Пирожки и пельмени

| пельмени | **peel'myenee** | stuffed dumplings |
| пирог/пирожки | **peerok/peerozhkee** | large pie/small pie |

пирог **peerok**
Large pie filled with meat, cabbage, mushroom, fish, etc. and topped with pastry.

пирожки **peerashkee**
Small pies with various fillings: meat, cabbage, mushrooms, onions, jam, etc.

хачапури **khachyapooree**
Georgian speciality: a kind of hot pancake filled with cheese (a popular snack).

вареники **varyeneekee**
Ukrainian dumplings filled with white cheese.

сырники со сметаной **sirneekee sa smeetanay**
White cheese fritters served with sour cream.

Dessert Сладкое

ватрушка	*vatrooshka*	cottage cheese pastry
кисель	*keesyel'*	fruit jelly
компот	*kampot*	fruit compote
оладьи с яблоками	*aladee с yablakamee*	small apple pancakes
рисовый пудинг	*reesaviy poodeeng*	rice pudding
ромовая баба	*romavaya baba*	rum baba
рулет	*roolyet*	sponge roll
яблоко в тесте	*yablaka v tyestye*	apple baked in pastry
взбитые сливки	*vzbeetiye sleefkee*	whipped cream

блинчики с вареньем *bleenchyeekee s varyeneeyam*
Small pancakes served with jam.

мороженое *marozhyenaye*
Ice cream – very popular everywhere and available in many flavors, including vanilla (ванильное *vaneel'naye*); fruit (фруктовое *frooktovaye*); and chocolate (шоколадное *shakalatnaye*).

пирог *peerok*
Pies or tarts served with a variety of fruit or cheese fillings, including lemon (с лимоном **s leemonam**); cottage cheese (творогом **tvaragom**); and fruit (фруктами *frooktamee*).

Pancakes Блины

Russian pancakes are made with yeast and served with different fillings. Smaller and thicker than Western pancakes, they are usually served with sour cream (сметана) and/or butter.

блины с икрой	*bleeni s eekroy*	pancakes with caviar
блины с сёмгой	*bleeni s syomgoy*	pancakes with salmon
блины со сметаной	*bleeni so smetanay*	pancakes with sour cream
блины с вареньем	*bleeni s varyenyem*	pancakes with jam
блины с брынзой	*bleeni s brinzoy*	pancakes with ewe's milk cheese

Drinks   Напитки

Wine   Вино

Wines from many countries are available throughout Russia. And it is sometimes easier to find French, California, and Italian wines than to find old favorites from Georgia such as **Tsinandali** (a dry, white wine), **Mukuzani** (a red table wine), and **Kindzmaraooli** (Stalin's favorite – red, a little sweet).

Russian champagne or sparkling wine is a popular drink. Dry, it can accompany almost any meal; sweet, it is usually enjoyed after meals or with dessert. Quality and price vary for wine with the same label. In general it is better to buy any drink from a liquor store than from a street kiosk.

I'd like a bottle of …	Я хотел(а) бы бутылку ... *ya khatyel(a) bi bootilkoo ...*
red wine	красного вина *krasnava veena*
white wine	белого вина *byelava veena*
champagne	шампанского *shampanskava*
blush [rosé] wine	розового вина *rozavava veena*
dry/sweet/sparkling wine	сухое/сладкое/шипучее вино *sookhoye/slatkaye/sheepoochyeeye veeno*

Beer   Пиво

It is often easier to buy imported beer than milk. There is no shortage of the former, from all over the world. Many Russian beers taste weak to the Western palate, but it is worthwhile trying some while you are in Russia. **Zhigulyovskoye** and **Stolichnoye** are reliable brands.

Russian beer	жигулёвское *zheegoolyevskaye*
Riga beer	рижское *rishskaye*
Moscow beer	московское *maskofskaye*
Please bring me a bottle of beer.	Принесите мне, пожалуйста, бутылку пива. *preeneeseetye mnye pazhalsta bootilkoo peeva*
Lager, please.	Светлого пива, пожалуйста. *svyetlava peeva pazhalsta*

Vodka   Водка

Vodka is served chilled and always neat in small glasses. The etiquette of vodka drinking is as follows: drain the glass in one gulp, then chase it down with a morsel of food (usually a piece of black bread or salted cucumber). It is common to propose a toast when raising your glass. The smallest measure of vodka you can order is 50 grams (equal to a single), the next measure being 100 grams (equal to a double).

Please give me 50 grams of vodka.	Дайте мне, пожалуйста, 50 грамм водки. *daytye mnye pazhalsta peedeesyat' gram votkee*
I would like …	Я хотел(а) бы... *ya khatyel(a) bi...*
brandy (cognac)/sherry	коньяк/херес *kanyak/khyeres*
whisky/gin/rum	виски/джин/ром *veeskee/dzhin/rom*
liqueur	ликёр *leekyor*
To your good health!	За ваше здоровье! *za vashe zdarov'ye*

Non-alcoholic drinks   Безалкогольные напитки

Stores and kiosks in big towns and cities are full of imported and locally produced soft drinks, fruit juices, and mineral water. The drink called a "cocktail" (коктейль **kakteyl'**), offered in ice-cream parlors, is a non-alcohol soft drink made from fruit juice or lemonade, to which ice cream and sometimes whipped cream is added – an ice-cream soda. Elsewhere this drink is called a "milk cocktail" (молочный коктейль **malochniy kakteyl'**) – a milk shake.

Kvass (квас) is a popular soft drink and a good thirst quencher in the summer when it is sold from small stalls in the street. Kvass, which looks like beer, is made from black bread and yeast.

Coffee   Кофе

Coffee is not a traditional Russian drink. If you want strong coffee, ask for "eastern-style coffee" (кофе по-восточному **kofee pa vastochynamoo**), similar to Turkish coffee. If you order coffee with milk, you'll often get a glass of very sweet coffee with condensed milk.

coffee	кофе *kofye*
black/with milk	чёрный/с молоком *chyorniy/s malakom*
decaffeinated	без кофеина *bees kafeyna*

Tea   Чай

Tea is the most popular Russian beverage. During your stay you will probably see one of the traditional Russian samovars (самовар **samavar**) used to heat the water for tea making. Tea is usually served in glasses, and it is often sweetened with honey or jam rather than sugar.

tea	чай *chyay*
black/with milk	чёрный/с молоком *chyorniy/s malakom*
with lemon	с лимоном *s leemonam*
iced tea	чай со льдом *chyay so l'dom*

Menu Reader

This Menu Reader gives listings under main food group headings. You will see that the Russian words are shown in large type. This is to help you to identify, from a menu that has no English, at least the basic ingredients making up a dish.

Meat, fish, and poultry

мясо	*myasa*	meat (general)
говядина	*gavyadeena*	beef
свинина	*sveeneena*	pork
телятина	*talyateena*	veal
молодая баранина	*maladaya baraneena*	lamb
кура	*koora*	chicken
утка	*ootka*	duck
рыба	*riba*	fish (general)
дары моря	*dari morya*	seafood (general)
икра	*eekra*	caviar
яйца	*yaytsa*	eggs (general)

Vegetables

овощи	_ovashchee_	vegetable(s) (general)
бобы/фасоль	_babi/fasol'_	beans
шпинат	_shpeenat_	spinach
картофель	_kartofeel'_	pototoes
помидоры	_pameedori_	tomatoes
салат	_salat_	lettuce
огурец	_agooryets_	cucumber
морковь	_markof'_	carrrots
лук	_look_	onions
брокколи	_brakolee_	broccoli
капуста	_kapoosta_	cabbage
свёкла	_svyokla_	beetroot

Fruit

фрукты	*frookti*	fruit (general)
яблоко	*yablako*	apple
апельсин	*apeel'seen*	orange
банан	*banan*	banana
дыня	*dinya*	melon
арбуз	*arboos*	watermelon
груша	*groosha*	pear
слива	*sleeva*	plum
клубника	*kloobneeka*	strawberries
киви	*keevee*	kiwi fruit
ананас	*ananas*	pineapple

Staples: bread, rice, pasta, etc.

хлеб	*khlyep*	bread
рис	*rees*	rice
лапша	*lap<u>sha</u>*	noodles
каша	*<u>ka</u>sha*	porridge
макароны	*maka<u>ro</u>ni*	pasta
спагетти	*spag<u>ye</u>tee*	spaghetti
бобовые	*ba<u>bo</u>viye*	beans [pulses]

Basics

соль	*sol'*	salt
перец	*<u>pye</u>reets*	pepper
горчица	*gar<u>chee</u>tsa*	mustard
сахар	*<u>sa</u>khar*	sugar
уксусная	*<u>oo</u>ksoosnaya*	vinaigrette
заправка	*<u>za</u>prafka*	[French dressing]

Basic styles

варёный	*var<u>yo</u>niy*	boiled
жареный	*zh<u>a</u>reeniy*	fried
жаренный на гриле	*zh<u>a</u>reeniy na <u>gree</u>lee*	grilled
жаркое	*zhark<u>oye</u>*	roasted
копчёный	*kap<u>chyo</u>niy*	smoked
паровой	*para<u>voy</u>*	steamed
отварной	*atavar<u>noy</u>*	poached
тушёный	*too<u>sho</u>niy*	stewed
соте	*sa<u>te</u>*	sautéed
фаршированный	*farshee<u>rova</u>niy*	stuffed
маринованный	*maree<u>no</u>vaniy*	marinated

Classic dishes

азу	*azoo*	chopped meat in a savory sauce
бефстроганов	*beefstroganaf*	Beef Stroganoff *strips of beef fillet* *cooked with shallots* *in cream and brandy*
говядина тушёная с кореньями	*gavyadeena* *toshonaya* *s karyenyami*	braised beef with aromatic vegetables
жаркое из свинины с черносливом	*zharkoyl ees* *sveeneeni* *cheernasleevam*	roast pork with plums
утка тушёная с яблоками	*ootka* *tooshonaya* *s yablakamee*	roast duck with apples
котлеты по-киевски	*katlyeti* *pa keeyefskee*	Chicken Kiev *breast of chicken* *stuffed with butter* *and garlic*

чахохбили из кур	*chakhakh<u>bee</u>lee ees koor*	Caucasian chicken casserole *served with tomatoes and lots of onions*
голубцы	*galoop<u>tsi</u>*	cabbage stuffed with rice and meat
пельмени	*peel'<u>mye</u>nee*	stuffed dumplings
шашлык	*shash<u>lik</u>*	Caucasian shashlik *pieces of lamb grilled on skewers*
осетрина под белым соусом	*asee<u>tree</u>na pat <u>bye</u>lim <u>soo</u>osam*	steamed sturgeon in white sauce
осетрина по-русски	*asee<u>tree</u>na pa <u>roo</u>skee*	poached sturgeon served with tomato sauce and vegetables
судак жаренный в тесте	*soo<u>dak</u> <u>zha</u>reeniy f <u>tye</u>stye*	battered pike perch deep fried in batter
судак отварной соус яичный	*soo<u>dak</u> atvarnoy sooos ya<u>eech</u>niy*	poached pike perch in an egg sauce

Drinks

вода	*va<u>da</u>*	water
молоко	*mala<u>ko</u>*	milk
чай	*chay*	tea
кофе	*<u>ko</u>fye*	coffee
шоколад	*shaka<u>lat</u>*	chocolate
водка	*<u>vo</u>tka*	vodka
виски	*<u>vee</u>skee*	whisky
джин	*dzheen*	gin
пиво	*<u>pee</u>va*	beer
вино	*vee<u>no</u>*	wine
шампанское	*sham<u>pan</u>skaya*	champagne
фруктовый сок	*frook<u>to</u>viy sok*	(fruit) juice

апельсиновый сок	*apeel'__see__navay sok*	orange juice
сок из грейпфрута	*sek ees greypf__roo__ta*	grapefruit juice
лимонад	*leema__nat__*	lemonade
кока-кола	*__ko__la*	cola
содовая вода	*__so__davaya va__da__*	soda water
тоник	*__to__neek*	tonic water
молочный коктейль	*malochniy kak__teyl__'*	milk shake
минеральная вода	*meenee__ral__'naya va__da__*	mineral water
квас	*kvas*	soft drink

Snacks

жареный картофель	*zhareeniy kartofeel'*	French fries [chips]
гамбургер	*gamboorgeer*	hamburger
колбаса	*kalbasa*	sausage
омлет	*amlyet*	omelet
бутерброд	*bootirbrot*	sandwich
чипсы	*cheepsi*	potato chips [crisps]
мороженое	*marozheenaya*	ice cream
блины	*bleeni*	pancakes
печенье	*peechyenye*	cookie [biscuit]
пирожное	*peerozhnaya*	cake (small)
торт	*tort*	cake (large)

Soups/soup-based dishes

борщ	**borshch**	borscht *a substantial soup made with beef and vegetables, chiefly beet, served with sour cream*
щи	**shchee**	shchee *cabbage soup with many regional varieties*
бульон	**boolyon**	broth or consommé made from a variety of ingredients
бульон из куры	**boolyon ees koori**	chicken soup
окрошка	**akroshka**	summer soup *cold soup made with cucumber, egg, onion, and sour cream*
суп	**soop**	thick soup usually made with either peas, mushrooms, or potatoes
уха	**ookha**	fish soup

Soups/soup-based dishes (continued)

харчо	*khar<u>cho</u>*	mutton soup – spicy Georgian soup made with mutton and rice
шурпа	*shoor<u>pa</u>*	an Uzbek soup made with mutton, bacon, and tomato

Dairy/soy products

сыр	*sir*	cheese
йогурт	*<u>yo</u>goort*	yogurt
сливки	*<u>slee</u>ftee*	cream
масло	*<u>ma</u>sla*	butter
молоко	*mala<u>ko</u>*	milk
соевый творог	*<u>so</u>yeviy tva<u>rok</u>*	tofu
кефир	*kee<u>feer</u>*	kefir *sour milk, similar to thinner types of plain yogurt*
топлёное молоко	*tap<u>lyo</u>naye mala<u>ko</u>*	baked milk served chilled, similar to junket
сырок	*si<u>rok</u>*	fresh white cheese

Desserts

ватрушка	*vatrooshka*	cottage cheese tart
кисель	*keesyel'*	fruit jelly topped with sugar, milk or cream
компот	*kampot*	fruit compote
оладьи с яблоками	*aladyee s yablakamee*	small apple pancakes
рисовый пудинг	*reesavay poodeeng*	rice pudding
ромовая баба	*romavaya baba*	rum baba
рулет	*roolyet*	sponge roll
яблоко в тесте	*yablaka b tyestye*	apple baked in pastry
блинчики с вареньем	*bleencheekee s varyenyem*	pancakes with jam
пирог	*peerok*	pie or tart served with a variety of fruit or cheese fillings

Travel

ESSENTIAL

1/2/3 ticket(s) to …	один билет/два/три билета в… *adeen beelyet/dva/tree beelyeta v …*
To …, please.	В …, пожалуйста *v … pazhalsta*
one-way [single]	в один конец *v adeen kanyets*
round-trip [return]	туда и обратно *tooda ee abratna*
How much …?	Сколько стоит …? *skol'ka stoeet*

Safety   Безопасность

Beware of pickpockets in crowded places. It is a good idea to keep your money in a money belt.

Would you accompany me to the bus stop?	Проводите меня до автобусной остановки, пожалуйста. *pravadeetye meenya da aftoboosnay astanofkee pazhalsta*
I don't want to … on my own.	Я не хочу … один/одна. *ya nee khachyoo … adeen/adna*
stay here	оставаться здесь *astavat'sa zdyes'*
walk home	идти домой *eettee damoy*
I don't feel safe here.	Я не чувствую себя здесь в безопасности. *ya nee choofsvooyoo seebya zdyes' f beezapasnastee*

Arrival   Прибытие

As well as a valid passport, you will need a visa to visit Russia. You can obtain one from the Russian Embassy, or, perhaps, your travel agent.

Some international airports in Russia now have red and green custom's channels. The red channels often have long lines, due to "shuttle" traders. However, if you need to have currency and customs declaration forms stamped to avoid being detained upon leaving Russia because of any valuable items, such as photographic equipment and jewelry, which you brought with you, you need to go through the red channel. Currently, declaration forms are not stamped if you go through the green channel. Check on current regulations before setting off.

If you intend to stay in Russia for more than three months, you must produce a medical certificate showing that you are not HIV positive. Keep your passport with you at all times, especially if you have a dark complexion. People who look as if they are from the Caucuses/Chechnya are frequently stopped by the police.

The chart below shows what duty-free items you can bring into the country.

Cigarettes	Cigars	Tobacco	Spirits	Wine
250	250	250 g.	1 l.	2 l.

Passport control   Паспортный контроль

Ваш паспорт, пожалуйста	Can I see your passport, please?
Цель Вашего визита?	What's the purpose of your visit?
С кем Вы здесь?	Who are you here with?

We have a joint passport.

У нас общий паспорт.
oo nas opshchiy pasport

The children are on this passport.

Дети вписаны в паспорт.
dyetee fpeesani f pasport

I'm here on vacation [holiday]/business.

Я здесь в отпуске/по делу.
ya zdyes' v otpooskye/pa dyeloo

I'm just passing through.

Я проездом. *ya prayezdam*

I'm going to …

Я еду в … *ya yedoo v …*

I'm on my own.

Я один (одна). *ya adeen (adna)*

I'm with my family.

Я с семьёй. *ya s seemyey*

I'm with a group.

Я с группой. *ya s groopay*

WHO ARE YOU WITH? ➤ 120

Customs   Таможня

I have only the normal allowances.	У меня только то, что разрешается. *oo meenya tol'ka to shto rasreeshayetsa*
It's a gift/for my personal use.	Это подарок/для личного пользования. *eta padarak/dlya leechnava pol'zavaneeya*

У Вас есть что-нибудь предъявить таможне?	Do you have anything to declare?
Вам надо платить пошлину.	You must pay duty on this.
Где Вы это купили?	Where did you buy this?
Откройте эту сумку.	Please open this bag.
У Вас есть ещё багаж?	Do you have any more luggage?

I would like to declare …	Я хочу предъявить ... таможне. *ya khachyoo preedyaveet' ... tamozhnye*
I don't understand.	Я не понимаю. *ya nee paneemayoo*
Does anyone here speak English?	Здесь кто-нибудь говорит по-английски? *zdyes' ktoneebood' gavareet pa angleeyskee*

ПАСПОРТНЫЙ КОНТРОЛЬ	PASSPORT CONTROL
ГРАНИЦА	BORDER CROSSING
ТАМОЖНЯ	CUSTOMS
СВОБОДНЫЙ КОРИДОР	NOTHING TO DECLARE
ТАМОЖЕННЫЙ ДОСМОТР	GOODS tTO DECLARE
МИЛИЦИЯ	POLICE
ТОВАРЫ БЕЗ ПОШЛИНЫ	DUTY-FREE GOODS

Duty-free shopping   Покупка товаров без пошлины

What currency is this in?	В какой это валюте? *f kakoy eta valyootye*
Can I pay in …	Можно платить в ... *mozhna plateet' v ...*
dollars/rubles/pounds	долларах/рублях/фунтах *dollarakh/rooblyakh/foontakh*

Plane   Самолёт

The former national airline, Aeroflot, has been broken up into many different companies, producing a confusing array of domestic carriers. International flights with an internal stopover are generally more realiable.

Tickets and reservations   Заказ билетов

When is the … flight to Moscow?	Когда … рейс в Москву? *kagda … reys v maskvoo*
first/next/last	первый/следующий/последний *pyerviy/slyedooyooshchyeey/paslyedneey*
I'd like two … tickets to Moscow.	Мне надо два билета … в Москву? *mnye nada dva beelyeta … v maskvoo*
one-way [single]	в один конец *v adeen kanyets*
round-trip [return]	туда и обратно *tooda ee abratna*
first class	первый класс *pyerviy klass*
business class	бизнес класс *beeznees klass*
economy class	пассажирский класс *passazhirskeey klass*
How much is a flight to …?	Сколько стоит билет в …? *skol'ka stoeet beelyet v …*
Are there any supplements/ discounts?	Есть какая-нибудь доплата/скидка? *yest' kakaya-neebood' daplata/skeetka*
I'd like to … my reservation for flight number …	Я хотел(а) бы … мой заказ на рейс номер … *ya khatyel(a) bi … moy zakas na reys nomeer …*
cancel	отменить *atmeeneet'*
change	поменять *pameenyat'*
confirm	подтвердить *pattveerdeet'*

Inquiries about the flight   Справки о полётах

How long is the flight?	Сколько длится полёт? *skol'ka dleetsa palyot*
What time does the plane leave?	Во сколько вылетает самолёт? *va skol'ka vileetayet samalyot*
What time will we arrive?	Во сколько мы прилетаем? *va skol'ka mi preeleetayem*
What time do I have to check in?	Во сколько регистрация? *va skol'ka reegeestratsiya*

Checking in   Регистрация

Where is the check-in desk for flight …?

Где регистрация на рейс в …? *gdye reegeestratsiya na reys v …*

I have …

У меня … *oo meenya …*

three cases to check in

три чемодана *tree chyeemadana*

two pieces of hand luggage

два места ручной клади *dva myesta roochnoy kladee*

How much luggage is allowed free?

Сколько багажа можно провести бесплатно? *skol'ka bagazha mozhna praveestee beesplatna*

Ваш билет/паспорт, пожалуйста.	Your ticket/passport, please.
Вам место у окна или боковое?	Would you like a window or an aisle seat?
Курящий или некурящий?	Smoking or non-smoking?
Проходите в зал ожидания.	Please go through to the departure lounge.
Сколько у Вас мест багажа?	How many pieces of baggage do you have?
У Вас перевес багажа.	You have excess baggage.
Вы должны заплатить … рублей.	You'll have to pay a supplement of … rubles.
Этот слишком тяжёлый/ большой для ручной клади.	That's too heavy/large for hand baggage.
Вы сами упаковывали багаж?	Did you pack these bags yourself?
Там есть острые или электрические предметы?	Do they contain any sharp or electronic items?

ПРИБЫТИЕ	ARRIVALS
ОТПРАВЛЕНИЕ	DEPARTURES
СЛУЖБА КОНТРОЛЯ	SECURITY CHECK
НЕ ОСТАВЛЯЙТЕ БАГАЖ БЕЗ ПРИСМОТРА	DO NOT LEAVE BAGS UNATTENDED

BAGGAGE ➤ 71

Information Справки

Is there any delay on flight …?	Рейс в … задерживается? *reys v … za<u>dy</u>erzhivaeetsa*
How late will it be?	На сколько задерживается? *na <u>skol</u>'ka za<u>dy</u>erzhivaeetsa*
Has the flight from … landed?	Самолёт из … прибыл? *samal<u>yot</u> eez … <u>pree</u>bil*
Which gate does flight … leave from?	С какого выхода посадка на рейс …? *s ka<u>ko</u>va <u>vi</u>khada pa<u>sa</u>tka na reys*

Boarding/In-flight Посадка/В полёте

Your boarding card, please.	Ваш посадочный талон, пожалуйста. *vash pa<u>sa</u>dachniy ta<u>lon</u> pa<u>zhal</u>sta*
Could I have a drink/ something to eat, please?	Можно что-нибудь попить/поесть? *mozhna shto<u>nee</u>bood' pa<u>peet</u>'/pa<u>yest</u>'*
Please wake me for the meal.	Разбудите меня, когда принесут еду. *razboo<u>dee</u>tye mee<u>nya</u> kag<u>da</u> preenee<u>soot</u> ee<u>doo</u>*
What time will we arrive?	Во сколько мы прилетаем? *va <u>skol</u>'ka mi preelee<u>ta</u>yem*
An air sickness bag, please.	Дайте гигиенический пакет, пожалуйста. *<u>day</u>tye geegeeye<u>nee</u>chyeeskeey pa<u>kyet</u> pa<u>zhal</u>sta*

Arrival Прибытие

Where is/are the …?	Где …? *gdye …*
currency exchange	обмен валюты *ab<u>myen</u> va<u>lyoo</u>ti*
buses	автобусы *af<u>to</u>boosi*
car rental [hire]	прокат автомобилей *pra<u>kat</u> aftama<u>bee</u>leey*
exit	выход *<u>vi</u>khat*
taxis	такси *tak<u>see</u>*
telephone	телефон *teelee<u>fon</u>*
Is there a bus into town?	Есть автобус в город? *yest' af<u>to</u>boos v <u>go</u>rat*
How do I get to the … hotel?	Как мне добраться до отеля …? *kak mnye da<u>brat</u>'sa da a<u>tye</u>lya*

Baggage Багаж

Porter! Excuse me!
Носильщик! Можно вас!
naseel'shchyeek mozhna vas

Could you take my luggage to …?
Подвезите мой багаж до …
padveezeetye moy bagash da …

a taxi/bus
такси/автобуса *taksee/aftoboosa*

Where is/are the …?
Где …? *gdye …*

luggage carts [trolleys]
багажные тележки
bagazhniye teelyeshkee

luggage lockers
камеры хранения
kameeri khranyeneeya

luggage check [left-luggage office]
багажное отделение
bagazhnaye addeelyeneeye

baggage reclaim
выдача багажа *vidachya bagazha*

Where is the baggage from flight …?
Где багаж рейса из …?
gdye bagash reysa eez …

Loss, damage, and theft Потеря, повреждение и кража

My luggage has been lost/stolen.
У меня пропал/украли багаж.
oo meenya prapal/ookralee bagazh

My suitcase was damaged.
Мне повредили чемодан.
mnye pavreedeelee chyeemadan

Our luggage has not arrived.
Наш багаж не прибыл.
nash bagash nee preebil

Do you have claim forms?
У Вас есть бланки?
oo vas yest' blankee

Как выглядит Ваш багаж?	What does your baggage look like?
У Вас есть багажный талон?	Do you have the claim check [reclaim tag]?
Ваш багаж …	Your baggage …
могли отправить в …	may have been sent to …
может прибыть сегодня позднее	may arrive later today
Пожалуйста, приходите завтра.	Please come back tomorrow.
Позвоните по этому номеру, чтобы узнать, прибыл ли багаж	Call this number to check if your baggage has arrived.

POLICE ➤ 152; COLOR ➤ 143

Train   Поезд

The Russian writer Nikolay Gogol (1809—1852) wrote that the roads in Russia were bad. They still are. But a very comprehensive rail network was built during the Soviet era.

Sadly, train stations can be frequented by drunks and homeless people, and are not the exciting and animated places they were a few years ago. Overnight trains — while remaining a wonderful way to travel around Russia — are not as safe as they used to be. So, check with your embassy or travel agent before traveling.

For long journeys make your reservations in advance. For short trips out to the suburbs check with your Intourist representative or ask at you hotel beforehand to see if there are any travel limits.

Экспресс *ehkspryes*

Long-distance express with luxury coaches; stops only at main stations.

Скорый поезд *skorriy poeezd*

Standard long-distance train; stopping at main stations.

Пассажирский поезд *passazhirskeey poeezd*

Inter-city train; doesn't stop at very small stations; regular fare. This type of train is seldom available for tourist travel.

Электричка *eeleektreechka*

Local train stopping at almost every station.

Международный вагон *meezhdoonarodniy vagon*

Sleeper with individual compartments (usually double) and washing facilities.

Купейный вагон *koopyeyniy vagon*

Car with compartments for four people; berths with blankets and pillows. You can choose between "soft" (first) class, and "hard" (second) class.

Мягкий вагон *myakhkeey vagon*

"Soft" (first) class; individual compartments for two or four people.

Жёсткий вагон *zhostkeey vagon*

"Hard" (second) class.

Плацкартный вагон *platskartniy vagon*

Second class only; no individual compartments, but with sleeping places.

To the station На вокзал

| How do I get to the train station? | Как мне добраться до вокзала? *kak mnye dabrat'sa da vagzala* |

| Do trains to Moscow leave from … station? *paeezda na* | Поезда на Москву отправляются с ... вокзала? *maskvoo atpravlyayootsa s ... vagzala* |

| Is it far? | Это далеко? *eta daleeko* |

| Can I leave my car here? | Можно здесь оставить машину? *mozhna zdyes' astaveet' mashinoo* |

At the station На вокзале

Where is/are the …?	Где …? *gdye …*
baggage check [left-luggage office]	багажное отделение *bagazhnaye addeelyeneeye*
currency exchange office	обмен валюты *abmyen valyooti*
information desk	справочное бюро *spravachnaye byooro*
lost-and-found office [lost-property office]	бюро находок *byooro nakhodak*
luggage lockers	камеры хранения *kameeri khranyeneeya*
platforms	платформы *platformi*
snack bar	буфет *boofyet*
ticket office	билетные кассы *beelyetniye kassi*
waiting room	зал ожидания *zal azhidaneeya*

ВХОД	ENTRANCE
ВЫХОД	EXIT
К ПЛАТФОРМАМ	TO PLATFORMS
ИНФОРМАЦИЯ	INFORMATION
ЗАКАЗ БИЛЕТОВ	RESERVATIONS
ПРИБЫТИЕ	ARRIVALS
ОТПРАВЛЕНИЕ	DEPARTURES

DIRECTIONS ➤ 94

Tickets Билеты

There are now many travel agencies in Russia where you can
buy train tickets. Many hotels can also obtain tickets for you.
Tickets purchased at a train station may be cheaper, but will
probably cost you more in time and nervous energy.

I'd like a ... ticket to St. Petersburg.	Я хотел(а) бы билет ... до Санкт-Петербурга. *ya khatyel(a) bi beelyet ... da sankt peeteerboorga*
one-way [single]	в один конец *v adeen kanyets*
round-trip [return]	туда и обратно *tooda ee abratna*
first/second class	мягкий/купейный вагон *myakhkeey/koopyeyniy vagon*
concessionary	плацкарта *platskarta*
I'd like to reserve a(n) ...	Я хотел(а) бы заказать ... *ya khatyel(a) bi zakazat' ...*
seat	место *myesta*
window seat	у окна *oo akna*
berth	полку *polkoo*
Is there a sleeping car [sleeper]?	Это купейный/плацкартный вагон? *eta koopyeyniy/platskartniy vagon*
I'd like a(n) ... berth.	Я хотел(а) бы ... полку. *ya khatyel(a) bi ... polkoo*
upper/lower	верхнюю/нижнюю *vyerkhnyooyoo/neezhnyooyoo*
Can I buy a ticket on board?	Можно купить билет в поезде? *mozhna koopeet' beelyet v poyezdye*

Price Цена

How much is that?	Сколько стоит? *skol'ka stoeet*
Is there a discount for ...?	Есть скидка на ...? *yest' skeetka na ...*
children/families	детей/семейные группы *deetyey/seemyeyniye groopi*
senior citizens	пенсионерам *peenseeanyeram*
students	студентам *stoodyentam*
Do you offer a cheap same-day round-trip [return] fare?	Можно купить дешёвый билет туда и обратно? *mozhna koopeet' deeshoviy beelyet tooda ee abratna*

Queries   Справки

Do I have to change trains?	Мне надо делать пересадку? *mnye **nada** **dyelat'** peereesatkoo*
Is it a direct train?	Это прямой поезд? *eta preemoy poeest*
You have to change at …	Вам надо делать пересадку в … *vam **nada** **dyelat'** peereesatkoo v …*
How long is this ticket valid for?	Сколько действителен этот билет? *skol'ka deestveeteeleen etat beelyet*
Can I take my bicycle on to the train?	Можно провезти велосипед в поезде? *mozhna praveestee veelaseepyet f poeezdye*
Can I return on the same ticket?	Это обратный билет? *eta abratniy beelyet*
In which car [coach] is my seat?	В каком вагоне моё место? *f kakom vagonye mayo myesta*
Is there a dining car on the train?	В поезде есть ресторан? *f poeezdye yest' reestaran*

> – ya khatyel(a) bi beelyet da vladeemeera, pazhalsta.
> – tol'ka tooda eelee tooda ee abratna?
> – tooda ee abratna pazhalsta.
> – s vas peedeesyat rooblyey.
> – mnye nada dyelat' peereesatkoo?
> – da eta s peereesatkay v maskvye.
> – spaseeba. da sveedaneeya.

Train times   Расписание поездов

Could I have a timetable, please?	Можно расписание, пожалуйста? *mozhna raspeesaneeye pazhalsta*
When is the … train to Vladimir?	Когда … поезд до Владимира? *kagda … poeezd da vladeemeera*
first/next/last	первый/следующий/последний *pyerviy /slyedooyooshchyeey/paslyedneey*
There's a train to Vladimir at …	Есть поезд до Владимира в … *yest' poeezd da vladeemeera v …*

How frequent are the trains to …?	Как часто идут поезда до …? *kak chyasta eedoot paeezda da …*
once/twice a day	один раз/два раза в день *adeen ras/dva raza v dyen'*
five times a day	пять раз в день *pyat' ras v dyen'*
every hour	каждый час *kazhdiy chyas*
What time do they leave?	Во сколько они отправляются? *va skol'ka anee atpravlyayootsa*
on the hour	каждый час *kazhdiy chyas*
20 minutes past the hour	каждые 20 минут *kazhdiye dvatsat' meenoot*
What time does the train stop at …?	Во сколько поезд останавливается в …? *va skol'ka poeezd astanavleevaeetsa v …*
What time does the train arrive in …?	Во сколько поезд прибывает в …? *va skol'ka poeezd preebivayet v …*
How long is the trip [journey]?	Сколько длится поездка? *skol'ka dleetsa payestka*
Is the train on time?	Поезд прибывает вовремя? *poeest preebivayet vovreemya*

Departures   Отправление

Which platform does the train to … leave from?	С какой платформы отходит поезд до …? *s kakoy platformi atkhodeet poeezd da …*
Where is platform 4?	Где платформа номер четыре? *gdye platforma nomeer chyeetiree*
over there	вон там *von tam*
on the left/right	налево/направо *nalyeva/naprava*
under the underpass	через подземный переход *chyeereez padzyemniy peereekhot*
Where do I change for …?	Где мне делать пересадку на …? *gdye mnye dyelat' peereesatkoo na …*
How long will I have to wait for a connection?	Сколько нужно ждать поезда на пересадку? *skol'ka noozhna zhdat' poeezda na peereesatkoo*

TIME ➤ 220; DIRECTIONS ➤ 94

Boarding Посадка

Is this the right platform for …?

Поезд до … отходит с этой платформы?
poeezd da … atkhodeet s etiy platformi

Is this the train to …?

Это поезд до …?
eta poeezd da …

Is this seat taken?

Это место занято? *eta myesta zaneeta*

I think that's my seat.

Мне кажется, это моё место.
mnye kazhetsa eta mayo myesta

Here's my reservation.

Вот мой билет. *vot moy beelyet*

Are there any seats/berths available?

Есть свободные места/полки?
yest' svabodniye meesta/polkee

Do you mind if …?

Не возражаете, если…?
nee vazrazhaeetye yeslee …

I sit here

я сяду здесь *ya syadoo zdyes'*

I open the window

я открою окно *ya atkroyoo akno*

On the journey В дороге

On long distance trains the attendant (проводник **pravadneek**) will check your ticket and may offer you some tea. There is often a dining car, but even if one is advertised it is still a good idea to bring food with you. And take plenty of soft drinks or mineral water. Trains can be very hot and stuffy. If you are in a separate compartment, secure the door from inside before you go to sleep. Take some strong string with you for this.

How long are we stopping here for?

Сколько мы здесь стоим?
skol'ka mi zdyes' staeem

When do we get to …?

Когда мы будем в …?
kagda mi boodyem v …

Have we passed …?

Мы проехали…? *mi prayekhalee …*

Where is the dining/ sleeping car?

В каком вагоне ресторан?
f kakom vagonye reestaran

Where is my berth?

Где моя полка? *gdye maya polka*

I've lost my ticket.

Я потерял(а) билет.
ya pateeryal(a) beelyet

СТОП-КРАН	EMERGENCY BRAKE
АВТОМАТИЧЕСКИЕ ДВЕРИ	AUTOMATIC DOORS
ВЫЗОВ ПРОВОДНИКА	ALARM

Long-distance bus [Coach]
Междугородный автобус

There are long-distance buses between towns in Russia, but the network is not as accessible as the rail network — you will need to ask around to find out where the terminus is for a particular destination.

Where is the bus [coach] station?	Где автобусная станция? *gdye aftoboosnaya stantsiya*
When's the next bus [coach] to …?	Когда следующий автобус до …? *kagda slyedooyooshchyeey aftoboos da …*
Which bus stop [bay] does it leave from?	С какой стоянки отправляется? *s kakoy stayankee atpravlyaeetsa*
Where are the bus stops [coach bays]?	Где стоянка автобусов? *gdye stayanka aftoboosaf*
Does the bus [coach] stop at …?	Этот автобус останавливается в …? *etat aftoboos astanavleevaeetsa v …*
How long does the trip [journey] take?	Сколько длится поездка? *skol'ka dleetsa payestka*

Bus/Streetcar [Tram]   Автобус/Трамвай

Buses are not as fast as the subway [metro], and run less frequently; on the other hand, you see more of the city. The fare is standard, regardless of the distance (but you can't change buses on the same ticket). It is a good idea to buy a booklet of tickets at a newsstand or subway station, although you can also get one on the bus, from the driver.

Where is the terminal [bus station]?	Где автобусная станция/кольцо? *gdye aftoboosnaya stantsiya/kal'tso*
Where can I get a bus/streetcar [tram] to …?	Где я могу сесть на автобус/трамвай до …? *gdye ya magoo syest' na aftoboos/tramvay da …*

Остановка вон там/вниз по улице.	You need that stop over there/down the road.
Вам нужен автобус номер …	You need bus number …
Вам нужно делать пересадку в …	You must change buses at …

АВТОБУСНАЯ ОСТАНОВКА	BUS STOP
ПО ТРЕБОВАНИЮ	REQUEST STOP
НЕ КУРИТЬ	NO SMOKING
(ЗАПАСНЫЙ) ВЫХОД	(EMERGENCY) EXIT

DIRECTIONS ➤ 94; TIME ➤ 220

Buying tickets   Покупка билетов

Where can I buy tickets?	Где можно купить билеты? _gdye mozhna koopeet' beelyeti_
A … ticket to the center, please.	Билет … до центра, пожалуйста. _beelyet … da tsyentra pazhalasta_
one-way [single]	в один конец _v adeen kanyets_
round-trip [return]	туда и обратно _tooda ee abratna_
day/weekly/monthly	на день/на неделю/ на месяц _na dyen'/na needyelyoo/na myeseets_
A booklet of tickets, please.	Книжку талонов, пожалуйста. _kneeshkoo talonaf pazhalasta_
How much is it to …?	Сколько стоит билет до …? _skol'ka stoeet beelyet da …_

Traveling   Поездка

Is this the right bus/streetcar [tram] to …?	Этот автобус/трамвай идёт до …? _etat aftoboos/tramvay eedyot da …_
Could you tell me when to get off?	Вы скажите мне где выходить? _vi skazhitye mnye gdye vikhadeet'_
Do I have to change buses?	Мне нужно делать пересадку? _mnye noozhna dyelat' peereesatkoo_
How many stops are there to …?	Сколько остановок до …? _skol'ka astanovak da …_
Next stop, please!	На следующей, пожалуйста. _na slyedooyooshchyee pazhalsta_

– eezveeneetye etat avtoboos eedyot da garsavyeta?
– da.
– adeen da garsavyeta pazhalsta.
– s vas adeen roobl'.
– vi skazheetye mnye gdye vikhadeet'?
– eta chyeetiree astanofkee atsyooda.

NUMBERS ➤ 216; DIRECTIONS ➤ 94

Subway [Metro]   Метро

The subway [metro] is the fastest and most convenient way of getting around in town. There are good networks in Moscow, St. Petersburg, and some other big cities. Moscow has the most extensive subway system, which is worth a visit for its fabulous décor alone. It runs from 6 a.m. to 1 a.m. The fare is standard, regardless of the distance traveled. You'll need to buy some tokens (жетоны **zhetoni**) at the counter and drop one in the token machine at the entrance. If you plan to travel around the city a lot, you may decide to buy a pass (единый билет **yedeeniy beelyet**), valid for 8 days, 16 days, or monthly, for travel on the subway, bus, trolleybus, and streetcar [tram].

General inquiries   Общие вопросы

Where's the nearest subway [metro] station?	Где ближайшая станция метро? *gdye bleezhayshaya stantsiya meetro*
Where can I buy a ticket?	Где можно купить билет? *gdye mozhna koopeet' beelyet*
Could I have a map of the subway [metro], please?	Где можно посмотреть схему метро? *gdye mozhna pasmatryet' skhyemoo meetro*

Traveling   Поездка

Which line should I take for …?	По какой линии ехать до …? *pa kakoy leeneeyee yekhat' da …*
Is this the right train for …?	Этот поезд идёт до …? *etat poeest eedyot da …*
Which stop do I get off at for …?	Где мне выходить у …? *gdye mnye vikhadeet' oo …*
How many stops is it to …?	Сколько остановок до …? *skol'ka astanovak da …*
Is the next stop …?	Следующая …? *slyedooyooshchyaya …*
Where are we?	Где мы находимся? *gdye mi nakhodeemsa*
Where do I change for …?	Где делать пересадку до …? *gdye dyelat' peereesatkoo da …*
What time is the last train to …?	Когда отправляется последний поезд до …? *kagda atpravlyaeetsya paslyedneey poyeezd da …*

ПЕРЕСАДКА НА …   TO OTHER LINES/TRANSFER

NUMBERS ➤ 216; BUYING TICKETS ➤ 74, 79

Ferry Паром

There are many rivers and lakes in Russia which have
regular ferry services. This is especially important in Siberia
where there are few roads.

When is the … car ferry to Volgograd?	Когда … паром до Волгограда? *kagda … param da Volgagrada*
first/next/last	первый/следующий/последний *pyerviy/slyedooyooshchyeey/paslyedneey*
hovercraft/ship	ракета/пароход *rakyeta/parakhot*
A round-trip [return] ticket for …	Билет до … туда и обрано. *beelyet da … tooda ee abratna*
one car and one trailer [caravan]	одна машина и один трейлер *adna mashina ee adeen tryeyleer*
two adults and three children	двое взрослых и трое детей *dvoye vzroslikh ee troye deetyey*
I want to reserve a … cabin.	Я хочу заказать … каюту. *ya khachyoo zakazat' … kayootoo*
single/double	одноместную/двухместную *adnamyestnooyoo/dvookhmyestnooyoo*

СПАСАТЕЛЬНЫЙ КРУГ	LIFE PRESERVER [LIFE BELT]
СПАСАТЕЛЬНАЯ ШЛЮПКА	LIFEBOAT
МЕСТО СБОРА	MUSTER STATION
ПРОХОД ЗАПРЕЩЁН!	NO ACCESS

Boat trips Водные экскурсии

Is there a …?	У вас есть…? *oo vas yest' …*
boat trip	водная экскурсия *vodnaya ekskoorseeya*
river cruise	речной круиз *reechnoy krooeez*
What time does it leave/return?	Когда она начинается/кончается? *kagda ana nacheenayeetsya/kanchayeetsya*
Where can we buy tickets?	Где можно купить билеты? *gdye mozhna koopeet' beelyeti*

TIME ➤ 220; BUYING TICKETS ➤ 74, 79

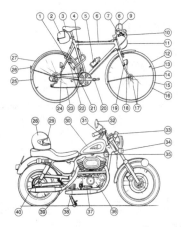

1 brake pad тормозная колодка f *tarmaznaya kalotka*
2 bicycle bag подседельная сумка f *patseedyel'naya soomka*
3 saddle седло n *seedlo*
4 pump насос m *nasos*
5 water bottle бутылка с водой f *bootilka s vadoy*
6 frame рама f *rama*
7 handlebars руль m *rool'*
8 bell звонок m *zvanok*
9 brake cable тросик тормоза m *troseek tormaza*
10 gear shift переключатель скоростей m *peereeklyoochateel' skarastyey*
11 gear cable тросик переключателя скоростей m *troseek peereeklyoochateelya skarastyey*
12 inner tube камера f *kameera*
13 front/back wheel переднее/заднее колесо n *peeryedneeye/zadneeye kaleeso*
14 axle ось f *os'*
15 tire протектор m *pratyektar*
16 wheel колесо n *kaleeso*
17 spokes спицы fpl *speetsi*
18 bulb лампа f *lampa*
19 headlight [headlamp] фара f *fara*
20 pedal педаль f *peedal'*
21 lock замок m *zamok*

22 generator генератор m *geeneeratar*
23 chain цепь f *tsyep'*
24 rear light задняя фара f *zadnyaya fara*
25 rim обод m *obat*
26 reflector отражатель m *atrazhateel'*
27 fender фартук m *fartook*
28 helmet шлем m *shlyem*
29 visor щиток m *shcheetok*
30 fuel tank топливный бак m *topleevniy bak*
31 clutch lever рычаг сцепления m *richak stseeplyeneeya*
32 mirror зеркало n *zyerkala*
33 ignition switch зажигание n *zazheeganeeya*
34 turn signal [indicator] указатель поворота m *ookazateel' pavarota*
35 horn звуковой сигнал m *zvookavoy seegnal*
36 engine двигатель m *dveegateel'*
37 gear shift [lever] рычаг переключения передач m *richak peereeklyoochateelya peereedach*
38 kick stand упор m *oopor*
39 exhaust pipe выхлопная труба f *vikhlapnaya trooba*
40 chain guard щиток цепи m s *hcheetok tsepee*

REPAIRS ➤ 89

Bicycle/Motorbike
Велосипеды/Мотоциклы

I'd like to rent [hire] a …	Я хотел(а) бы взять напрокат … *ya khatyel(a) bi vzyat' naprakat …*
3-/10-speed bicycle	3-/10-скоростной велосипед *tryokh/deesateeskarastnoy veelaseepyet*
moped	мопед *mapyet*
motorbike	мотоцикл *matatseekal*
How much does it cost per day/week?	Сколько это стоит в день/неделю? *skol'ka eta stoeet v dyen'/needyelyoo*
Do you require a deposit?	Нужно платить аванс? *noozhna plateet' avans*
The brakes don't work.	Тормоза не работают. *tarmaza nee rabotayoot*
There are no lights.	Нет фар. *nyet far*
The front/rear tire [tyre] has a flat [puncture].	Передняя/задняя шина проколота. *peeryednyaya/zadnyaya shina prakolota*

Hitchhiking   Голосовать на дороге

Hitchhiking in Russia can be dangerous and is not recommended for foreigners, except in cases of extreme emergency.

Where are you heading?	Куда Вы едете? *kooda vi yedeetye*
I'm heading for …	Я еду в … *ya yedoo v …*
Can you give me/us a lift?	Вы можете меня/нас подвезти? *vi mozhetye meenya/nas padveestee*
Is that on the way to …?	Это по пути в …? *eta pa pootee …*
Could you drop me off …?	Высадите меня …, пожалуйста. *visadeetye meenya … pazhalsta*
here	здесь *zdyes'*
at the … exit	у поворота *oo pavarota*
downtown	в центре *f tsentrye*
Thanks for the lift.	Спасибо, что подвезли. *spaseeba shto padveezlee*

DIRECTIONS ➤ 94; NUMBERS ➤ 216

Taxi/Cab Такси

In the early 1990s taxis, which were all state owned, almost disappeared. Now more and more private taxi companies are being set up. Despite this there are still few taxis on the streets.

Most people hail private cars in the street. If you do this, make sure that the driver understands where you want to go. In addition, fix the price before getting in. Warning: Never get into a car if somebody else is in it with the driver. Be especially careful after dark.

Where can I get a taxi?	Где можно взять такси? *kak vizvat' taksee pa teeleefonoo*
Do you have the number for a taxi?	Как вызвать такси по телефону? *kak vizvat' taksee pa teeleefonoo*
I'd like a taxi …	Мне нужно такси … *mnye noozhna taksee …*
now	сейчас *seechyas*
in an hour	через час *chyeereez chyas*
for tomorrow at 9:00	на завтра на 9:00 *na zaftra na devyat*
The pick-up address is …, going to …	Заберите по адресу ..., и езжайте по адресу … *zabeereetye pa adreesoo …, ee eezzhzhaytye pa adreesoo …*

СВОБОДНО	FOR HIRE

Please take me to (the) …	Пожалуйста, отвезите меня … *pazhalsta atveezeetye meenya …*
airport	в аэропорт *v aeraport*
train station	на вокзал *na vagzal*
this address	по этому адресу *pa etamu adreesoo*
How much will it cost?	Сколько это будет стоить? *skol'ka eta boodeet stoeet'*
How much is that?	Сколько с меня? *skol'ka s meenya*
You said … rubles.	Вы сказали … рублей. *vi skazalee … rooblyey*
Keep the change.	Оставьте сдачу. *astaf'tye zdachyoo*

> – na vagzal, pazhalsta.
> – sadeetyees'.
> – skol'ka eta boodeet stoeet'?
> – sorak pyat' rooblyey. … preeyekhalee
> – astaf'tye zdachyoo.

Car/Automobile Машина

If you want to rent a car you must be 21 and have an international driver's license ▶ 86. If you are coming from Europe and want to take your car, you will need an international driving license, car registration papers, and insurance. It is essential to obtain up-to-date information on precisely what documents you need, so check with your travel agent or with the Russian Embassy. In both cases, however, be aware that car theft is big business in Russia, and that anything left unattended in the car is likely to be stolen. If you have a removable radio-cassette player, take it with you. It is also a good idea to take the windshield [windscreen] wipers!

When driving you must have an international driver's license and the car's registration papers. You should also check with your travel agent or the Russian Embassy as to what other documents you may need.

Russian drivers do not give way to pedestrians at pedestrian crossings. So if you are on foot, beware! And if you are driving, remember that the trucks and cars behind you will not stop!

Be especially careful at traffic-light controled intersections. Some drivers go through red lights well after they have changed. Others set off before their lights have turned to green.

In addition, you should observe speed limits as there are lots of radar traps. And always wear a seat belt — it is compulsory.

Conversion chart

km	1	10	20	30	40	50	60	70	80	90	100	110	120	130
miles	0.62	6	12	19	25	31	37	44	50	56	62	68	74	81

Speed limits

Speed limits	Cars	Motorbikes
Residential/ Built-up areas	60 km/h	60 km/h

Fuel

Gasoline	Premium [super]/Regular	Diesel
бензин	бензин А-93/бензин А-98	дизельное топливо
bee<u>nzeen</u>	*bee<u>nzeen</u> a deevee<u>nos</u>ta tree/ bee<u>nzeen</u> a deevee<u>nos</u>ta <u>vos</u>eem*	*<u>dee</u>zeel'naya <u>top</u>leeva*

85

Car rental   Прокат автомобилей

If you plan on renting a car, try to make arrangements in advance via your travel agent. Cars can be rented on the spot through Intourist and at some hotels. Locally published English-language newspapers, available free from many hotels and foreign-currency stores (Берёзка **beeryoska**), advertise car rental companies. Credit cards are accepted by the large car rental companies. To rent a car you must be 21 and have an international driver's license.

Where can I rent a car?	Где можно взять машину напрокат? *gdye <u>mozh</u>na vzyat' mashinoo napra<u>kat</u>*
I'd like to rent a(n) …	Я хотел(а) бы взять машину … напрокат. *ya kha<u>tyel</u>(a) bi vzyat' mashinoo … napra<u>kat</u>*
2-/4-door car	с двумя/четырьмя дверями *z dvoo<u>mya</u>/chyeetir'<u>mya</u> dvee<u>rya</u>mee*
automatic	с автоматической трансмиссией *s afta<u>ma</u>teecheeskay trans<u>mee</u>seeyey*
car with 4-wheel drive	с полным приводом *s <u>pol</u>nim <u>pree</u>vadam*
car with air conditioning	с кондиционером *s kandeetsiany<u>e</u>ram*
I'd like it for a day/week.	Я хотел(а) бы на день/неделю. *ya kha<u>tyel</u>(a) bi na dyeny/need<u>ye</u>lyoo*
How much does it cost per day/week?	Сколько стоит на день/неделю? *<u>skol</u>'ka <u>sto</u>eet na dyen'/need<u>ye</u>lyoo*
Is mileage/insurance included?	Километраж/страховка входит? *keelameet<u>rash</u>/strah<u>of</u>ka <u>fkho</u>deet*
Are there special weekend rates?	Есть особый тариф по выходным? *yest' a<u>so</u>biy ta<u>reef</u> pa vikhad<u>nim</u>*
Can I leave the car at …?	Можно возвратить машину в …? *<u>mozh</u>na vazvra<u>teet</u>' mashinoo v …*
What kind of fuel does it take?	Какой бензин нужен? *ka<u>koy</u> been<u>zeen</u> <u>noo</u>zheen*
Where is high [full]/ low [dipped] beam?	Где дальний/ближний свет? *gdye <u>dal</u>'neey/<u>bleezh</u>neey svyet*
Could I have full insurance, please?	Можно полную страховку, пожалуйста? *<u>mozh</u>na <u>pol</u>nooyoo strah<u>of</u>koo pa<u>zhal</u>sta*

86

Gas [Petrol] station Автосервис

New gas [petrol] stations are springing up like mushrooms,
and gas is now usually available in urban areas. However,
many Russians keep a full 20-liter gas container on board
when going on long trips, just in case.

Where's the next gas [petrol] station?	Где ближайшая заправочная станция? gdye blee_zhay_shaya za_pra_vachnaya stantsiya
Is it self-service?	Здесь самообслуживание? zdyes' samaap_sloo_zhivaneeye
Fill it up, please.	Полный бак, пожалуйста. _polniy_ bak pa_zhal_sta
… liters, please.	… литров бензина, пожалуйста. … _leetraf_ been_zeena_ pa_zhal_sta
premium [super]/regular	бензин 98/бензин 93 been_zeen_ _nomeer_ deevee_nosta_ _voseem_'/ been_zeen_ _nomeer_ deevee_nosta_ tree
unleaded/diesel	очищенный/дизельное топливо a_chyeeshchyeeniy_/_deezeel'naye topleeva_
Where is the air pump/water?	Где воздух/вода? gdye _vozdookh_/va_da_

○ ЦЕНА ЗА ЛИТР	PRICE PER LITER ○

Parking Автостоянка

Parking is usually unrestricted, except in central areas in Moscow and
St. Petersburg where one can now encounter not only parking meters and
restricted zones but also booting [clamping] and tow-away vehicles.

Is there a parking lot [car park] nearby?	Здесь рядом есть автостоянка? zdyes' _ryadam_ yest' aftasta_yanka_
What's the charge per hour/day?	Сколько стоит в час/день? _skol'ka_ _stoeet_ f chyas/dyen'
Do you have some change for the parking meter?	Разменяйте для автомата, пожалуйста. razmee_nyaytye_ dlya af_tamata_ pa_zhal_sta
My car has been booted [clamped]. Who do I call?	Моя машина заблокирована. Кого нужно вызвать? _Maya ma_shina zablakeerovana. Kavo noozhna vis_bat'_

NUMBERS ➤ 216; DIRECTIONS ➤ 94

Breakdown Поломка

The state vehicle inspection authority patrols the traffic on
highways [motorways] and gives roadside assistance.

Where is the nearest garage?	Где ближайшая станция обслуживания? *gdye bleezhayshaya stantsiya aploozhivaneeya*
My car broke down.	У меня сломалась машина. *oo meenya slamalas' mashina*
Can you send a mechanic/ tow [breakdown] truck?	Можно прислать механика/буксир? *mozhna preeslat' meekhaneeka/bookseer*
I belong to a recovery service.	Я из службы технической помощи. *ya ees sloozhbi teekhneecheeskay pomashchee*
My registration number is …	Мой номер … *moy nomeer …*
The car is …	Машина … *mashina …*
on the highway [motorway]	на шоссе *na shasse*
2 km from …	в 2 км от … *v dvookh keelamyetrah at …*
How long will you be?	Как долго Вы будете? *kak dolga vi boodeetye*

What's wrong? Что случилось?

I don't know what's wrong.	Я не знаю, что-то не в порядке. *ya nee znayoo shtoto nee f paryatkee*
My car won't start.	Мотор не заводится. *mator nee zavodeetsa*
The battery is dead.	Аккумулятор сел. *akkoomoolyatar syel*
I've run out of gas [petrol].	Бензин кончился. *beenzeen konchyeelsa*
I have a flat [puncture].	Шина проколота. *shina prakolota*
There is something wrong with …	Что-то не в порядке с … *shtoto nee f paryatkye s …*
I've locked the keys in the car.	Я закрыл(а) ключи в машине. *ya zakril(a) klyoochyee v mashinye*

Repairs   Ремонт

Do you do repairs?	Вы ремонтируете машины? *vi reemanteerooeetye mashini*
Could you take a look at my car?	Посмотрите мою машину, пожалуйста. *pasmatreetye mayoo mashinoo pazhalsta*
Can you repair it?	Можно починить? *mozhna pachyeeneet'*
Please make only essential repairs.	Пожалуйста, сделайте только основной ремонт. *pazhalsta zdyelaytye tol'ka asnavnoy reemont*
Can I wait for it?	Мне подождать? *mnye padazhdat'*
Can you repair it today?	Вы отремонтируете её сегодня? *vi atreemanteerooeetye yeyo seevodnya*
When will it be ready?	Когда будет готово? *kagda boodyet gatova*
How much will it cost?	Сколько это будет стоить? *skol'ka eta boodyet stoeet'*
That's outrageous!	Это возмутительно! *eta vazmooteeteel'na*
Can I have a receipt for my insurance?	Можно квитанцию для страховки? *mozhna kveetantsiyoo dlya strakhofkee*

... не работает.	The ... isn't working.
У меня нет запасных частей.	I don't have the necessary parts.
Нужно будет заказать части.	I will have to order the parts.
Это можно починить только временно.	I can only repair it temporarily.
Вашу машину можно списать.	Your car is beyond repair.
Это нельзя починить.	It can't be repaired.
Будет готово ...	It will be ready ...
сегодня попозже	later today
завтра	tomorrow
через ... дня (дней).	in ... days

DAYS OF THE WEEK ➤ *218; NUMBERS* ➤ *216*

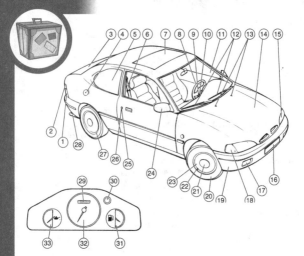

1 tail lights [back lights] задние огни
mpl *zadnee agnee*

2 brakelights тормозные огни mpl
tarmaznie agnee

3 trunk [boot] багажник m *bagazhneek*

4 gas tank door [petrol cap] крышка
бензобака f *krishka beenzabaka*

5 window окно n *akno*

6 seat belt ремень безопасности m
reemyen' beezapasnasti

7 sunroof люк m *lyook*

8 steering wheel рулевое колесо n
rooleevoye kaleeso

9 ignition зажигание n *zazheeganeeye*

10 ignition key ключ зажигания m
klyooch zazheeganeeya

11 windshield [windscreen] ветровое
стекло n *veetravoye steeklo*

12 windshield [windscreen] wipers
очистители ветрового стекла mpl
acheesteeteelee veetrayova steekla

13 windshield [windscreen] washer
омыватель ветрового стекла m
amiyateel' veetrayova steekla

14 hood [bonnet] капот m *kapot*

15 headlights фары переднего света fpl
fari peeryedneeva svyeta

16 license [number] plate номерной знак
m *nameernoy znak*

17 fog lamp противотуманная фара f
prateevatoomanaya fara

18 turn signals [indicators] указатели
поворота mpl *ookazateelee pavarota*

19 bumper бампер m *bampeer*

20 tires [tyres] шины fpl *sheeni*

21 wheel cover [hubcap] колпак m *kalpak*

22 valve клапан m *klapan*

23 wheels колеса npl *kalyosa*

24 outside [wing] mirror боковое зеркало
n *bakavoye zyerkala*

25 cental locking центральный замок m
tseetral'niy zamok

26 lock замок двери m *zamok dvyeree*

27 wheel rim обод m *obat*

28 exhaust pipe выхлопная труба f
vikhlapnaya trooba

29 odometer [milometer] одометр m
adometar

30 warning light контрольная лампа f
kantrol'naya lampa

31 fuel gauge расход топлива m
raskhot topleeva

32 speedometer спидометр m
speedmeetar

33 oil gauge расход масла m
raskhot masla

34 backup [reversing] lights фара заднего
хода f *fara zadneeva khoda*

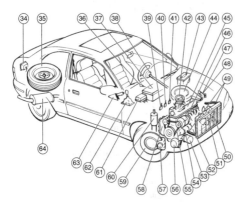

35 spare wheel запасное колесо n
zapasnoye kaleeso

36 choke воздушная заслонка f
vazdooshnaya zaslonka

37 heater обогреватель m
abagreevateel'

38 steering column рулевая колонка f
rooleevaya kalonka

39 accelerator акселератор m
akseeleeratar

40 pedal педаль f *peedal'*

41 clutch сцепление n *stseeplyeneeye*

42 carburetor карбюратор m
karbyooratar

43 battery аккамулятор m
akamoolyatar

44 alternator генератор m *geeneeratar*

45 camshaft распределительный вал
m *raspreedeeleeteel'niy val*

46 air filter воздушный фильтр m
vazdooshniy feel'tar

47 distributor распределитель m
raspreedeeleeteel'

48 points контакты mpl *kantakti*

49 radiator hose (top/bottom) шланг
радиатора (верхний, нижний) m
shlang radeegatara (verkhneey, neezhneey)

50 radiator радиатор m *radeegtar*

51 fan вентилятор m *veenteelyatar*

52 engine двигатель m *dveegateel'*

53 oil filter масляный фильтр m
maslyaniy feel'tar

54 starter [motor] стартер m *startyor*

55 fan belt ремень вентилятора m
reemyen' veenteelyatara

56 horn звуковой сигнал m
zvookavoy seegnal

57 brake pads тормозные колодки fpl
tarmazniye kalotkee

58 transmission [gearbox] коробка
передач f *karopka peereedach*

59 brakes тормоза mpl
tarmaza

60 shock absorbers амортизаторы mpl
amarteezatari

61 fuses предохранители mpl
preedakhraneeteelee

62 gear shift [lever] рычаг
переключения передач m *richak
peereeklyoochyeneeya peereedach*

63 handbrake ручной тормоз m
roochnoy tormas

64 muffler [silencer] глушитель m
gloosheeteel'

Accidents Авария

Insurance is not obligatory, but it is advisable to make sure that you, your passengers, any third party, and the car are covered. Try to arrange insurance before setting off for Russia. It may be possible to do so via agents of the state insurance agency **Ingosstrakh** (Ингосстрах).

There has been an accident.	Произошла авария. *praeezashla avareeya*
It's …	Это … *eta*
on the highway [motorway]	на шоссе *na shasse*
near …	около … *okala*
Where's the nearest telephone?	Где ближайший телефон? *gdye bleezhayshiy teeleefon*
Call …	Вызовите … *vizaveetee*
an ambulance	скорую помощь *skorooyoo pomashch'*
a doctor	врача *vrachya*
the fire department [brigade]	пожарную команду *pazharnooyoo kamandoo*
the police	милицию *meeleetseeyoo*
Can you help me, please?	Помогите, пожалуйста. *pamageetee pazhalsta*

Injuries Травмы

There are people injured.	Люди получили травмы. *lyoodee paloochyeelee travmi*
He's seriously injured/bleeding.	У него серьёзная травма/кровотечение. *oo neevo seeryoznaya travma/ kravateechyeneeya*
She's unconscious.	Она без сознания. *ana byes saznaneeya*
He can't breathe.	Он не может дышать. *on nee mozheet dishat'*
He can't breathe/move.	Он не двигается. *on nee dveegayetsa*
Don't move him.	Не трогайте его. *nee trogaytye eevo*

ACCIDENT & INJURY ➤ 162; DIRECTIONS ➤ 94

Legal matters   Юридические вопросы

What's your insurance company?	Кто ваш страхователь? *kto vash strakhavateel'*
What's your name and address?	Ваша фамилия и адрес? *vasha fameeleeya ee adrees*
He ran into me.	Он врезался в меня. *on vryezalsa v meenya*
She was driving too fast/ too close.	Она ехала слишком быстро/близко. *ana yekhala sleeshkam bistra/bleeska*
I had the right of way.	У меня было право проезда. *oo meenya bila prava prayezda*
I was (only) driving at … kmph.	Я ехал(а) со скоростью (всего) … км в час. *ya yekhal(a) sa skorastyoo (fsyevo) … keelamyetraf f chyas*
I'd like an interpreter.	Мне нужен переводчик. *mnye noozhen peereevotchyeek*
I didn't see the sign.	Я не видел(а) знака. *ya nee veedyel(a) znaka*
He/She saw it happen.	Он/она видел(а), как это случилось. *on/ana veedyel(a) kak eta sloochyeelas'*
The registration number was …	Номер … *nomeer*

Ваш(е/и) …. пожалуйста?	Can I see your …, please?
водительские права	driver's license [licence]
страховое свидетельство	insurance card
регистрационные документы	vehicle registration document
Во сколько это случилось?	What time did it happen?
Где это случилось?	Where did it happen?
Кто-нибудь ещё был там?	Was anyone else involved?
Есть свидетели?	Are there any witnesses?
Вы превышали скорость.	You were speeding.
Фары не работают	Your lights aren't working.
Вы должны заплатить штраф.	You'll have to pay a fine (on the spot).
Вам придётся дать показания в отделении.	We need you to make a statement at the station.

Asking directions   Как проехать

Excuse me, please.	Извините, пожалуйста. *eezveeneetye pazhalsta*
How do I get to …?	Как мне доехать до …? *kak mnye dayekhat' da …*
Where is …?	Где …? *gdye …*
Can you show me on the map where I am?	Покажите на карте, где я? *pakazhitye na kartye gdye ya*
I've lost my way. *zabloodeelsa(las')*	Я заблудился(-лась). *ya*
Can you repeat that, please?	Повторите, пожалуйста. *paftareetye pazhalsta*
More slowly, please.	Помедленнее, пожалуйста. *pamyedleennee pazhalsta*
Thanks for your help.	Спасибо за помощь. *spaseeba za pomashch'*

Traveling by car   Поездка на машине

Is this the right road for …?	Это дорога на …? *eta daroga na …*
How far is it to … from here?	Далеко до … отсюда? *daleeko da … atsyooda*
Where does this road lead?	Куда ведёт эта дорога? *kooda veedyot eta daroga*
How do I get onto the highway [motorway]?	Как мне выехать на шоссе? *kak mnye viyekhat' na shasse*
What's the next town called?	Как называется следующий город? *kak nazivaeetsa slyedooyooshchyeey gorat*
How long does it take by car?	Сколько времени ехать туда на машине? *skol'ka vryemeenee yekhat'* *tooda na mashinye*

– *eezveeneetye pazhalsta. kag mnye*
dayekhat' da vagzala?
– *tryeteey pavarot nalyeva ee patom preeyama.*
– *tryeteey pavarot nalyeva. eta dalyeeko?*
– *da nyet, dyeseet' meenoot khad'bi.*
– *spaseeba za pomashch'.*
– *pazhalsta.*

Location   Как искать дорогу

Это ...	It's ...
прямо	straight ahead
налево	on the left
направо	on the right
на другой стороне улицы	on the other side of the street
на углу/за углом	on the corner/around the corner
по направлению к ...	in the direction of ...
напротив .../позади ...	opposite .../behind ...
рядом с .../после ...	next to .../after ...
Поезжайте вниз по ...	Go down the ...
боковой улице/главной улице	side street/main street
Поезжайте через площадь/мост.	Cross the square/bridge.
Вам нужен третий поворот направо.	Take the third right.
Поверните налево ...	Turn left ...
после первого светофора	after the first traffic light
у второго перекрёстка	at the second intersection [crossroad]

By car   На машине

Это к ... от сюда.	It's ... of here.
северу/югу/востоку/западу	north/south/east/west
Поезжайте по дороге на ...	Take the road for ...
Это не та дорога.	You're on the wrong road.
Поезжайте назад до ...	You'll have to go back to ...
Следуйте дорожным знакам на ...	Follow the signs for ...

How far?   Это далеко?

Это ...	It's ...
близко/недалеко/очень далеко	close/not far/a long way
5 минут ходьбы	5 minutes on foot
10 минут на машине	10 minutes by car
около 100 м вниз по дороге	about 100 meters down the road
примерно в 10 километрах	about 10 kilometers away

TIME ➤ 220; NUMBERS ➤ 216

Road signs   Дорожные знаки

ПРОЕЗД	ACCESS ONLY
ВАРИАНТ МАРШРУТА	ALTERNATIVE ROUTE
ОБЪЕЗД	DETOUR [DIVERSION]
УСТУПИ ДОРОГУ	YIELD [GIVE WAY]
ОСТОРОЖНО, НИЗКИЙ ПРОЛЁТ	LOW DRIDGE
ОДНОСТОРОННЕЕ ДВИЖЕНИЕ	ONE-WAY STREET
ДОРОГА ЗАКРЫТА	ROAD CLOSED

Town plans   План города

аэропорт	airport
автобусный маршрут	bus route
автобусная остановка	bus stop
церковь	church
справочное бюро	information office
главная/центральная улица	main [high] street
кинотеатр	movie theater [cinema]
старый город	old town
парк	park
автостоянка	parking lot [car park]
переход	pedestrian crossing
пешеходная зона	pedestrian zone [precinct]
спортплощадка	playing field [sports ground]
отделение милиции	police station
почта	post office
стадион	stadium
вокзал	station
станция метро	subway [metro] station
стоянка такси	taxi stand [rank]
театр	theater
подземный переход	underpass
Вы вот здесь.	You are here.

DICTIONARY ➤ 169; SIGHTSEEING ➤ 97–107

Sightseeing

Intourist hotels have service bureaus (бюро обслуживания **byooro apsloozheevaneeya**) manned by multilingual staff who provide information, arrange outings and excursions, make reservations, and give general assistance. Other useful sources of information are the English-language newspapers, *Moscow Times* and *Where in St. Petersburg?*, found in many hotels and at kiosks.

Tourist information office
Туристическое бюро

Where's the tourist office?	Где справки? *gdye sprafkee*
What are the main attractions?	Какие главные достопримечательности? *kakeeye glavniye dastapreemeechyateelnastee*
We're here for ...	Мы здесь на ... *mi zdyes' na ...*
only a few hours	несколько часов *nyeskal'ka chyasof*
a day	на один день *na adeen dyen'*
a week	на неделю *na needyelyoo*
Can you recommend ...?	Вы можете порекомендовать ...? *vi mozheetye pareekameendavat' ...*
a sightseeing tour	обзорную экскурсию *abzornooyoo ekskoorseeyoo*
an excursion	экскурсию *ekskoorseeyoo*
a boat trip	водную экскурсию *vodnooyoo ekskoorseeyoo*
Are these leaflets free?	Эти брошюры бесплатно? *etee brashyoori beesplatna*
Do you have any information on ...?	У Вас есть информация по ...? *oo vas yest' eenfarmatsiya pa ...*
Are there any trips to ...?	Есть экскурсии в ...? *yest' ekskoorseeyee v ...*

Excursions   Экскурсии

How much does the tour cost?	Сколько стоит эта экскурсия?
	skol'ka stoeet eta ekskoorseeya
Is lunch included?	Цена включает обед?
	tseena fklyoochayeet abyet
Where do we leave from?	Откуда мы отправляемся?
	atkooda mi atpravlyayemsa
What time does the tour start?	Во сколько начинается экскурсия?
	va skol'ka nachyeenayetsa ekskoorseeya
What time do we get back?	Во сколько мы возвращаемся?
	va skol'ka mi vazvrashchyayemsa
Do we have free time in …?	У нас будет свободное время в …?
	oo nas boodyet svabodnaye vryemya v …
Is there an English-speaking guide?	У вас есть говорящий по-английски гид?
	oo vas yest' gavaryashcheey pa angleeyskee geet

On tour   На экскурсии

Public lavatories are rare and horrible. If you must go, try a supermarket, a large store, or a pharmacy. Toilet paper is not to be found in most toilets, so carry some tissues with you.

Are we going to see …?	Мы увидим …? *mi ooveedeem …*
We'd like to have a look at the …	Нам хотелось бы посмотреть …
	nam khatyelas' bi pasmatryet' …
Can we stop here …?	Можно здесь остановиться, чтобы …?
	mozhna zdyes' astanaveet'sa shtobi …
to take photographs	фотографировать *fatagrafeeravat'*
to buy souvenirs	купить сувениры *koopeet' sooveeneeri*
to use the bathrooms [toilets]	сходить в туалет *skhadeet' f tooalyet*
Would you take a photo of us, please?	Сфотографируйте нас, пожалуйста.
	sfatagrafeerooeetye nas pazhalta
How long do we have here/in …?	Сколько времени у нас здесь/в …?
	skol'ka vryemeenee oo nas zdyes'/v …
Wait! … isn't back yet.	Подождите! … ещё не пришёл (пришла).
	padazhdeetye … eeshcho nee preeshol (preeshla)
Stop the bus! My child is feeling sick.	Остановите автобус – ребёнка тошнит.
	astanaveetye aftoboos – reebyonka tashneet

Sights   Достопримечательности

Probably the best maps are the *New City Map and Guide* range, which sell for around $7. Maps in Cyrillic are cheaper, but the transliterated versions tend to be more up to date. (Maps printed before 1992 will have outdated street names.)

Where is the …	Где находится ...? *gdye na<u>kho</u>deetsa ...*
art gallery	картинная галерея *kart<u>ee</u>nnaya galeer<u>ye</u>ya*
battle site	место сражения *m<u>ye</u>sta sra<u>zhe</u>neeya*
botanical garden	ботанический сад *bata<u>nee</u>chyeeskee sat*
castle	замок *<u>za</u>mak*
cathedral/church	собор/церковь *s<u>a</u>bor/<u>tse</u>rkaf'*
downtown area	центр города *tsentr <u>go</u>rada*
fountain	фонтан *fan<u>ta</u>n*
library	библиотека *beebleeat<u>ye</u>ka*
market	рынок *<u>ri</u>nak*
(war) memorial	мемориал *meemar<u>ee</u>al*
monastery	монастырь *mana<u>stir'</u>*
museum	музей *moo<u>zyay</u>*
old town	старый город *<u>sta</u>riy <u>go</u>rat*
opera house	оперный театр *<u>o</u>peerniy tee<u>atr</u>*
palace	дворец *dva<u>ryets</u>*
park	парк *park*
parliament building	здание парламента *<u>zda</u>neeye parl<u>a</u>meenta*
ruins	развалины *raz<u>va</u>leeni*
shopping area	торговый центр *tar<u>go</u>viy tsentr*
statue/tower	статуя/башня *st<u>a</u>tooya/<u>ba</u>shnya*
theater	театр *tee<u>atr</u>*
town hall	горсовет *garsa<u>vyet</u>*
viewpoint	смотровая площадка *smatra<u>va</u>ya plashch<u>ya</u>tka*
Can you show me on the map?	Покажите мне на карте. *paka<u>zhi</u>tye mnye na <u>kar</u>tye*

DIRECTIONS ➤ 94

Admission Вход

Museums are usually open from 9 – 10 a.m. to 5 – 6 p.m. You'll find that they are invariably closed at least one day a week (usually Monday) and, in addition, one day a month will be set aside as "cleaning day."

Is the … open to the public?	… открыт(а) для всех? … *atkrit (a) dlya fsyekh*
Can we look around?	Можно посмотреть? *mozhna pasmatryet'*
What are the opening hours?	В какие часы работает? *f kakeeye chyasi rabotayet*
When does it close?	Когда закрывается? *kagda zakrivayetsa*
Is … open on Sundays?	… открыт(а) по воскресеньям? … *atkrit (a) pa vaskreesyenyeem*
When's the next guided tour?	Во сколько следующая экскурсия? *va skol'ka slyedooyooshchaya*
Do you have a guidebook (in English)?	У Вас есть путеводитель (на английском)? *oo vas yest' pooteevadeeteel' (na angleeskam)*
Can I take photos?	Можно фотографировать? *mozhna fatagrafeeravat'*
Is there access for the disabled?	Инвалидам можно? *eenvaleedam mozhna*
Is there an audioguide in English?	Есть запись экскурсии на английском? *yest' zapees' ekskoorseeyee na angleeskam*

Paying/Tickets Оплата/Билеты

How much is the entrance fee?	Сколько стоит входной билет? *skol'ka stoeet fkhadnoy beelyet*
Are there discounts for …?	Есть скидка для …? *yest' skeetka dlya …*
children/students	детей/студентов *deetyey/ stoodyentaf*
disabled/groups	инвалидов/групп *eenvaleedaf/groop*
senior citizens	пенсионеров *peenseeanyeraf*
1 adult and 2 children, please.	1 взрослый и 2 детских, пожалуйста. *adeen vzrosli ee dva dyetskeek pazhalsta*
I've lost my ticket.	Я потерял(а) билет. *ya pateeryal(a) beelyet*

TIME ➤ 220

– pyat' bee<u>lye</u>taf pazha<u>l</u>sta. oo vas
yest' <u>skeet</u>ka?
– da yest'. dlya deet<u>ye</u>y ee peenseeyan<u>ye</u>raf
cheet<u>i</u>ree roob<u>lya</u>.
– dva <u>vzros</u>likh ee tree <u>dyet</u>skeekh pazha<u>l</u>sta.
– s vas <u>dvat</u>tsat' <u>vo</u>seem' roob<u>lye</u>y pazha<u>l</u>sta.

ВХОД СВОБОДНЫЙ	FREE ADMISSION
ЗАКРЫТО	CLOSED
СУВЕНИРЫ	GIFT SHOP
ПОСЛЕДИЙ ВПУСК В 5 ЧАСОВ	LATEST ENTRY AT 5 P.M.
СЛЕДУЮЩАЯ ЭКСКУРСИЯ В ...	NEXT TOUR AT …
ВХОДА НЕТ	NO ENTRY
ФОТОГРАФИРОВАТЬ СО ВСПЫШКОЙ ЗАПРЕЩАЕТСЯ	NO FLASH PHOTOGRAPHY
НЕ ФОТОГРАФИРОВАТЬ!	NO PHOTOGRAPHY
ОТКРЫТО	OPEN
ЧАСЫ РАБОТЫ	VISITING HOURS

Impressions   Впечатления

It's …	Это … *eta* …
amazing	поразительно *para<u>zee</u>teel'na*
beautiful	прекрасно *pree<u>kras</u>na*
bizarre	причудливо *pree<u>choo</u>dleeva*
incredible	невероятно *neeveera<u>ya</u>tna*
interesting/boring	интересно/скучно *eentee<u>rye</u>sna/<u>skooch</u>na*
magnificent	великолепно *veeleeka<u>lye</u>pna*
romantic	романтично *raman<u>tee</u>chna*
strange/superb	странно/превосходно *<u>stran</u>na/preevas<u>kho</u>dna*
terrible/ugly	ужасно/безобразно *oo<u>zhas</u>na/ beeza<u>bra</u>zna*
It's good value.	Это стоит того. *eto <u>sto</u>eet ta<u>vo</u>*
It's a rip-off.	Это слишком дорого. *eta <u>slee</u>shkam <u>do</u>raga*
I like/don't like it.	Мне нравится/не нравится. *mnye <u>nra</u>veetsa/nee <u>nra</u>veetsa*

Tourist glossary
Словарь туриста

церковь/храм	*tsyerkaf'/khram*	church/temple
собор	*sabor*	cathedral
дворец	*dvar'yets*	palace
купол	*koopal*	dome
купол-луковка	*koopal-lookafka*	onion dome
английский парк	*angleeyskeey park*	formal garden
склеп	*sklyep*	crypt
икона/образ	*eekona/obraz*	icon
старинные вещи	*stareeniye vyeshchee*	antiquities
мавзолей	*mavzolyey*	mausoleum
башня	*bashnya*	tower

архитектура	*arkheeteektoora*	architecture
искусство	*eeskoostva*	art
керамика/фарфор	*keerameeka/ farfor*	ceramics/ porcelain
гончарные изделия	*gancharniye eezdyeleeya*	pottery
коллекция	*kalyektseeya*	collection
выставка	*vistafka*	exhibition
картина	*karteena*	painting
акварель	*akvaryel'*	watercolor painting
рукопись	*rookapees'*	manuscript
скульптура	*skool'ptoora*	sculpture
гобелен	*gabeelyen*	tapestry
ремёсла	*reemyosla*	crafts

Who?/What?/When?
Кто?/Что?/Когда?

What's that building?	Что это за здание?	*shto eta za zdaneeye*
Who was the architect/artist/sculptor?	Кто архитектор/художник/скульптор?	*kto arkheetyektar/khoodozhneek/skool'ptar*
When was it built/painted?	Когда это было построено/написано?	*kagda eta bila pastroyeena/napeesana*
What style is that?	Какой это стиль?	*kakoy eta steel'*
What period is that?	Какой это период?	*kakoy eta peereeat*

Moscow   Москва

The city of Moscow covers an area of 900 square kilometers. However, despite its size, the layout of the city is easily grasped – a series of concentric circles and radial lines, emanating from the Kremlin. The center of the city is compact enough to explore on foot.

Red Square and the **Kremlin** are the nucleus of the city. Here you'll find Lenin's Mausoleum and St. Basil's Cathedral, the famous GUM department store, and the Kremlin itself, whose splendid cathedrals and Armory museum head the list of attractions. The Kremlin is surrounded by two quarters, **Beliy Gorod** and **Zemlyanoy Gorod,** which are defined by circular boulevards built over the original medieval ramparts. In both quarters there are museums and art galleries. Beyond the historic core of the city, to the northwest of the Kremlin, there is the area called **Krasnaya Presnya** where the White House (the Russian Parliament building) is situated. South across the river from the Kremlin is **Zamoskvareche**, the home of the Tretyakov Gallery of Russian art, and Gorky Park.

St. Petersburg   Санкт-Петербург

Founded by Peter the Great in 1703, the city has been known as St. Petersburg, Petrograd, Leningrad, and now again, St. Petersburg. It is a city built on a grand scale in keeping with its original status as the capital of the Tsarist Empire. The **River Neva** and its tributaries divide the city. The center lies on the south bank with its southern boundary marked by the **River Fontanka**. Some of the greatest sights and monuments are in and around **Nevsky Prospekt**. Here you will find the **Winter Palace** and the art collections of the **Hermitage**, the Mikhailovsky Palace and Russian Museum, the Summer Palace and Garden, and the cathedrals of St. Isaac and Kazan. Across the **Palace Bridge** from the Winter Palace, on Vasilevsky Island in the area called the **Strelka**, are some of the city's oldest institutions and a number of fascinating museums.

On the north side of the River Neva is the **St. Peter and Paul Fortress**, whose construction anticipated the foundation of the city. Besides its strategic and military significance, it housed St. Petersburg's first prison and cathedral.

Rulers   Правители

Ivan III, Ivan the Great   1462–1505
Ruler of Muscovy, the first clear emergence of a nation-state.

Ivan IV, Ivan the Terrible   1547–1584
The first Muscovite ruler to make official and regular use of the
title **tsar**, a Slavonic form of "Caesar."

The Time of Troubles   1598–1682
Peasant wars and foreign intervention; reign of Boris Godunov.
Nominally ending with the first Romanov tsar.

Peter 1, Peter the Great   1682–1725
Foundation of St. Petersburg.

Catherine 11, Catherine the Great   1762–1796

Alexander I   1801–1825
1812 invasion of Russia by Napoleon.

Nicholas I   1825–1855
Crimean War.

Alexander II   1855–1881
Sale of Alaska to the United States. Serfs emancipated. Tsar assassinated.

Alexander III   1881–1894
Industrialization of Russia. *Communist Manifesto* translated into Russian.

Nicholas II   1894–1917
War with Japan. 1905 revolution. First World War. Abdication of the
Tsar (1917). Tsar executed (1918).

1917–1991
Two revolutions in 1917 culminating in the *October Revolution* lead to the
establishment of the Soviet government under Lenin.

1991–present
Breakup of the U.S.S.R. Establishment of the Russian Federation under
Boris Yeltsin.

Places of worship   Храмы

Russian Orthodox ch urches are being restored all over the country. Most
are open to the public during services only. You will also find Protestant
and Catholic churches.

Orthodox/Catholic/ Protestant church	православная/католическая/ протестанская церковь *prava<u>slav</u>naya/ kata<u>lee</u>chyeeskaya/pratee<u>stant</u>skaya <u>tser</u>kaf'*
mosque/synagogue	мечеть/синагога *mee<u>chyet</u>'/seena<u>go</u>ga*
What time is …?	Когда будет …? *ka<u>gda</u> boo<u>deet</u> …*
the mass/service	месса/служба *<u>mye</u>ssa/<u>sloo</u>zhba*

In the countryside За городом

I'd like a map of …	Я хотел(а) бы карту … *ya khatyel(a) bi kartoo …*
this region	этого района *etava rayona*
walking routes	пешеходных маршрутов *peesheekhodnikh marshrootaf*
cycle routes	велосипедных маршрутов *veelaseepyedneekh marshrootaf*
How far is it to …?	Сколько километров до …? *skol'ka keelamyetraf da …*
Can I walk there?	Можно пройти туда пешком? *mozhna praytee tooda peeshkom*
Is there a trail/scenic route to …?	Есть просёлочная дорога/живописный маршрут до …? *yest' prasyolachnaya daroga/zhivapeesniy marshroot da …*
Can you show me on the map?	Покажите мне на карте. *pakazhitye mnye na kartye*
I'm lost.	Я заблудился(лась). *ya zabloodeelsa(las')*

Organized walks/hikes Походы

When does the guided walk start?	Когда будет поход? *kagda boodyet pakhot*
When will we return?	Когда мы вернёмся? *kagda mi veernyomsa*
What's the walk/hike like?	Какой это поход? *kakoy eta pakhot*
gentle/medium/tough	лёгкий/средний/трудный *lyokhkeey/sryeneey/troodniy*
Where do we meet?	Где мы встречаемся? *gdye mi fstreechyayemsa*
I'm exhausted.	Я устал(а). *ya oostal(a)*
How high is that mountain?	Какая высота этой горы? *kakaya visata etay gari*
What kind of … is that?	Что это за …? *shto eta za …*
animal/bird	животное/птица *zhivotnaye/pteetsa*
flower/tree	цветок/дерево *tsveetok/dyereeva*

Geographic features
Географические особенности

bridge	мост *most*
cave	пещера *peeshchyera*
cliff	обрыв *abriv*
farm	ферма *fyerma*
field	поле *polye*
footpath	тропинка *trapeenka*
forest	лес *lyes*
hill	холм *kholm*
lake	озеро *ozeera*
mountain	гора *gara*
mountain pass	перевал *peereeval*
mountain range	хребет *khreebyet*
nature reserve	заповедник *zapavyedneek*
panorama	панорама *panarama*
park	парк *park*
pass	проход *prakhot*
path	тропинка *trapeenka*
peak	пик *peek*
picnic area	площадка для привала *plashchyatka dlya preevala*
pond	пруд *proot*
rapids	пороги *parogee*
ravine	овраг *avrak*
river	река *reeka*
sea	море *morye*
spa	минеральные воды *meeneeral'niye vodi*
stream	ручей *roochyey*
valley	долина *daleena*
viewpoint	смотровая площадка *smatravaya plashchyatka*
village	деревня *deeryevnya*
vineyard/winery	виноградник *veenagradneek*
waterfall	водопад *vadapat*
wood	лес *lyes*

Leisure

Events   Развлечения

Intourist hotels have service bureaus manned by multilingual staff who provide information, arrange outings and excursions, make reservations, and give general assistance. You can also find listings of events in the various English-language entertainment guides available ➤ 97.

During your stay, try to get tickets to the circus цирк (**tseerk**), especially the Moscow Circus or the Circus on Ice.

Do you have a program of events?	У Вас есть программа? *oo vas yest' pragramma*
Can you recommend a ...?	Вы можете порекомендовать ...? *vi mozheetye pareekameendavat' ...*
ballet/concert	балет/концерт *balyet/kantsert*
movie [film]	фильм *feel'm*
opera	оперу *opeeroo*
play	спектакль *speektakal'*

Availability   В продаже

When does it start/end?	Когда начинается/кончается? *kagda nachyeenayetsa/kanchyayetsa*
Where can I get tickets?	Где можно купить билеты? *gdye mozhna koopeet' beelyeti*
Are there any seats for tonight?	Есть билеты сегодня на вечер? *yest' beelyeti seevodnya na vyechyeer*
There are ... of us.	Нас ... *nas ...*

Tickets Билеты

How much are the seats?	Сколько стоят эти места? *skol'ka stoyet etee meesta*
Do you have anything cheaper?	Есть что-нибудь подешевле? *yest' shtoneebood' padeeshevlye*
I'd like to reserve …	Я хотел(а) бы заказать … *ya khatyel(a) bi zakazat' …*
three tickets for Sunday evening	3 на воскресенье вечером *tree na vaskreesyenye vyecheeram*
one ticket for the Friday matinée	1 на пятницу на дневное представление *adeen na pyatneetsoo na dnevnoye predstavlyeneeye*

Какой … кредитной карточки?	What's your credit card …?
номер	number
тип	type
срок действия	expiration [expiry] date
Пожалуйста, выкупите билеты …	Please pick up the tickets …
к … часам	by … p.m.
в кассе	at the reservations desk

May I have a program, please?	Можно программу, пожалуйста? *mozhna programoo pazhalsta*
Where's the coatcheck [cloakroom]?	Где гардероб? *gdye gardeerop*

– ya vas *slooshayoo?*
– ya *khatyel* bi dva *beelyeta* na *seevodnyashneey kantsert.*
– *pazhalsta.*
– ya *magoo zaplateet' kreedeetnay kartachkay?*
– da.
– *tagda* ya *vaspol'zooyoos' veezay.*
– *spaseeba* … *raspeesheetees' pazhalsta?*

ЗАКАЗ БИЛЕТОВ	ADVANCE RESERVATIONS
БИЛЕТЫ ПРОДАНЫ	SOLD OUT
БИЛЕТЫ НА СЕГОДНЯ	TICKETS FOR TODAY

NUMBERS ➤ 216

Movies [Cinema] В кино

You should be able to find several movie theaters [cinemas]
showing films in their original language.

Is there a multiplex cinema near here?	Здесь есть многозальный кинотеатр поблизости? *zdyes' yest' mnagazalniy keenateeatr pableezastee*
What's playing at the movies [on at the cinema] tonight?	Что идёт в кинотеатре сегодня вечером? *shto eedyot f keenateeatrye seevodnya vyechyeeram*
Is the film dubbed/subtitled?	Этот фильм дублирован/с субтитрами? *etat feel'm doobleeravan/s soopteetramee*
Is the film in the original English?	Этот фильм на английском? *etat feel'm na angleeskam*
Who's the main actor/actress?	Кто играет главную роль? *kto eegrayet glavnooyoo rol'*
A …, please.	…, пожалуйста. *pazhalsta*
box [carton] of popcorn	пакет воздушной кукурузы *pakyet vazdooshniy kookooroozi*
chocolate ice cream [choc-ice]	шоколадное мороженое *shakaladnaye marozzhenaye*
hot dog	хот-дог *khot dok*
soft drink	напиток/газированную воду *napeetak/gazeerovannooyoo vodoo*
small/regular/large	маленький/средний/большой *maleen'keey/sryedneey/bal'shoy*

Theater Театр

What's playing at the … theater?	Что идёт в … театре? *shto eedyot v … teeatre*
Who's the playwright?	Чья постановка? *chya pastanofka*
Do you think I'd enjoy it?	Вы думаете, мне понравится? *vi doomayetye mnye panraveetsa?*
I don't know much Russian.	Я плохо понимаю по-русски. *ya plokha paneemayoo pa rooskee*

Opera/Ballet/Dance
Опера/Балет/Танец

Where's the opera house?

Где находится оперный театр? *gdye nakhodeetsa opeerniy teeatar*

Who's the composer/soloist?

Кто композитор/солист? *kto kampazeetar/saleest*

Is formal dress required?

Вечернее платье обязательно? *veechyerneeye platye abeezateel'na*

Who's dancing?

Кто танцует? *kto tantsooyet*

I'm interested in contemporary dance.

Меня интересует современный балет. *meenya eenteereesooyet savreemyenniy balyet*

Music/Concerts Музыка/Концерты

Where's the concert hall?

Где находится концертный зал? *gdye nakhodeetsa kantsertniy zal*

Which orchestra/band is playing?

Какой(-ая) оркестр/группа играет? *kakoy(aya) arkyestr/groopa eegrayet*

What are they playing?

Что они исполняют? *shto anee eespalnyayoot*

Who is the conductor/soloist?

Кто дирижёр/солист? *kto deereezhor/saleest*

Who is the support band?

В сопровождении какого оркестра? *f sapravazhdyeneeye kakova arkyestra*

I really like …

Мне нравится … *mnye nraveetsa …*

country music

музыка кантри *moozika kantree*

folk music

народная музыка *narodnaya moozika*

jazz

джаз *dzhas*

music of the sixties

музыка 60-x *moozika shesteedeesatikh*

pop

поп-музыка *popmoozika*

rock music

рок-музыка *rok moozika*

soul music

музыка соул *moozika soool*

Have you ever heard of her/him?

Вы слышали о ней/нём? *vi slishalee a nyey/nyom*

Are they popular?

Они популярны? *anee papoolyarniy*

111

Nightlife Ночная жизнь

You'll find many nightclubs and discos. You can also join in with the locals enjoying a dinner-dance at most restaurants.

What is there to do in the evenings?	Что здесь можно делать по вечерам? *shto zdyes' mozhna dyelat' pa veercheeram*
Can you recommend a …?	Вы можете порекомендовать ...? *vi mozhetye pareekameendavat' ...*
Is there a … in town?	В городе есть ...? *v gorodye yest' ...*
bar	бар *bar*
casino	казино *kazeeno*
discotheque	дискотека *deeskatyeka*
gay club	гей-клуб *gyeykloob*
nightclub	ночной клуб *nachnoy kloop*
restaurant	ресторан *reestaran*
Is there a floor show/cabaret?	Здесь есть кабаре? *zdyes' yest' kabare*
What type of music do they play?	Какую музыку они играют? *kakooyoo moozikoo anee eegrayoot*
How do I get there?	Как туда попасть? *kak tooda papast'*

Admission Вход

What time does the show start?	Во сколько начинается представление? *va skol'ka nachyeenayetsa preedstavlyeneeye*
Is evening dress required?	Вечернее платье обязательно? *veechyerneeye platye abyazateel'na*
Is there a cover charge?	Есть наценка? *Yest' natsyenka*
Is a reservation necessary?	Нужно заказывать заранее? *noozhna zakazivat' zaraneeye*
Do we need to be members?	Нужно быть членами клуба? *noozhna bit' chlyenamee klooba*
How long will we have to stand in line [queue]?	Как долго стоять в очереди? *kak dolga stayat' v ocheereedee*
I'd like a good table.	Я хотел(а) бы хороший столик. *ya khatye(l)a bi kharoshiy stoleek*

TIME ➤ 220; TAXI ➤ 84

Children Дети

Can you recommend something for the children?	Что Вы рекомендуете для детей? *shto vi reekameendooyetye dlya deetyey*
Are there changing facilities here for babies?	Где можно перепеленать ребёнка? *gdye mozhna peereepeeleenat' reebyonka*
Where are the bathrooms [toilets]?	Где здесь туалет? *gdye zdyes' tooalyet*
amusement arcade	зал аттракционов *zal atraktseeonaf*
fairground	луна-парк *loonapark*
kiddie [paddling] pool	детский бассейн *dyetskeey bassyeyn*
playground	детская площадка *dyetskaya plashchyatka*
play group	детская группа *dyetskaya grooppa*
zoo	зоопарк *zapark*

Baby-sitting Присмотр за ребёнком

Can you recommend a reliable baby-sitter?	Вы можете порекомендовать хорошую няню? *vi mozhetye pareekamendavat' kharoshooyoo nyanyoo*
Is there constant supervision?	Дети постоянно под присмотром? *dyetee pastayanna pad preesmotram*
Are the staff properly trained?	Няни специально обучены? *nyanee speetsial'na aboochyeeni*
When can I drop them off?	Когда я могу их привести? *kagda ya magoo eekh preeveestee*
I'll pick them up at …	Я заберу их в … *ya zabeeroo eekh v …*
We'll be back by …	Мы вернёмся к … *mi veernyomsa k …*
What age is he/she?	Какой возраст? *kakoy vozrast*
She's 3 and he's 18 months.	Ей 3, а ему 18 месяцев. *yey tree a eemoo vaseemnatsat' myeseetseef*

Sports Спорт

Most of the sports common in the West are also played in Russia. The most popular in winter are ice hockey, skiing, and skating; in summer soccer, volleyball, and riding. Water sports, especially swimming, are very popular all year round, as are hunting and fishing.

Turkish-style public baths баня (**banya**) are a very popular form of relaxation and are a good way to meet people.

Spectating Спортивные зрелища

Is there a soccer [football] game [match] this Saturday?	Есть футбол в это воскресенье? *yest' foodbol' v eta vaskreesyeneeye*
Which teams are playing?	Какие команды играют? *kakeeye kamandi eegrayoot*
Can you get me a ticket?	Вы можете достать мне билет? *vi mozhetye dastat' mnye beelyet*
What's the admission charge?	Сколько стоит входной билет? *skol'ka stoeet fkhadnoy beelyet*
Where's the racetrack [race course]?	Где находится ипподром? *gdye nakhodeetsa eeppadrom*
Where can I place a bet?	Где я могу сделать ставку? *gdye ya magoo sdyelat' stafkoo*
What are the odds on …?	Какие шансы на ...? *kakeeye shansi na ...*
athletics	атлетика *atlyeteeka*
basketball	баскетбол *baskeedbol*
cycling	велоспорт *veelasport*
golf	гольф *gol'f*
horse racing	скачки *skachkee*
soccer [football]	футбол *foodbol*
swimming	плавание *plavaneeye*
tennis	теннис *tyenees*
volleyball	волейбол *valeebol*

Playing Спортивные игры

Where's the nearest …?	Где здесь поблизости …? *gdye zdyes' pableezastee …*
golf course	корт для гольфа *kort dlya gol'fa*
sports club	спортклуб *spartkloop*
Where are the tennis courts?	Где теннисные корты? *gdye tyenneesniye korti*
What's the charge per …?	Сколько стоит билет на …? *skol'ka stoeet beelyet na*
day/hour	день/час *dyeny/chyas*
game/round (golf)	партия/раунд *parteeya/raoont*
Do I need to be a member?	Обязательно быть членом клуба? *abeezateel'na bit' chlyenam klooba*
Where can I rent [hire] …?	Где можно взять напрокат …? *gdye mozhna vzyat' naprakat*
boots	спортивную обувь *sparteevnooyoo oboof'*
clubs	клюшки *klyoopkee*
equipment	снаряжение *snareezheneeye*
a racket	ракетку *rakyetkoo*
Can I get lessons?	Можно брать уроки? *mozhna brat' oorokee*
Is there an aerobic class?	Здесь есть класс аэробики? *zdyes' yest' klass ayerobeekee*
Do you have a fitness room?	У Вас есть тренажёрный зал? *oo vas yest' reenazhorniy zal*
Can I join in?	Можно мне вступить? *mozhna mnye fstoopeet'*

Извините, всё занято.	I'm sorry, we're booked up.
Нужен залог …	There is a deposit of …
Какой у Вас размер?	What size are you?
Нужна фотография размером на паспорт.	You need a passport-size photo.

РАЗДЕВАЛКА	CHANGING ROOM
РЫБНАЯ ЛОВЛЯ ЗАПРЕЩЕНА	NO FISHING
ТОЛЬКО ПО СПЕЦИАЛЬНОМУ РАЗРЕШЕНИЮ	PERMIT HOLDERS ONLY

At the beach   На пляже

Although the Russian summer is short, it can be hot, and there are a number of popular resorts on the Black Sea.

Is the beach …?	На пляже … *na plyazhee* …
pebbly/sandy	галька/песок *gal'ka/peesok*
Is there a … here?	Здесь есть …? *zdyes' yest'* …
children's pool	детский бассейн *dyetskeey bassyeyn*
swimming pool	бассейн *bassyeyn*
indoor/open-air	закрытый/открытый *zakritiy/atkritiy*
Is it safe to swim/dive here?	Здесь неопасно плавать/нырять? *zdyes' neeapasna plavat'/niryat'*
Is it safe for children?	Здесь неопасно для детей? *zdyes' neeapasna dlya deetyey*
Is there a lifeguard?	Здесь есть спасатели? *zdyes' yest' spasateelee*
I want to rent [hire] a/some …	Я хочу взять … напрокат. *ya khachyoo vzyat' … naprakat*
deck chair	шезлонг *shezlonk*
jet-ski	водный мотоцикл *vodniy matatseekal*
motorboat	моторную лодку *matornooyoo lotkoo*
rowboat	лодку *lotkoo*
sailboat	яхту *yakhtoo*
diving equipment	акваланг *akvalank*
umbrella [sunshade]	зонт *zont*
surfboard	доску *doskoo*
water skis	водные лыжи *vodniye lizhi*
windsurfer	виндсёрфинг *veentsyorfeenk*
For … hours.	На … час(-а, -ов). *na … chyas(-a, -of)*

Skiing   Лыжи

Skiing, particularly cross-country, is a popular sport in Russia. The *Russian Ski Club* can be a source of detailed information (http://www.poseidon.aha.ru/~ski/). Skating is also very popular. There are ice rinks in large parks and squares. Russians also love traditional horse-driven sleighs.

Is there much snow?	Сегодня много снега? *seevodnya mnoga snyega*
What's the snow like?	Какой сегодня снег? *kakoy seevodnya snyeg*
heavy/icy	тяжёлый/со льдом *tyazholiy/sa l'dom*
powdery/wet	жёсткий/влажный *zhyoskeey/vlazhniy*
I'd like to hire …	Я хотел(а) бы взять … напрокат. *ya khatyel(a) bi vzyat' … naprakat*
poles	лыжные палки *lizhniye palkee*
skates	коньки *kan'kee*
ski boots/skis	лыжные ботинки/лыжи *lizhniye bateenkee/lizhi*
These are too …	Это слишком … *eta sleeshkam …*
big/small	велико/мало *veeleeko/mala*
A lift pass for a day/ five days, please.	Проездной на день/пять дней, пожалуйста. *praeezdnoy na dyen'/ pyat' dnyey pazhalsta*
I'd like to join the ski school.	Я хотел(а) бы записаться в лыжную школу. *ya khatyel(a) bi zapeesat'sa v lizhnooyoo shkoloo*
I'm a beginner.	Я новичок. *ya naveechyok*
I'm experienced.	Я опытный лыжник. *ya opitniy lizhneek*

ВАГОН ПОДВЕСНОЙ ДОРОГИ	CABLE CAR/GONDOLA
ПОДВЕСНОЙ ПОДЪЁМНИК	CHAIR LIFT

Making Friends

Introductions   Знакомство

You can use the Russian equivalent of Mr. (господин **gaspadeen**) and Mrs. or Miss/Ms. (госпожа **gaspazha**) along with the person's surname. However, these were not used during the communist era, when "comrade" (товарищ **tavareeshch**) was used for both men and women. As a result, today Russian people often don't know how to address each other!

It is polite to address people you know by their first name and patronymic, derived from the father's name. So, Nikolay, whose father's name is Ivan, would be called *Nikolay Ivanovich*; Natalia, whose father's name is Alexander, would be called *Natalia Alexandrovna*.

In Russian there are two forms of "you" (taking different forms of the verb): ты (**ti**) is used between members of the same family, close friends, and when talking to young children; Вы (**vi**) is the polite form of address when you are talking to a person you do not know or to an acquaintance. When you are addressing more than one person, вы must always be used.

Hello, we haven't met.	Здравствуйте, мы не знакомы? *zdrastvooytye mi nee znakomi*
My name is …	Меня зовут … *meenya zavoot* …
May I introduce …?	Познакомьтесь … *paznakomtees'* …
John, this is …	Джон, это … *Dzhon eta* …
Pleased to meet you.	Очень приятно. *ochyeen' preeyatna*
What's your name?	Как Вас зовут? *kak vas zavoot*
How are you?	Как дела? *kak deela*
Fine, thanks. And you?	Спасибо, хорошо. А как Вы?* *spaseeba kharasho a kak vi*

* The question "And you?" is given here in the polite form with "Вы." In the dialog you will see the same question in the familiar form with "ты."

> – *preevyet. kag deela?*
> – *spaseeba kharasho. a kak ti?*
> – *spaseeba kharasho.*

118

Where are you from? Откуда Вы?

Where do you come from?	Откуда Вы приехали? *atkooda vi preeyekhalee*
Where were you born?	Где Вы родились? *gdye vi radeelees'*
I'm from (the) ...	Я из ... *ya eez ...*
Australia	Австралии *afstraleeyee*
Britain	Великобритании *veeleekabreetaneeyee*
Canada	Канады *kanadi*
England	Англии *angleeyee*
Ireland	Ирландии *eerlandeeyee*
Scotland	Шотландии *shatlandeeyee*
United States	Соединённых Штатов *sayeedeenyonikh shtataf*
Wales	Уэльса *ooel'sa*
Where do you live?	Где Вы живёте? *gdye vi zhivyotye*
What part of ... are you from?	В каком районе ... Вы живёте? *f kakom rayonye ... vi zhivyotye*
Russia	России *rasseeyee*
Ukraine	Украины *ookraeeni*
Belarus	Белоруссии *beelarooseyee*
We come here every year.	Мы приезжаем сюда каждый год. *mi pree eezzhzhayem syooda kazhdiy got*
It's my/our first visit.	Это мой/наш первый приезд. *eta moy/nash pyerviy preeyest.*
Have you ever been to ...?	Вы бывали в ...? *vi bivalee v ...*
Britain/the United States	Великобритании/Соединенных Штатах *veeleekabreetaneeyee/ sayeedeenyonikh shtatakh*
Do you like it here?	Вам нравится здесь? *vam nraveetsa zdyes'*
What do you think of the ...?	Что Вы думаете о ...? *shto vi doomayetye a ...*
I love the ... here.	Мне очень нравится ... здесь. *mnye ochyeen' nraveetsa ... zdyes'*
I don't care for the ... here.	Мне не нравится ... здесь. *mnye nee nraveetsa ... zdyes'*
food/people	кухня/люди *kookhnya/lyoodee*

Who are you with?   С кем Вы?

Who are you with?	С кем Вы? *s kyem vi*
I'm on my own.	Я один (одна). *ya adeen (adna)*
I'm with a friend.	Я с другом. *ya z droogam*
I'm with …	Я с … *ya s …*

my wife
моей женой *mayey zheenoy*

my husband
моим мужем *mayeem moozhem*

my family
моей семьёй *mayey seemyoy*

my children
моими детьми *mayeemee deet'mee*

my parents
моими родителями
mayeemee radeeteelyamee

my boyfriend/my girlfriend
моей подругой *mayey padroogay*

my father/my mother
моим отцом/моей матерью
mayeem atsom/mayey mateeryoo

my son/my daughter
моим сыном/моей дочерью
mayeem sinam/mayey docheeryoo

my brother/my sister
моим братом/моей сестрой
mayeem bratam/mayey seestroy

my uncle/my aunt
моим дядей/моей тетей
mayeem dyadeey/mayey tyoteey

What's your son's/
wife's name?
Как зовут Вашего сына/Вашу жену?
kak zavoot vasheva sina/vashoo zheenoo

Are you married?
Вы женаты? (to a man)/Вы замужем?
(to a woman) *vi zhenati/vi zamoozhem*

I'm married.
Я женат (man)/замужем (woman).
ya zhenat /zamoozhem

I'm single.
Я холост (man)/не замужем (woman).
ya kholast/nee zamoozhem

I'm divorced/separated.
Я разведён(a)/не живу с мужем (женой).
*razveedyon (razveedeena)/nee zhivoo s
moozhem (zhenoy)*

I'm engaged.
Я обручён(a). *abroochyon (abroochyeena)*

We live together.
Мы живём вместе. *mi zhivyom vmyestye*

Do you have any children?
У вас есть дети? *oo vas yest' dyetee*

Two boys and a girl.
Два мальчика и девочка.
dva mal'cheeka ee dyevachka

How old are they?
Сколько им лет? *skol'ka eem lyet*

They're ten and twelve.
Им десять и двенадцать.
eem dyeseet' ee dveenattsat'

What do you do?   Ваша профессия?

What do you do?	Ваша профессия? *vasha prafyeseeya*
What are you studying?	Что Вы изучаете? *shto vi eezoochayeetee*
I'm studying …	Я изучаю … *ya eezoochyayoo*
I'm in business.	Я занимаюсь бизнесом. *ya zaneemayoos' beezneesam*
I'm in sales.	Я занимаюсь торговлей. *ya zaneemayoos' targovleey*
Who do you work for?	Где Вы работаете? *gdye vi rabotayetye*
I work for …	Я работаю в/на … *ya rabotayoo v/na …*
I'm a(n) …	Я … *ya …*
accountant	бухгалтер *bookhgalteer*
engineer	инженер *eenzhenyer*
housewife	домохозяйка *damakhazyayka*
student	студент *stoodyent*
I'm …	Я … *ya …*
retired	на пенсии *na pyenseeyee*
self-employed	работаю на себя *rabotayoo na seebya*
between jobs	временно не работаю *vryemeenna nee rabotayoo*
What are your interests/ hobbies?	Какие у Вас интересы/хобби? *kakeeye oo vas eenteeryesi/khobbee*
I like …	Я люблю … *ya lyooblyoo*
music	музыку *moozikoo*
reading	читать *chyeetat'*
sports	спорт *sport*
I play …	Я играю в … *ya eegrayoo v …*
Would you like to play …?	Хотите сыграть в …? *khateetye sigrat' v …*
cards	карты *karti*
chess	шахматы *shakhmati*

What weather!   Какая хорошая погода!

What a lovely day!	Какой прекрасный день! **ka<u>koy</u> preek<u>ras</u>niy dyen'**
What terrible weather!	Какая ужасная погода! **ka<u>ka</u>ya oo<u>zhas</u>naya pagoda**
It's cold/hot today.	Как холодно/жарко сегодня. **kak <u>kho</u>ladna/<u>zhar</u>ka see<u>vo</u>dnya**
Is it usually this warm?	Здесь обычно такая тёплая погода? **zdyes' a<u>bich</u>na ta<u>ka</u>ya <u>tyo</u>playa pagoda**
Do you think it's going to ... tomorrow?	Как Вы думаете, завтра будет ...? **kak vi <u>doo</u>mayetye <u>zaf</u>tra <u>boo</u>dyet ...**
be a nice day	хороший день **kha<u>ro</u>shiy dyen'**
rain	дождь **dozhd'**
snow	снег **snyek**
What is the weather forecast?	Какой прогноз погоды? **ka<u>koy</u> pra<u>gnos</u> pagodi**
It's ... today.	Сегодня ... **see<u>vo</u>dnya ...**
cloudy	облачно **<u>ob</u>lachna**
foggy	туман **too<u>man</u>**
frosty	мороз **ma<u>ros</u>**
icy	гололёд **gala<u>lyot</u>**
rainy	дождь **dozhd'**
snowy	снег **snyek**
stormy	гроза **gra<u>za</u>**
windy	ветер **<u>vye</u>teer**
Has the weather been like this for long?	Давно стоит такая погода? **da<u>vno</u> sta<u>eet</u> ta<u>ka</u>ya pagoda**
What's the water temperature?	Как температура воды? **Kak teempeera<u>too</u>ra va<u>di</u>**
hot/warm/cold	горячая/тёплая/холодная **gar<u>ya</u>chyaya/<u>tyo</u>playa/<u>kho</u>ladnaya**
Will it be good weather for skiing?	Какой прогноз для лыжных прогулок? **ka<u>koy</u> pra<u>gnos</u> dlya <u>li</u>zhnikh pra<u>goo</u>lok**

ПРОГНОЗ ПОГОДЫ   WHEATHER FORECAST

Enjoying your trip?
Вам здесь нравится?

Вы в отпуске?	Are you on vacation?
На чём Вы приехали сюда?	How did you get here?
Как прошла поездка?	How was your trip?
Где Вы остановились?	Where are you staying?
Сколько Вы уже здесь?	How long have you been here?
Сколько Вы пробудете здесь?	How long are you staying?
Что удалось посмотреть?	What have you done so far?
Какие у Вас планы?	Where are you going next?
Вам здесь нравится?	Are you enjoying your vacation?

I'm here on …	Я здесь … *ya zdyes' …*
business	в командировке *f kamandeerofkye*
vacation [holiday]	в отпуске/на каникулах *v otpooskye/na kaneekoolakh*
We came by …	Мы приехали на … *mi preeyekhalee na …*
train/bus/plane	поезде/автобусе/самолёте *poeezdye/aftoboosye/samalyotye*
car/ferry	машине/пароме *mashinye/paromye*
I have a rental [hire] car.	Я взял(а) машину напрокат. *ya vzyal(a) mashinoo naprakat*
We're staying …	Мы остановились … *mi astanaveelees' …*
in an apartment	на квартире *na kvarteerye*
at a hotel/campsite	в отеле/кемпинге *vatyelye/kyempeengye*
with friends	у друзей *oo droozyey*
Can you suggest …?	Посоветуйте, …? *pasavyetooytye …*
things to do	что здесь можно делать *shto zdyes' mozhna dyelat'*
places to eat	где можно поесть *gdye mozhna payest'*
places to visit	куда можно поехать *kooda mozhna payekhat'*
We're having a great/terrible time.	Нам здесь очень нравится/совсем не нравится. *nam zdyes' ochyeen' nraveetsa/savsyem nee nraveetsa*

Invitations Приглашения

Would you like to have dinner with us on …?	Можно пригласить вас к нам на ужин в …? *mozhna preeglaseet' vas k nam na oozhin v …*
Are you free for lunch?	Можно пригласить вас на обед? *mozhna preeglaseet' vas na abyet*
Can you come for a drink this evening?	Может быть посидим где-нибудь сегодня вечером? *mozhet bit' paseedeem gdye neebood' seevodnya*
We are having a party. Can you come?	У нас вечеринка. Придёте? *oo nas veechyeereenka preedyotye*
May we join you?	Можно к вам присоединиться? *mozhna k vam preesaeedeeneet'sa*
Would you like to join us?	Не хотите к нам присоединиться? *nee khateetye k nam preesaeedeeneet'sa*

Going out Прогулка

What are your plans for …?	Какие у вас планы на …? *kakeeye oo vas plani na …*
today/tonight	сегодня/сегодня вечером *seevodnya/seevodnya vyechyeeram*
tomorrow	завтра *zaftra*
Are you free this evening?	Вы свободны сегодня вечером? *vi sfabodni seevodnya vyechyeeram*
Would you like to …?	Хотите …? *khateetye …*
go dancing	пойти потанцевать *paytee patantsevat'*
go for a drink/meal	пойти в ресторан *paytee v reestaran*
go for a walk	пойти погулять *paytee pagoolyat'*
go shopping	пойти по магазинам *paytee pa magazeenam*
Where would you like to go?	Куда Вы хотите пойти? *kooda vi khateetye paytee*
I'd like to go to …	Я хотел(а) бы пойти в … *ya khatyel(a) bi paytee v …*
I'd like to see …	Я хотел(а) бы посмотреть … *ya khatyel(a) bi pasmatryet' …*
Do you enjoy …?	Вам понравилось …? *vam panraveelas' …*

Accepting/Declining
Принять/Отказать

Thank you. I'd love to.	Спасибо. Я с удовольствием. *spaseeba. ya s oodovol'stveeyem*
Thank you, but I'm busy.	Спасибо, но я занят(а). *spaseeba no ya zanyat(a)*
May I bring a friend?	Можно с другом? *mozhna z droogam*
Where shall we meet?	Где встретимся? *gdye fstryeteemsa*
I'll meet you …	Я буду ждать Вас .... *ya boodoo zhdat' vas ...*
in the bar	в баре *v barye*
in front of your hotel	перед входом в отель *pyereet fkhodam v atyel'*
I'll call for you at 8.	Я зайду за Вами в 8. *ya zaydoo za vamee v voseem'*
Could we make it a bit later/earlier?	Можно чуть позже/раньше? *mozhna chyoot' pozzhe/ran'she*
How about another day?	Как-нибудь в другой раз. *kakneebood' v droogoy ras*
That will be fine.	Договорились. *dagavareelees'*

Dining out/in   Ужин в ресторане/дома

If you are invited to a person's home for a visit or a meal, it will be much appreciated if you take a gift – flowers, chocolates, wine – or perhaps a small souvenir from your own country.

Let me buy you a drink.	Позвольте вам предложить что-нибудь выпить. *pazvol'tee vam preedlazheet' shto-neebood' vipeet'*
Do you like …?	Вы любите ...? *vi lyoobeetye ...*
What are you going to have?	Что Вы будете? *shto vi boodyetye*
That was a lovely meal.	Это был прекрасный ужин. *eta bil preekrasniy oozhin*

Encounters В гостях

Are you waiting for someone?	Вы ждёте кого-нибудь? vi zhdyotye kavoneebood'
Do you mind if I …?	Вы не возражаете, если я …? vi nee vazrazhayetye yeslee ya …
sit here/smoke	сяду здесь/закурю syadoo zdyes' zakooryoo
Can I get you a drink?	Вам принести что-нибудь выпить? vam preeneestee shtoneebood' vipeet'
I'd love to have some company.	Я люблю быть в компании. ya lyooblyoo bit' f kampaneeyee
Why are you laughing?	Почему Вы смеётесь? pachyeemoo vi smeeyotyes'
Is my Russian that bad?	Что, мой русский так плох? shto moy roosskeey tak plokh
Shall we go somewhere quieter?	Давайте пойдём куда-нибудь, где потише. davaytye paydyom koodaneebood' gde pateeshi
Leave me alone, please!	Оставьте меня в покое, пожалуйста. astaf'tye meenya f pakoye pazhalsta
You look great!	Ты прекрасно выглядишь! ti preekrasna vigleedeesh
May I kiss you?	Можно тебя поцеловать? mozhna teebya patselavat'
I'm not ready for that.	Я не готов(а) к этому. ya nee gotof(va) k etamoo
I'm afraid we have to leave now.	Боюсь, что нам пора идти. bayoos' shto nam para eettee
Thanks for the evening.	Спасибо за вечер. spaseeba za vyechyeer
It was great.	Всё было прекрасно. fsyo bila preekrasna
Can I see you again tomorrow?	Может, увидимся завтра? mozhet ooveedeemsa zaftra
See you soon.	Пока. paka
Can I have your address?	Можно твой адрес? mozhna tvoy adrees

Telephoning Телефон

One of the biggest changes in the "New Russia" has been in internal and international telecommunications. It is now possible to dial direct to almost anywhere in the world from a private or hotel phone.

The public telephone system is changing rapidly in the big towns and cities. However, public telephones can only be used for local calls. There are two types of public phone – those requiring brown plastic tokens (жетоны **zhetoni**) and those requiring telephone cards (карточки **kartochkee**). Both can be bought at subway [metro] stations. There are small telephone directories available in Moscow and St. Petersburg, listing numbers of organizations, shops, restaurants, and hotels. However, there are still no telephone directories listing numbers of private individuals.

Can I have your telephone number?	Можно Ваш номер телефона? *mozhna vash nomeer teeleefona*
Here's my number.	Вот мой телефон. *vot moy teeleefon*
Please call me.	Пожалуйста, звоните. *pazhalsta zvaneetye*
I'll give you a call.	Я позвоню Вам. *ya pazvanyoo vam*
Where's the nearest telephone booth?	Где здесь телефон-автомат? *gdye zdyes' teeleefon aftamat*
May I use your phone?	Можно от Вас позвонить? *mozhna at vas pazvaneet'*
It's an emergency.	Это срочно. *eta srochna*
I'd like to call someone in England.	Я хочу позвонить в Англию. *ya khachyoo pazvaneet' v angleeyoo*
What's the area [dialling] code for …?	Какой код в …? *kakoy kod v …*
What's the number for Information [Directory Enquiries]?	Какой номер справочной службы? *kakoy nomeer spravachniy sloozhb*
I'd like the number for …	Мне нужен номер … *mnye noozhen nomeer …*
I'd like to call collect [reverse the charges].	Я хочу позвонить за счёт вызываемого абонента. *ya khachyoo pazvaneet' za shchyot vizivayeemava abanyenta*

Speaking   Разговор по телефону

Hello. This is …	Алло. Это … *allo eta* …
I'd like to speak to …	Можно …. к телефону. *mozhna … k teeleefonoo*
Extension …	Добавочный номер … *dabavachniy nomeer* …
Speak louder, please.	Говорите громче, пожалуйста. *gavareetye gromchye pazhalsta*
Speak more slowly, please?	Говорите медленнее, пожалуйста. *gavareetye myedleennyeye pazhalsta*
Could you repeat that, please.	Повторите, пожалуйста. *paftareetye pazhalsta*
I'm afraid he's/she's not in.	Боюсь, что его/её нет. *bayoos' shto eevo/eeyo nyet*
You have the wrong number.	Вы неправильно набрали номер. *vi neepraveel'na nabralee nomeer*
Just a moment.	Минуточку. *meenootachkoo*
Hold on, please.	Подождите, пожалуйста. *padazhdeetye pazhalsta*
When will he/she be back?	Когда он/она будет? *kagda on/ana boodyet*
Will you tell him/her that I called?	Передайте ему/ей, что я звонил(а). *peereedaytye eemoo/yey shto ya zvaneel(a)*
My name is …	Моя фамилия … *maya fameeleeya* …
Would you ask him/her to phone me?	Попросите его/её позвонить мне. *papraseetye eevo/eeyo pazvaneet' mnye*
Would you take a message, please?	Что передать? *shto peereedat'*
I must go now.	Мне пора. *mnye para*
Nice to speak to you.	Приятно было поговорить. *preeyatna bila pagavareet'*
I'll be in touch.	Я еще позвоню. *ya eshchyo pazvanyoo*
Bye.	Пока. *Paka*

128

Stores & Services

All stores used to be state owned. Now privatization is in full swing. However, there are still long lines [queues] in state-owned food stores, where prices tend to be lower. You can buy almost anything in Moscow and St. Petersburg, although imported goods are more expensive. Street markets are fun places to shop – and don't be afraid to bargain! Ask at your hotel about the nearest, or best, street market. Foreign-currency stores (Берёзка **beeryoska**) were set up in Soviet times to profit from tourist hard currency, and to offer a selection of luxury goods not generally available. And they are still good places to find souvenirs and gifts.

ESSENTIAL

I'd like …	Я хотел(а) бы … *ya khatyel(a) bi …*
Do you have …?	У Вас есть …? *oo vas yest' …*
How much is that?	Сколько стоит? *skol'ka stoeet*
Thank you.	Спасибо. *spaseeba*

ОТКРЫТО	OPEN
ЗАКРЫТО	CLOSED
РАСПРОДАЖА	SALE

Stores and services
Товары и услуги

Where is …? Где …?

Where's the nearest …?	Где ближайший …? *gdye blee<u>zhay</u>shiy …*
Where's there a good …?	Где здесь есть хороший ...? *gdye zdyes' yest' kha<u>ro</u>shiy …*
Where's the main shopping mall [centre]?	Где здесь торговый центр? *gdye zdyes' tar<u>go</u>viy tsentr*
Is it far from here?	Это далеко отсюда? *<u>e</u>ta da<u>lee</u>ko at<u>syoo</u>da*
How do I get there?	Как туда добраться? *kak too<u>da</u> da<u>brat'</u>sa*

Stores Товары

Most stores just carry the name of the article sold, e.g., ХЛЕБ (bread), РЫБА (fish), ОБУВЬ (shoes), ЦВЕТЫ (flowers), etc.

antique store	антикварный магазин *antee<u>kvar</u>niy maga<u>zeen</u>*
bakery	булочная *<u>boo</u>lachnaya*
bank	банк *bank*
bookstore	книжный магазин *<u>kneezh</u>niy maga<u>zeen</u>*
butcher	мясной магазин *mees<u>noy</u> maga<u>zeen</u>*
camera store	фототовары *fatata<u>va</u>ri*
cigarette kiosk [tobacconist]	табачный киоск *ta<u>bach</u>niy kee<u>osk</u>*
clothing store	одежда *a<u>dyezh</u>da*
delicatessen	магазин деликатесов *maga<u>zeen</u> deeleeka<u>tyess</u>af*
department store	универмаг *ooneevee<u>rmak</u>*
drugstore	аптека *ap<u>tyeka</u>*
fish store [fishmonger]	рыба *<u>ri</u>ba*
florist	цветы *tsvee<u>ti</u>*
gift store	подарки *pa<u>dar</u>kee*
greengrocer	овощи и фрукты *<u>o</u>vashchyee ee <u>froo</u>kti*
health food store	диетические продукты *deeee<u>tee</u>chyeeskeeye pra<u>doo</u>kti*
jeweler	ювелирный магазин *yoovee<u>leer</u>niy maga<u>zeen</u>*

liquor store [off-licence]	винный магазин **veen<u>niy</u> maga<u>zeen</u>**
market	рынок **<u>ri</u>nak**
pastry store	кондитерская **kan<u>dee</u>teerskaya**
pharmacy [chemist]	аптека **ap<u>tye</u>ka**
produce [grocery] store	бакалея **baka<u>lye</u>ya**
record [music] store	пластинки **pla<u>steen</u>kee**
shoe store	обувь **<u>o</u>boof'**
shopping mall [centre]	торговый центр **tar<u>go</u>viy <u>tsen</u>tar**
souvenir store	сувениры **sooveen<u>ee</u>ri**
sporting goods store	спорттовары **spartta<u>va</u>ri**
supermarket	универсам **ooneevee<u>rsam</u>**
toy store	игрушки **ee<u>groosh</u>kee**

Services   Обслуживание

clinic	поликлиника **palee<u>klee</u>neeka**
dentist	зубной врач **zoob<u>noy</u> vrach'**
doctor	врач **vrach'**
dry cleaner	химчистка **kheem<u>chees</u>tka**
hairdresser/barber	парикмахерская **pareek<u>ma</u>kheerskaya**
hospital	больница **bal'<u>neet</u>sa**
laundromat	прачечная **<u>pra</u>chyeechnaya**
library	библиотека **beeblee<u>a</u>tyeka**
optician	оптика **<u>op</u>teeka**
police station	отделение милиции **atdee<u>lye</u>neeye mee<u>leet</u>siyee**
post office	почта **<u>poch</u>ta**
travel agency	бюро путешествий **byoo<u>ro</u> pootee<u>shes</u>tveey**

Opening hours   Часы работы

State-owned stores are usually open from 8 a.m. – 8 p.m. with a lunch break from 1 p.m. – 2 p.m. Monday to Saturday, with shorter hours on Sundays. Most privately owned stores keep similar hours, but do not close for lunch.

When does the ... open/shut?	Когда ... открывается/закрывается? *ka**gda** ... atkriv**ae**etsa/zakriv**ae**etsa*
Are you open in the evening?	Вы вечером работаете? *vi **vye**cheeram rab**o**taeetye*
Do you close for lunch?	Вы закрываетесь на обед? *vi zakriv**ae**etyes' na a**byet***
Where is the ...	Где ... *gdye ...*
cashier [cash desk]	касса *k**a**ssa*
elevator [lift]	лифт *leeft*
escalator	эскалатор *eska**la**tar*
store directory [guide]	перечень отделов *pyer**ee**cheen' at**dye**laf*
It's in the basement.	Это в подвале. *eta f pad**va**lye*
It's on the ... floor.	Это на ... этаже. *eta na ... eta**zhe***
first [ground (*Brit.*)] floor	первом *pye**rvam***
second [first (*Brit.*)] floor	втором *fta**rom***
Where's the ... department?	Где ... отдел? *gdye ... at**dyel***

ЗАКРЫТО НА ОБЕД	CLOSED FOR LUNCH
БЕЗ ПЕРЕРЫВА НА ОБЕД	OPEN ALL DAY
ЧАСЫ РАБОТЫ	BUSINESS HOURS
ВХОД	ENTRANCE
ВЫХОД	EXIT
ЗАПАСНЫЙ ВЫХОД	EMERGENCY EXIT
ПОЖАРНЫЙ ВЫХОД	FIRE EXIT
ЛЕСТНИЦА	STAIRS

Service   Обслуживание

Can you help me?	Помогите мне, пожалуйста. *pamageetye mnye pazhalsta*
I'm looking for …	Я ищу … *ya eeshchyoo …*
I'm just browsing.	Я просто смотрю. *ya prosta smatryoo*
It's my turn.	Это моя очередь. *eta maya ochyeereed'*
Do you have any …?	У Вас есть …? *oo vas yest' …*
I'd like to buy …	Я хочу купить … *ya khachyoo koopeet' …*
Could you show me …?	Покажите мне …, пожалуйста. *pakazhitye mnye … pazhalsta*
How much is this/that?	Сколько это/то стоит? *skol'ka eta/to stoeet*
That's all, thanks.	Это всё, спасибо. *eta fsyo spaseeba*

Доброе утро/Добрый день госпожа/господин.	Good morning/afternoon, madam/sir.
Я вас слушаю?	Can I help you?
Что Вы хотите?	What would you like?
Я сейчас посмотрю.	I'll just check that for you.
Это всё?	Is that everything?
Что ещё?	Anything else?

– *shto vi khateetye?*

– *spaseeba neechyeevo. ya prosta smatryoo.*

– *kharasho.*

– *eezveeneetye.*

– *da slooshayoo vas.*

– *skol'ka eta stoeet?*

– *ya seechyas pasmatryoo … deeveenosta voseem rooblyey.*

ОБСЛУЖИВАНИЕ	CUSTOMER SERVICE
САМООБСЛУЖИВАНИЕ	SELF- SERVICE
РАСПРОДАЖА	CLEARANCE

Preference   Выбор

I want something …	Я хочу что-нибудь … *ya khachyoo shto-neebood'…*
It must be …	Это должно быть … *eta dolzhno bit'…*
big/small	большой/маленький *bal'shoy/maleen'keey*
cheap/expensive	дешёвый/дорогой *deeshoviy/daragoy*
dark/light	тёмный/светлый *tyomniy/svyetliy*
light/heavy	лёгкий/тяжёлый *lyokhkeey/teezholiy*
oval/round/square	овальный/круглый/квадратный *aval'niy/kroogliy/kvadratniy*
I don't want anything too expensive.	Я не хочу ничего дорогого. *ya nee khachyoo neechyeevo daragova*
In the region of … rubles.	Примерно … рублей. *preemyerna … rooblyey*

Какого … Вы хотите?	What … would you like?
цвета/покроя	color/shape
качества/количества	quality/quantity
Какого плана Вы хотите?	What sort would you like?
За какую цену?	What price range are you thinking of?

Do you have anything …?	У Вас есть …? *oo vas yest'* …
larger	побольше *pabol'she*
better quality	лучшего качества *loochsheva*
cheaper	подешевле *padeeshevlye*
smaller	поменьше *pamyen'she*
Can you show me …?	Покажите мне …? *pakazhitye mnye* …
that/this one	то/это *to/eta*
these/those ones	эти/те *etee/tye*
the one in the window/ display case	то, что в витрине/ в горке *to shto v veetreenye/f gorkee*
some others	другие *droogeeye*

Conditions of purchase
Условия покупки

Is there a guarantee?	Есть гарантия? *yest' garanteeya*
Are there any instructions with it?	Есть инструкция? *yest' een<u>strook</u>tsiya*

Out of stock Продано

Извините, у нас нет.	I'm sorry, we don't have any.
Извините, продано.	We're out of stock.
Показать Вам что-нибудь ещё?	Can I show you something else / a different sort?
Хотите это заказать?	Shall we order it for you?

Decision Решение

That's not quite what I want.	Это не совсем то, что я хочу. *<u>e</u>ta nee saf<u>sye</u>m to shto ya kha<u>chy</u>oo*
No, I don't like it.	Нет, это мне не нравится. *nyet <u>e</u>ta mnye nee <u>nra</u>veetsa*
That's too expensive.	Это очень дорого. *<u>e</u>ta <u>o</u>chyeen' <u>do</u>raga*
I'd like to think about it.	Надо подумать. *<u>na</u>da pa<u>doo</u>mat'*
I'll take it.	Я возьму это. *ya vaz'<u>moo</u> <u>e</u>ta*

– *z<u>dra</u>stvooytye. ya kha<u>chy</u>oo koo<u>pee</u>t' roo<u>bash</u>koo pa<u>zhal</u>sta.*

– *ka<u>koo</u>yoo roo<u>bash</u>koo vi kha<u>tee</u>tye?*

– *a<u>ran</u>zhiviyoo pa<u>zhal</u>sta. ee saf<u>sye</u>m bal'shova raz<u>mye</u>ra.*

– *vot. <u>e</u>ta sto <u>dva</u>ttsat' roob<u>lyey</u>.*

– *hmm. <u>e</u>ta nee saf<u>sye</u>m to shto ya kha<u>chy</u>oo. spa<u>see</u>ba.*

Paying Оплата

When shopping in foreign-currency stores, you pay in the normal way. In other stores, however, you have to memorize the price of the item you want to buy, pay that amount at the cash desk, and then using the receipt you have obtained, pick up the item you want from the counter.

International credit cards are accepted in many stores. However, it is illegal to pay in foreign currency, although prices are often given in U.S. dollars and converted to rubles at the current exchange rate.

Where do I pay?	Куда платить? **kooda plateet'**
How much is that?	Сколько это стоит? **skol'ka eta stoeet**
Could you write it down, please?	Напишите, пожалуйста. **napeeshitye pazhalsta**
Do you accept …?	Вы принимаете ...? **vi preeneemaeetye** ...
traveler's checks [cheques]	аккредитивы **akreedeeteevi**
I'll pay …	Я заплачу ... **ya zaplachoo** ...
by cash/by credit card	наличными/по кредитной карточке **naleechnimee/pa kreedeetniy kartachkee**
I don't have any smaller change.	У меня нет сдачи. **oo meenya nyet zdachyee**
Sorry, I don't have enough money.	Извините, у меня не хватает денег. **eezveeneetee oo meenya nee khvatayeet dyeneek**
Could I have a receipt, please?	Можно чек, пожалуйста? **mozhna chyek pazhalsta**
I think you've given me the wrong change.	Мне кажется, что Вы неправильно дали сдачу. **mnye kazhetsa shto vi neepraveel'na dalee zdachyoo**

Как будете платить?	How are you paying?
... рублей, пожалуйста.	That's … rubles, please.
Это мы не принимаем.	This transaction has not been approved/accepted.
Эта карточка недействительна.	This card is not valid.
Можно Ваше удостоверение?	May I have additional identification?
У Вас есть деньги мельче?	Do you have any smaller change?

ПЛАТИТЬ ЗДЕСЬ	PLEASE PAY HERE
КРАЖА ТОВАРОВ ПРЕСЛЕДУЕТСЯ ПО ЗАКОНУ	SHOPLIFTERS WILL BE PROSECUTED

Complaints Жалобы

This doesn't work.	Это с браком. *eta z brakam*
Where can I make a complaint?	Куда я могу пожаловаться? *kooda ya magoo pazhalavat'sa*
Can I exchange this, please?	Можно это поменять? *mozhna eta pameenyat'*
I'd like a refund.	Я хотел(а) бы получить деньги назад. *ya khatyel(a) bi paloocheet' dyen'gee nazat*
Here's the receipt.	Вот чек. *vot chyek*
I don't have the receipt.	У меня нет чека. *oo meenya nyet chyeka*
I'd like to see the manager.	Я хотел(а) бы видеть администратора. *ya khatyel(a) bi veedyet' admeeneestratara*

Repairs/Cleaning Ремонт/Химчистка

This is broken. Can you repair it?	Это сломано. Можно это починить? *eta slomana. mozhna eta pachyeeneet'*
Do you have … for this?	У Вас есть …? *oo vas yest' …*
a battery	батарейка *bataryeyka*
replacement parts	запасные части *zapasniye chyastee*
There's something wrong with …	Что-то не в порядке с … *shtoto nee f paryatkye s …*
Can you … this?	Вы можете это …? *vi mozhetye eta …*
clean	почистить *pachyeesteet'*
press	погладить *pagladeet'*
alter	переделать *peereedyelat'*
patch	заштопать *zashtopat'*
When will it/they be ready?	Когда будет готово? *kagda boodyet gatova*
Can I collect it …?	Можно забрать это …? *mozhna zabrat' eta …*
later today/tomorrow	сегодня позже/завтра *seevodnya pozhzhe/zaftra*
on Friday/next week	в пятницу/на следующей неделе *f pyatneetsoo/na slyedooyooshchyee needyelye*
This isn't mine.	Это не моё. *eta nee mayo*
There's … missing.	Здесь не хватает … *zdyes' nee khvatayet …*

Bank/Currency exchange
Банк/Обмен валюты

Check with your travel agent or the Russian embassy before your trip on the latest regulations regarding how much foreign currency you can bring in.

In big towns and cities there are many currency exchange offices in banks, hotels, stores, and even street kiosks. Some work non-stop, 24 hours a day. Others are open from early morning to late evening, with a break for lunch. You may be required to show your passport.

All currency exchange offices accept U.S. dollars. However, they will not take dirty notes or notes with writing on them. You may have difficulty changing notes issued before 1993, so try to obtain clean, post-1993 notes. Some currency exhange offices also accept clean German marks. For other currencies and traveler's checks use the banks and big hotels. But remember: U.S. dollars are your best bet!

Where's the nearest …?	Где ближайший …? *gdye bleezhayshiy …*
bank	банк *bank*
currency exchange office [bureau de change]	обмен валюты *abmyen valyooti*

Changing money   Обмен денег

Warning: You may be approached by someone on the street offering normal or slightly better rates. It is easy to be cheated, so stick to the official places.

Can I exchange foreign currency here?	Можно обменять валюту здесь? *mozhna abmeenyat' valyootoo zdyes'*
I'd like to change some dollars/ pounds into rubles.	Я хотел(а) бы обменять доллары/фунты на рубли. *ya khatyel(a) bi abmeenyat' dollari/foonti na rooblee*
I want to cash some traveler's checks [cheques].	Я хочу обменять аккредитивы. *ya khachyoo abmeenyat' akreedeeteevi*
What's the exchange rate?	Какой курс? *kakoy koors*
How much commission do you charge?	Сколько процентов комиссионный сбор? *skol'ka pratsentaf kameesseeonniy zbor*
I've lost my traveler's checks. These are the numbers.	Я потерял(а) аккредитивы. Вот номера. *ya pateeryal(a) akreedeeteevi. vot nameera*

КАССЫ	CASHIERS
ВСЕ ОПЕРАЦИИ	ALL TRANSACTIONS
ОТ СЕБЯ/НА СЕБЯ/НАЖМИТЕ	PUSH/PULL/PRESS

Security Служба безопасности

Можно ...?	Could I see ...?
Ваш паспорт	your passport
удостоверение	some identification
Вашу кредитную карточку	your bank card
Ваш адрес?	What's your address?
Где вы остановились?	Where are you staying?
Заполните этот бланк, пожалуйста.	Fill in this form, please.
Распишитесь здесь.	Please sign here.

ATMs [Cash machines] Банкоматы

Can I withdraw money on my credit card here?	Можно здесь снять деньги по кредитной карточке? *mozhna zdyes' snyat' dyen'gee pa kreedeetniy kartachkye*
Where are the ATMs [cash machines]?	Где здесь банкоматы? *gdye zdyes' bankamati*
Can I use my ... card in the cash machine?	Можно мне использовать мою ... карточку в этом автомате? *mozhna mnye eespol'zavat' mayoo ... kartachkoo v etam aftomatye*
The cash machine has eaten my card.	У меня застряла карточка в автомате. *oo menya zastryala kartachka v aftomatye*

КОМИССИОННЫЙ СБОР	BANK CHARGES
ИНОСТРАННАЯ ВАЛЮТА	FOREIGN CURRENCY
БАНКОМАТ	AUTOMATED TELLER (ATM) [CASH MACHINE]

The monetary unit is the ruble (рубль), which until recently was divided into 100 kopecks. Due to recent mass inflation, however, the kopeck is now worthless. To cope with this inflation, the Russian currency was "denominated," i.e., divided by 1,000. Hence 1,000 rubles (about 20 cents U.S./10 pence Sterling) are now worth 1 ruble. At the moment, both prices are being quoted to give Russians a chance to adapt.

Pharmacy   Аптека

You can buy medicine at a pharmacy (аптека **aptyeka**) or from private foreign/joint-venture hospitals. Although medical treatment is free in Russian state hospitals, it is customary to give the doctor a present – a box of chocolates or a bottle of wine, for example. However, you will have to pay for medicine. Also, be sure to get medical insurance before you go.

For toiletries, you have to go to a парфюмерия (**parfyoomyereeya**). You can find a wide range of toiletries and cosmetics in big towns and cities. But prices are high, so stock up before going.

Where's the nearest (all-night) pharmacy?	Где ближайшая (ночная) аптека? *gdye bleezhayshaya (nachnaya) aptyeka*
What time does the pharmacy open/close?	Во сколько аптека открывается/ закрывается? *va skol'ka aptyeka atkrivaeetsa/zakrivaeetsa*
Can you make up this prescription for me?	Вы можете приготовить это лекарство? *vi mozhetye preegatoveet' eta leekarstva*
Shall I wait?	Мне подождать? *mnye padazhdat'*
I'll come back for it.	Я приду за ним. *ya preedoo za neem*

Dosage instructions   Дозы и инструкции

How much should I take?	Сколько нужно принимать? *skol'ka noozhna preeneemat'*
How often should I take it?	Как часто нужно принимать? *kak chyasta noozhna preeneemat'*
Is it suitable for children?	Это можно детям? *eta mozhna dyeteem*

Принимайте ... таблетки/ ... ложки ...	Take ... tablets/... teaspoons ...
перед едой/после еды	before/after meals
с водой	with water
целые	whole
утром/вечером	in the morning/at night
в течение ... дней	for ... days

ЯД	POISON
НАРУЖНОЕ	FOR EXTERNAL USE ONLY
НЕ ДЛЯ ВНУТРЕННЕГО УПОТРЕБЛЕНИЯ	NOT TO BE TAKEN INTERNALLY

Asking advice Лекарства

What would you recommend for …?	Что Вы рекомендуете от …? *shto vi reekameend<u>oo</u>eetye at …*
a cold	простуды *pr<u>a</u>stoodi*
a cough	кашля *k<u>a</u>shlya*
diarrhea	поноса *pan<u>o</u>sa*
a hangover	похмелья *pakhm<u>ye</u>lya*
hay fever	сенной лихорадки *seen<u>oy</u> leekhar<u>a</u>tkee*
insect bites	укусов насекомых *ook<u>oo</u>saf nasee<u>ko</u>mikh*
a sore throat	воспаления горла *vaspal<u>ye</u>neeye <u>go</u>rla*
sunburn	солнечного ожёга *s<u>o</u>lneechnava az<u>ho</u>ga*
motion [travel] sickness	морской болезни *marsk<u>oy</u> bal<u>ye</u>znee*
an upset stomach	расстройства желудка *rasstr<u>oy</u>stva zhee<u>loo</u>tka*
Can I get it without a prescription?	Можно это получить без рецепта? *m<u>o</u>zhna eta palooch<u>yee</u>t' byez reets<u>e</u>pta*
Can I have a(n)/some …?	Дайте, пожалуйста, … *d<u>ay</u>tye pazh<u>a</u>lsta …*
antiseptic cream	антисептическую мазь *anteeseept<u>ee</u>chyeeskooyoo maz'*
aspirin	аспирин *aspeer<u>ee</u>n*
gauze [bandages]	бинт *beent*
adhesive bandages [plasters]	пластыри *pl<u>a</u>stiree*
condoms	презервативы *preezeervat<u>ee</u>vi*
cotton [cotton wool]	вату *v<u>a</u>too*
insect repellent	средство от комаров *sry<u>e</u>tstva at kam<u>a</u>raf*
painkillers	болеутоляющее *baleeootal<u>ya</u>yooshchyeye*
vitamin tablets	витамины в таблетках *veetam<u>ee</u>ni f tabl<u>ye</u>tkakh*

Toiletries Туалетные принадлежности

I'd like a(n)/some … Дайте, пожалуйта …
daytye pa_zhalsta_ …

after shave	лосьон после бритья **las'on _poslye_ bree_tya_**
deodorant	дезодорант **deezada_rant_**
razor blades	лезвия **_lyez_veeya**
sanitary napkins [towels]	гигиенические салфетки **geegeeee_nee_chyeeskeeye sal_fyet_kee**
sunscreen	крем для загара **kryem dlya za_gara_**
soap	мыло **_mila_**
tampons	тампоны **tam_poni_**
tissues	бумажные салфетки **boo_mazh_niye sal_fyet_kee**
toilet paper	туалетную бумагу **tooa_lyet_nooyoo boo_magoo_**
toothpaste	зубную пасту **zoob_nooyoo pas_too**

Haircare Уход за волосами

comb	расчёска **ra_shchyos_ka**
conditioner	кондиционер **kandeetsia_nyer_**
hair brush	щётка для волос **_shchyot_ka dlya va_los_**
hair mousse	мусс для волос **mooss dlya va_los_**
hair spray	лак для волос **lak dlya va_los_**
shampoo	шампунь **sham_poon'_**

For the baby Для ребёнка

baby food	детское питание **_dyet_skaye pee_ta_neeye**
baby wipes	гигиенические салфетки **geegeenee_che_skeeye sal_fyet_kee**
diapers [nappies]	пелёнки **pee_lyon_kee**
sterilizing solution	стерилизующий раствор **steereelee_zoo_yooshchyeey ras_tvor_**

Clothing Одежда

Street markets are cheaper than stores. Don't be afraid to bargain – it's part of the fun.

Duty-free shopping is found at the airports and large hotels.

General Общие вопросы

| I'd like … | Я хотел(а) бы … *ya khatyel(a) bi* … |
| Do you have any …? | У Вас есть…? *oo vas yest'* … |

ЖЕНСКАЯ ОДЕЖДА	LADIESWEAR
МУЖСКАЯ ОДЕЖДА	MENSWEAR
ДЕТСКАЯ ОДЕЖДА	CHILDRENSWEAR

Color Цвет

I'm looking for something in …	Я ищу что-нибудь … *ya eeshchyo shtoneebood'* …
beige	бежевое *byezhevaye*
black	чёрное *chyornaye*
blue	синее *seenyeeye*
brown	коричневое *kareechneevaye*
green	зелёное *zeelyonaye*
gray [grey]	серое *syeraye*
orange	оранжевое *aranzhevaye*
pink	розовое *rozavaye*
purple	алое *alaye*
red	красное *krasnaye*
white	белое *byelaye*
yellow	жёлтое *zholtaye*
light …	светло-… *svyetla-…*
dark …	тёмно-… *tyomna-…*
I want a darker/lighter shade.	Я хочу темнее/светлее. *ya khachyoo teemnyeye/sveetlyeye*
Do you have the same in …?	У Вас есть такое же по …? *oo vas yest' takoye zhe pa* …

Clothes and accessories
Одежда и аксессуары

belt	ремень/пояс *reemyen'/poees*
bikini	бикини *beekeenee*
blouse	блузка *blooska*
bra	бюстгальтер *byoostgal'teer*
briefs	трусики *trooseekee*
coat	пальто *pal'to*
dress	платье *plat'e*
handbag	сумка *soomka*
hat	шапка *shapka*
jacket	пиджак *peedzhak*
jeans	джинсы *dzheensi*
leggings	лосины *laseeni*
pants (U.S.)	брюки *bryookee*
pantyhose [tights]	колготки *kalgotkee*
raincoat	плащ *plashch*
scarf	шарф *sharf*
shirt	рубашка *roobashka*
shorts	шорты *shorti*
skirt	юбка *yoopka*
socks	носки *naskee*
stockings	чулки *chyoolkee*
suit	костюм *kastyoom*
sunglasses	солнечные очки *solneechniye achkee*
sweater	пуловер *pooloveer*
sweatshirt	рубашка (футболка) *roobashka (footbolka)*
swimming trunks/swimsuit	плавки/купальник *plafkee/koopal'neek*
T-shirt	майка *mayka*
tie	галстук *galstook*
trousers	брюки *bryookee*
underpants	трусы *troosi*
with long/short sleeves	с длинными/короткими рукавами *z dleennimee/karotkeemee rookavamee*
with a V-/round neck	с вырезом/круглым воротом *s vireezam/krooglim voratam*

Shoes Обувь

a pair of …	пара … *para* …
boots	сапоги *sapagee*
flip-flops	шлёпанцы *shlyopantsi*
running [training] shoes	кроссовки *krassofkee*
sandals	сандалии *sandaleeyee*
shoes	туфли *tooflee*
slippers	тапочки *tapachkee*

Walking/Hiking gear В походе

hiking boots	ботинки *bateenkee*
knapsack	рюкзак *ryoogzak*
waterproof jacket/anorak	дождевик *dazhdeeveek*
windbreaker [cagoule]	куртка *koortka*

Fabric Ткани

I want something in …	Я хочу что-нибудь из … *ya khachyoo shtoneebood' eez* …
cotton	хлопка *khlopka*
denim	джинсовой ткани *dzheensoviy tkanee*
lace	кружев *kroozhef*
leather	кожи *kozhi*
linen	льна *l'na*
wool	шерсти *sherstee*
Is this …?	Это …? *eta* …
pure cotton	чистый хлопок *chyeestiy khlopak*
synthetic	синтетика *seentyeteeka*
Is it hand washable/ machine washable?	Это стирать вручную/в машине? *eta steerat' vroochnooyoo/v mashinye*

ХИМЧИСТКА ТОЛЬКО	DRY CLEAN ONLY
РУЧНАЯ СТИРКА	HANDWASH ONLY
НЕ ГЛАДИТЬ	DO NOT IRON
СТИРАТЬ ОТДЕЛЬНО	COLORFAST

Does it fit?   Подходит?

Can I try this on?	Можно это примерить? *mozhna eta preemyereet'*
Where's the fitting room?	Где примерочная? *gdye preemyerachnaya*
It fits well. I'll take it.	Подходит. Я возьму. *patkhodeet. ya vaz'moo*
It doesn't fit.	Не подходит. *nee patkhodeet*
It's too …	Слишком … *sleeshkam …*
short/long	коротко/длинно *koratka/dleenna*
tight/loose	тесно/свободно *tyesna/sfabodna*
Do you have this in size …?	У Вас есть … размера? *oo vas yest' … razmyera*
What size is this?	Какой это размер? *kakoy eta razmyer*
Could you measure me, please?	Вы можете снять мерку? *vi mozhetye snyat' myerkoo*
What size do you take?	Какой у Вас размер? *kakoy oo vas razmyer*
I don't know Russian sizes.	Я не знаю русских размеров. *ya nee znayoo roosskeekh razmyeraf*

Size   Размер

	Dresses/Suits						Women's shoes			
American	8	10	12	14	16	18	6	7	8	9
British	10	12	14	16	18	20	$4^{1/2}$	$5^{1/2}$	$6^{1/2}$	$7^{1/2}$
Russian	36	38	40	42	44	46	36	37	38	40

	Shirts				Men's shoes								
American British }	15	16	17	18	5	6	7	8	$8^{1/2}$	9	$9^{1/2}$	10	11
Russian	38	41	43	45	38	39	41	42	43	43	44	44	45

ОЧЕНЬ БОЛЬШОЙ	EXTRA LARGE (XL)
БОЛЬШОЙ	LARGE (L)
СРЕДНИЙ	MEDIUM (M)
МАЛЫЙ	SMALL (S)

1 centimeter (cm.) = 0.39 in.   1 inch = 2.54 cm.
1 meter (m.) = 39.37 in.   1 foot = 30.5 cm.
10 meters = 32.81 ft.   1 yard = 0.91 m.

Health and beauty
Здоровье и красота

I'd like a …	Я хотела бы сделать … *ya khatyel(a) bi zdyelat' …*
facial	чистку лица *cheestkoo leetsa*
manicure	маникюр *maneekyoor*
massage	массаж *massash*
waxing	эпиляцию воском *eepeelyatseeyoo voskam*

Hairdresser/Hairstylist   В парикмахерской

I'd like to make an appointment for …	Я хотел(а) бы записаться на … *ya khatyel(a) bi zapeesat'sa na …*
Can you make it a bit earlier/later?	Можно пораньше/попозже? *mozhna paran'she/papozhzhe*
I'd like a …	Я хочу … *ya khachyoo …*
cut and blow-dry	стрижку и посушить феном *streeshkoo ee pasooshit' fyenam*
shampoo and set	вымыть и уложить *vimit' ee oolazhit'*
trim	подстричься *padstreeh'sa*
I'd like my hair …	Я хотел(а) бы … волосы. *ya khatyel(a) bi … volasi*
colored/tinted	покрасить/тонировать *pakraseet'/taneeravat'*
highlighted	осветлить *asveetleet'*
permed	сделать химическую завивку *zdyelat' kheemeecheeskooyoo zaveefkoo*
Don't cut it too short.	Не слишком коротко, пожалуйста. *nee sleeshkam korotka pazhalsta*
A little more off the …	Снимите ещё немного … *sneemeetye eeshchyo neemnoga …*
back/front	сзади/спереди *zzadee/spyereedee*
neck/sides	с шеи/боков *s sheyee/bakof*
top	с затылка *s zatilka*
That's fine, thanks.	Очень хорошо, спасибо. *ochyeen' kharasho spaseeba*

Household articles
Хозяйственные товары

I'd like a(n)/some …	Мне нужен(а) … *mnye noozhen (noozhna) …*
adapter	адаптер *adapteer*
alumin(i)um foil	фольга *fol'ga*
bottle opener	открывалка *atkrivalka*
can [tin] opener	открывалка *atkrivalka*
candles	свечи *svyechyee*
clothes pins [pegs]	прищепки *preeshchyepkee*
corkscrew	штопор *shtopar*
light bulb	лампочка *lampachka*
matches	спички *speechkee*
paper napkins	бумажные салфетки *boomazhniye salfyetkee*
plastic wrap [cling film]	продуктовая плёнка *pradooktovaya plyonka*
plug	штепсель *shtyepseel'*
scissors	ножницы *nozhneetsi*
screwdriver	отвёртка *atvyortka*

Cleaning items   Уборка

bleach	отбеливатель *atbyeleevateel'*
dish cloth	тряпка *tryapka*
dishwashing [washing-up] liquid	жидкость для мытья посуды *zhidkast' dlya mitya pasoodi*
garbage [refuse] bags	полиэтиленовые мешки *palee-eteelyenaviye meeshkee*
detergent [washing powder]	стиральный порошок *steeral'niy parashok*

Crockery/Cutlery   Посуда

cups	чашки *chashkee*
knives/forks	ножи/вилки *nazhi/veelkee*
spoons	ложки *loshkee*
glasses	стаканы *stakani*
mugs	кружки *krooshkee*
plates	тарелки *taryelkee*

Jeweler   Ювелирные изделия

Russia is well-known for its amber (янтарь **eentar'**), and
you will find amber jewelry and that jewelry made from
other semi-precious stones in foreign-currency stores.

Could I see …?	Можно посмотреть …? _mozhna_ pas_matryet'_ …
this/that	это/то _eta/to_
It's in the window/ display cabinet.	что в витрине/в горке _shto v_ vee_tree_nye/f _gorkye_
I'd like a(n)/some …	Я хочу купить … _ya_ kha_chyoo_ koo_peet'_ …
bracelet	браслет _braslyet_
brooch	брошь _brosh_
clock	часы _chyasi_
earrings	серьги _syer'gee_
necklace/chain	ожерелье/цепочку _azheryelye/_tse_pochkoo_
ring	кольцо _kal'tso_
watch	наручные часы _naroochniye chasi_

Materials   Материалы

Is this real silver/gold?	Это настоящее серебро/золото? _eta_ nasto_yashchyeye_ seereе_bro/_zo_lata_
Is there a certificate for it?	На это есть сертификат? _na eta yest'_ seertee_feekat_
Do you have anything in …?	У Вас есть изделия из …? _oo vas yest' eezdyeleeya eez_ …
copper	меди _myedee_
crystal (quartz)	хрусталя _khroostalya_
cut glass	резного стекла _reeznova steekla_
diamond	брильянтов _breelyantaf_
enamel	эмали _emalee_
gold/gold-plate	золота/позолоты _zolata/_paza_loti_
pearl	жемчуга _zhemchyooga_
platinum	платины _plateeni_
silver/silver-plate	серебра/посеребрённые _seereebra/paseereebryonniye_
stainless steel	нержавеющей стали _neerzhavyeyooshchyeey stalee_

Newsstand [Newsagent]/
Tobacconist   Газетный киоск/Табак

Russian newspapers and magazines can be bought near subway [metro] stations (marked with a large M for Метро **meetro**) and at kiosks with the sign Печать. The latter may also sell envelopes and postcards.

Locally published English-language newspapers are offered free in many hotels, supermarkets, and stores. For foreign language newspapers and magazines, your best bet is the newsstand in your hotel.

Lots of imported and Russian brands of cigarettes are sold in stores and kiosks – and are much cheaper than in Western countries.

Do you sell English-language books/newspapers?	Есть в продаже английские книги/газеты? *yest' f pradazhe angleeyskeeye kneegee/gazyeti*
I'd like a(n)/some …	Дайте, пожалуйста … *daytye pazhalsta …*
book	книгу *kneegoo*
candy [sweets]	конфеты *kanfyeti*
chewing gum	жевательную резинку *zheevateel'nooyoo reezeenkoo*
chocolate bar	шоколадку *shakalatkoo*
cigarettes (pack of)	пачку сигарет *pachkoo seegaryet*
cigars	сигары *seegari*
dictionary	словарь *slavar'*
English-Russian	англо-русский *anglo/roosskee*
guidebook of …	путеводитель по … *pooteevadeeteel' pa …*
lighter	зажигалку *zazheegalkoo*
magazine	журнал *zhoornal*
map of the town	карту города *kartoo gorada*
matches	спички *speechkee*
newspaper	газету *gazyetoo*
American	американскую *ameereekanskooyoo*
English	английскую *angleeskooyoo*
pen/paper	ручку/бумагу *roochkoo/boomagoo*
road map of …	карту автомобильных дорог … *kartoo aftamabeel'nikh darok…*
stamps	марки *markee*
tobacco	табак *tabak*

Photography   Фотография

Film is probably more expensive in Russia than where you live, so it may be worthwhile taking some with you.
Warning: Don't photograph objects of a military nature, airports, or harbors.

I'm looking for a(n) ... camera.	Я ищу ... фотоаппарат. *ya eeshchyoo ... fataapparat*
automatic	автоматический *aftamateechyeeskeey*
compact	компактный *kampaktniy*
disposable	одноразовый *adnarazaviy*
SLR	зеркальный *zeerkal'niy*
battery	батарейка *bataryeyka*
camera case	футляр *footlyar*
electronic flash	вспышка *fspishka*
filter	фильтр *feel'tar*
lens	объектив *ab'ekteef*
lens cap	крышка объектива *krishka ab'ekteeva*

Film/Processing   Фотография /Обработка

I'd like a ... film.	Дайте, пожалуйста, ... плёнку. *daytye pazhalsta ... plyonkoo*
black and white	чёрно-белую *chyorna byelooyoo*
color	цветную *tsvyetnooyoo*
I'd like this film developed, please.	Я хотел(а) бы проявить плёнку. *ya khatyel(a) bi praeeveet' plyonkoo*
Would you enlarge this, please?	Можно это увеличить? *mozhna eta ooveeleechyeet'*
How much do ... exposures cost?	Сколько стоит сделать ... фото? *skol'ka stoeet zdyelat' ... fota*
When will the photos be ready?	Когда фотографии будут готовы? *kagda fatagrafeeyee boodoot gatovi*
I'd like to collect my photos.	Я хочу забрать фотографии. *ya khachyoo zabrat' fatagrafeeyee*
Here's the receipt.	Вот квитанция. *vot kveetantsiya*

Police Милиция

Crime is a big problem all over Russia, and particularly in Moscow and St. Petersburg. Sensible precautions include making photocopies of your passport and visa, leaving tickets and valuables in your hotel safe, and taking out only the money you need. Crime that affects tourists is mostly of a "petty" nature: theft from cars and hotel rooms, and pickpocketing. The police are recognized by their blue-gray uniforms with red lapels and cap bands. To contact the police in an emergency ☎ 02.

Where's the nearest police station?	Где ближайшее отделение милиции? *gdye bleezhaysheye addeelyeneeye meeleetsiee*
Does anyone here speak English?	Здесь кто-нибудь говорит по-английски? *zdyes' ktoneebood' gavareet pa angleeyskee*
I want to report a(n) …	Я хочу заявить о … *ya khachyoo zaeeveet' a …*
accident/attack	несчастном случае/нападении *neeshchyastnam sloochyaye/napadyeneeye*
mugging/rape	краже/изнасиловании *krazhe/eeznaseelavaneeye*
My child is missing.	У меня пропал ребёнок. *oo meenya prapal reebyonak*
Here's a photo of him/her.	Вот его/её фотография. *vot eevo/eeyo fatagrafeeya*
I need an English-speaking lawyer.	Мне нужен адвокат, говорящий по-английски. *mnye noozhen advakat gavaryashchyeey pa angleeyskee*
I need to make a phone call.	Мне нужно позвонить. *mnye noozhna pazvaneet'*
I need to contact the … Consulate.	Мне нужно связаться с … консульством. *mnye noozhna sveezat'sa s … konsool'stvam*
American/British	американским/британским *ameereekanskeem/breetanskeem*

Вы можете описать его/её?	Can you describe him/her?
мужчина/женщина	male/female
блондин(ка)/брюнет(ка)	blond(e)/brunette
рыжий(-ая)/седые волосы	red-headed/gray haired
длинные/короткие волосы/лысый	long/short hair/balding
рост …/возраст …	height …/aged …
Был(а) одет(а) в …	He/She was wearing …

CLOTHES ➤ 144; COLORS ➤ 143

Lost property/Theft Пропажа/Кража

I want to report a theft/break-in.
Я хочу заявить о краже/взломе. *ya khachyoo zaeeveet' a krazhe/vzlomye*

My car's been broken into.
У меня взломали машину. *oo meenya vzlamalee mashinoo*

I've been robbed/mugged.
Меня обокрали. *meenya abakralee*

I've lost my ...
Я потерял(а) ... *ya pateeryal(a) ...*

My ... has been stolen.
У меня украли ... *oo meenya ookralee ...*

bicycle
велосипед *veelaseepyet*

camera
фотоаппарат *fataapparat*

(rental) car
машину *mashinoo*

credit card
кредитную карточку *kreedeetnooyoo kartachkoo*

handbag
сумочку *soomachkoo*

money
деньги *dyen'gee*

passport
паспорт *paspart*

purse
кошелёк *kasheelyok*

wallet
бумажник *boomazhneek*

watch
часы *chyasi*

What shall I do?
Что мне делать? *shto mnye dyelat'*

I need a police report for my insurance claim.
Мне нужно свидетельство из милиции для получения страховки. *mnye noozhna sveedyeteel'stva eez meeleetsiee dlya paloochyeneeya strakhofkee*

Что пропало?	What's missing?
Когда украли?	When was it stolen?
Когда это случилось?	When did it happen?
Где Вы остановились?	Where are you staying?
Откуда украли?	Where was it taken from?
Где Вы были в это время?	Where were you at the time?
Мы пригласим Вам переводчика	We're getting an interpreter for you.
Мы всё проверим.	We'll look into the matter.
Пожалуйста, заполните эту форму.	Please fill out this form.

Post office   Почта

The main post offices in Moscow and St. Petersburg offer round-the-clock service. Other post offices are generally open Monday through Saturday from 8 a.m. to 7 p.m. and Sunday from 9 a.m. to 7 p.m. Major hotels have their own branches for postal, telegraph, and telephone services. Note: International money orders can only be cashed at banks. Also, both incoming and outgoing postal services are slow, so allow plenty of time.

General queries   Общие вопросы

Where is the nearest/main post office?	Где здесь ближайшая почта/главпочтамт? *gdye zdyes' bleezhayshaya pochta/glavpachtamt*
What time does the post office open/close?	Во сколько почта открывается/ закрывается? *va skol'ka pochta atkrivaeetsa/zakrivaeetsa*
Does it close for lunch?	Закрывается на обед? *zakrivaeetsa na abyet*
Where's the mailbox [postbox]?	Где здесь почтовый ящик? *gdye zdyes' pachtoviy yashchyeek*
Is there any mail for me? My name is …	Есть почта для меня? Моя фамилия … *yest' pochta dlya meenya. maya fameeleeya …*

Buying stamps   Марки

A stamp for this postcard/ letter, please.	Дайте марку на эту открытку/это письмо, пожалуйста. *daytye markoo na etoo atkritoo/eto pees'mo pazhalsta*
A … ruble stamp, please.	Марку за … рублей, пожалуйста. *markoo za … rooblyey pazhalsta*
What's the postage for a postcard/letter to …?	Сколько стоит послать открытку/ письмо в …? *skol'ka stoeet paslat' atkritkoo/pees'mo v …*

– *zdrastvooytye. ya khachyoo paslat' etee atkritkee v ameereekoo.*

– *skol'ka atkritok?*

– *dyeveet' pazhalsta.*

– *tak pa tree rooblya dyeveet' ras. s vas dvatsats syem' rooblyey.*

Sending packages Посылки

I want to send this package [parcel] by …	Я хочу послать эту посылку … *ya khachyoo paslat' etoo pasilkoo…*
air mail	авиапочтой *aveeyapochtay*
special delivery [express]	экспресс-почтой *ekspryess-pochtay*
registered mail	заказной почтой *zakaznoy pochtay*
It contains …	Там … *tam …*

Пожалуйста, заполните таможенную декларацию.	Please fill in the customs declaration.
Какая стоимость?	What's the value?
Что там?	What's inside?

Other services Другие услуги

I'd like a phone card, please.	Я хочу телефонную карточку, пожалуйста. *Ya khachoo teeleefonooyoo kartochkoo pazhalsta*
10/20/50 units	на десять/двадцать/пятьдесят единиц *na dyesyat'/dvattsat'/peedeesyat' yedeeneets*
Do you have a photocopier/ fax machine here?	Здесь есть ксерокс/факс? *zdyes' yest' ksyeraks/ faks*
I'd like to send a telex/fax.	Мне нужно послать телекс/факс. *mnye noozhna paslat' tyeleeks/faks*
I'd like to send a message by e-mail.	Мне нужно послать сообщение по электронной почте. *mnye noozhna paslat' sapshchyeneeye pa eeleektronay pochtee*
What's your e-mail address?	Какой у вас адрес электронной почты? *kakoy oo vas adrees eeleektronay pochtee*
Can I access the Internet here?	Можно ли здесь войти в Интернет? *mozhna lee zdyes' vayetee v eenteernyet?*
What are the charges per hour?	Сколько стоит в час? *skol'ka stoyeet f chyas*

МАРКИ	STAMPS
ТЕЛЕГРАММЫ	TELEGRAMS
ДО ВОСТРЕБОВАНИЯ	GENERAL DELIVERY [POSTE RESTANTE]
ВЫЕМКА ПОЧТЫ В …	NEXT COLLECTION …
ПОСЫЛКИ	PACKAGES

Souvenirs Сувениры

When buying antiques remember that anything dating from before 1917 is likely to be considered a national treasure not to be taken out of the country. Thus, you can only export antique paintings, sculptures, antique samovars, and icons after securing permission from the Ministry of Culture and upon payment of customs duties. Rules and regulations are subject to change. Obtain up-to-date information from your travel agent or the Russian embassy before setting off.

amber	янтарь *eentar'*
balalaika	балалайка *balalayka*
caviar	икра *eekra*
chess set	шахматы *shakhmati*
fur hat	меховая шапка *meekhavaya shapka*
icon	икона *eekona*
nesting dolls	матрёшка *matryoshka*
Palekh boxes	палехские шкатулки *paleekhskeeye shkatoolkee*
poster	плакат *plakat*
rugs from *Tekin*	текинские ковры *teekeenskeeye kavri*
samovar	самовар *samavar*
shawl	шаль *shal'*
wood carving	резьба по дереву *reez'ba pa dyereevoo*
wooden spoons	деревянные ложки *deereevyaniye loshkee*

Gifts Подарки

bottle of wine	бутылка вина *bootilka veena*
box of chocolates	коробка шоколада *karopka shakalada*
calendar	календарь *kaleendar'*
key ring	брелок *breelok*
postcard	открытка *atkritka*
souvenir guide	путеводитель *pooteevadeeteel'*
tea towel	кухонное полотенце *kookhonnaye palatyentse*
T-shirt	футболка *footbolka*

Music Музыка

Locally produced audio- and videocassettes and compact discs are inexpensive, especially for classical music.

I'd like a …	Я хочу купить … *ya khachyoo koopeet'* …
cassette	кассету *kasyetoo*
compact disc	компакт-диск *kampakt deesk*
record	пластинку *plasteenkoo*
videocassette	видеокассету *veedeeakasyetoo*
Who are the popular native singers/bands?	Кто сейчас популярные певцы/группы? *kto seechyas papoolyarniye peevtsi/grooppi*

Toys and games Игрушки и игры

I'd like a toy/game …	Я хочу купить игрушку/игру … *ya khachyoo koopeet' eegrooshkoo/eegroo* …
for a boy	для мальчика *dlya mal'cheeka*
for a 5-year-old girl	для пятилетней девочки *dlya peeteelyetnee dyevachkee*
chess set	шахматы *shakhmati*
doll	куклу *kookloo*
electronic game	электронную игру *eleektronnooyoo eegroo*
pail and shovel [bucket and spade]	ведёрко и совок *veedyorka ee savok*
teddy bear	мишку *meeshkoo*

Antiques Старинные вещи

How old is this?	Какой это век? *kakoy eta vyek*
Do you have anything of the … era?	У Вас есть что-нибудь … века? *oo vas yest' shtoneebood' … vyeka*
Can you send it to me?	Вы можете переслать это мне по-почте? *vi mozhetye peereeslat' eta mnye pa pachtye*
Will I have problems with customs?	Могут быть проблемы на таможне? *mogoot bit' prablyemi na tamozhnye*
Is there a certificate of authenticity?	Есть сертификат подлинности? *yest' seerteefeekat padlyeennastyee*

Supermarket/Minimart
Универсам/Павильон

There are big supermarkets with a wide choice of food and Western imports in large cities which only accept cash. Credit cards can only be used in Western-owned shops. However, many of the large supermarkets have ATMs which accept Visa and MasterCard. For beer, spirits, and tobacco, it is better to go to kiosks or minimarts, where prices are lower.

At the supermarket   В универсаме

Excuse me. Where can I find (a) …?	Извините. Где можно купить ...? *eezveeneetye gdye mozhna koopeet'* ...
Do I pay for this here or at the checkout?	Где платить: здесь или в кассу? *gdye plateet' zdyes' eelee f kassoo*
Where are the shopping carts [trolleys]/baskets?	Где здесь тележки/корзинки? *gdye zdyes' teelyeshkee/karzeenkee*
Is there a … here?	Здесь есть ...? *zdyes' yest'* ...
bakery	булочная *boolachnaya*
delicatessen	магазин деликатесов *magazeen deeleekatyessaf*
pharmacy	аптека *aptyeka*

ХЛЕБ И КОНДИТЕРСКИЕ ИЗДЕЛИЯ	BREAD AND CAKES
МОЛОЧНЫЕ ПРОДУКТЫ	DAIRY PRODUCTS
РЫБА	FRESH FISH
МЯСО/ПТИЦА	FRESH MEAT/POULTRY
СВЕЖИЕ ПРОДУКТЫ	FRESH PRODUCE
МОРОЖЕНЫЕ ПРОДУКТЫ	FROZEN FOODS
ХОЗЯЙСТВЕННЫЕ ТОВАРЫ	HOUSEHOLD GOODS
КОНСЕРВИРОВАННЫЕ ФРУКТЫ/ОВОЩИ	CANNED FRUIT/VEGETABLES
ВИНА И КРЕПКИЕ НАПИТКИ	WINES AND SPIRITS

Weights and measures
- 1 kilogram or kilo (kg.) = 1000 grams (g.); 100 g. = 3.5 oz.;
  1 kg. = 2.2 lb.; 1 oz. = 28.35 g.; 1 lb. = 453.60 g.
- 1 liter (l.) = 0.88 imp. quart or 1.06 U.S. quart; 1 imp. quart = 1.14 l.
  1 U.S. quart = 0.951 l.; 1 imp. gallon = 4.55 l.; 1 U.S. gallon = 3.8 l.

Food hygiene   Гигиена питания

УПОТРЕБИТЬ В ТЕЧЕНИЕ ... ДНЕЙ ПОСЛЕ ОТКРЫТИЯ	EAT WITHIN ... DAYS OF OPENING
ХРАНИТЬ В ХОЛОДИЛЬНИКЕ	KEEP REFRIGERATED
ДЛЯ МИКРОВОЛНОЙ ПЕЧИ	MICROWAVEABLE
ПОДОГРЕТЬ ПЕРЕД УПОТРЕБЛЕНИЕМ	REHEAT BEFORE EATING
ДИЕТИЧЕСКОЕ ПИТАНИЕ	SUITABLE FOR VEGETARIANS
ГОДЕН ДО ...	USE BY ...

At the minimart   В павильоне

I'd like some of that/those.	Дайте, пожалуйста, вон то/вот это. *daytye pazhalsta von to/vot eta*
I'd like ...	Дайте, пожалуйста, ... *daytye pazhalsta ...*
this one/these	вон эту/вон эти *von etoo/von etee*
that one/those	вон ту/вон те *von too/von tye*
on the left/right	направо/налево *naprava/nalyeva*
over there/here	вон там/вон здесь *von tam/von zdyes'*
Where is/are the ...?	Где у вас ...? *gdye oo vas ...*
a kilo of apples	килограмм яблок *keelagram yablak*
a half-kilo of tomatoes	полкило помидоров *palkeelo pameedoraf*
100 grams of cheese	100 грамм сыра *sto gramm sira*
a liter of milk	литр молока *leetr malaka*
10 eggs	десяток яиц *deesyatak eeeets*
... slices of ham	... ломтиков ветчины *... lomteekaf veetchyeeni*
a piece of cake	кусочек торта *koosochyeek torta*
a bottle of wine	бутылку вина *bootilkoo veena*
a carton of milk	пакет молока *pakyet malaka*
a jar of jam	банку варенья *bankoo varyenya*
a bag of potato chips [crisps]	пакет чипсов *pakyet chyeepsaf*

Provisions/Picnic   Продукты/Пикник

beer	пиво **peeva**
butter	масло **masla**
cheese	сыр **sir**
cold meats	мясные изделия **meesniye eezdyeleeya**
cookies [biscuits]	печенье **peechyenye**
eggs	яйца **yaytsa**
grapes	виноград **veenagrat**
ice cream	мороженое **marozhenaye**
instant coffee	растворимый кофе **rastvareeniy kofye**
loaf of bread	булка хлеба **boolka khlyeba**
margarine	маргарин **margareen**
milk	молоко **malako**
oranges	апельсины **apeel'seeni**
potato chips [crisps]	чипсы **cheepsi**
rolls	булочки **boolachkee**
sausages	сосиски **saseeskee**
soft drinks	безалкогольные напитки **beezalkagol'niye napeetkee**
wine	вино **veeno**

Russian bakeries and supermarkets sell a rich variety of black and white bread. In addition, each region has its own special varieties and forms of bread. Well-known types of bread include Московский (**maskofskeeye**), Рижский (**reezhskeeye**), and Бородинский (**boradeenskeeye**). Sliced bread is available in many supermarkets.

MEAT ➤ 46; VEGETABLES ➤ 47

Health

Medical treatment is supposed to be free in Russia, but it is customary to offer the doctor a present: a box of chocolates or a bottle of something. State hospitals are generally run-down and uncomfortable. Food may not be provided. And you will have to pay for medicine.

More and more private hospitals and clinics are opening in big towns and cities with imported drugs and equipment. These charge American rates, so it is advisable to take out medical insurance before traveling.

Visitors to Russia are advised to get booster shots for diphtheria, tetanus, and polio. If you are on prescription medication, you should bring sufficient supplies with you.

Doctor (General)   Врач/(Общие вопросы)

Where can I find a hospital/dentist?	Мне нужен врач/зубной врач. *mnye noozhen vrach/zoobnoy vrach*
Where's there a doctor who speaks English?	Где есть врач, говорящий по-английски? *gdye yest' vrach gavaryashchyeey pa angleeyskee*
What are the office [surgery] hours?	Когда открыта поликлиника? *kagda atkrita paleekleeneeka*
Could the doctor come to see me here?	Можно вызвать врача на дом? *mozhna vizvat' vrachya na dam*
Can I make an appointment for …?	Можно записаться к врачу на …? *mozhna zapeesat'sa k vrachyoo na …*
today/tomorrow	сегодня/завтра *seevodnya/zaftra*
as soon as possible	как можно скорее *kak mozhna skaryeye*
It's urgent.	Это срочно. *eta srochna*
I've got an appointment with Doctor …	Я по записи к доктору … *ya pa zapeesee k doktaroo …*

TIME ➤ 220; DATES ➤ 218

– <u>mozh</u>na zapee<u>sat'</u>sa k vra<u>chyoo</u>?

– za<u>pees'</u> na pree<u>yom</u> za<u>kon</u>cheena
see<u>vod</u>nya. <u>e</u>ta <u>sroch</u>na?

– da.

– kha<u>ra</u>sho. <u>mozh</u>eem vam preedla<u>zheet'</u> na
<u>dye</u>seet' peet<u>nat</u>sat' k <u>dok</u>taroo Sheev<u>chyen</u>koo.
na <u>dye</u>seet' peet<u>nat</u>sat'.
– spa<u>see</u>ba vam bal<u>shoye</u>.

Accident and injury
Несчастный случай и травма

My … is hurt/injured.	Мой(-я) … ушибся(-лась). *moy (maya) … ooshipsa (ooshiblas')*
husband/wife	муж/жена *moosh/zhena*
son/daughter	сын/дочь *sin/doch'*
friend	друг *drook*
child	ребёнок *reebyonak*
He/She is unconscious.	Он/она без сознания. *on/ana byes saznaneeya*
He/She is bleeding (heavily).	У него/неё кровотечение (сильное). *oo neevo/neeyo kravateechyeneeye (seel'naye)*
He/She is (seriously) injured.	Он/она (тяжело) ранен(а). *on/ana (teezhelo) ranyen(a)*
I have a(n) …	У меня … *oo meenya …*
blister	волдырь *valdir'*
boil	нарыв *nariv*
bruise	синяк *seenyak*
burn	ожог *azhok*
cut/graze	порез/ссадина *paryes/ssadeena*
insect bite	укус *ookoos*
lump	шишка *shishka*
rash	сыпь *sip'*
strained muscle	растянута мышца *rastyanootaya mishtsa*
My … is swollen.	У меня распухло … *oo meenya raspookhla …*
My … hurts.	У меня болит … *oo meenya baleet …*

Symptoms   Симптомы

I've been feeling ill for … days.	Я заболел(а) … дня/дней назад. *ya zabalyel(a) … dnya/dnyey nazat*
I feel …	У меня … *oo meenya* …
faint	слабость *slabast*
feverish	жар *zhar*
sick	тошнота *tashnata*
I've been vomiting.	Меня тошнило. *meenya tashneela*
I have diarrhea.	У меня понос. *oo meenya panos*
It hurts here.	Мне больно вот здесь. *mnye bol'na vot zdyes'*
I have (a/an) …	У меня … *oo meenya* …
backache	болит спина *baleet speena*
cold	простуда *prastooda*
cramps	судороги *soodaragee*
earache	болит ухо *baleet ookha*
headache	болит голова *baleet galava*
stomachache	болит живот *baleet zhivot*
sore throat	болит горло *baleet gorla*
sunstroke	солнечный удар *solneechniy oodar*

Health conditions   Состояние здоровья

I have arthritis.	У меня артрит. *oo meenya artreet*
I have asthma.	У меня астма. *oo meenya astma*
I am …	Я … *ya* …
deaf	глухой(-ая) *glookhoy (-aya)*
diabetic	диабетик *deeabyeteek*
epileptic	эпилептик *epeelyepteek*
handicapped	инвалид *eenvaleet*
(… months) pregnant	(… месяца) беременна *(… myeseetsa) beeryemeenna*
I have a heart condition/ high blood pressure.	У меня больное сердце/высокое кровяное давление. *oo meenya bolynoye syerttse/visokaye kravyanoye davlyeneeye*
I had a heart attack … years ago.	У меня был сердечный приступ … года/лет назад. *oo meenya bil seerdyechniy preestoop … goda/lyet nazat*

Doctor's inquiries   Вопросы врача

Давно Вы себя так чувствуете?	How long have you been feeling like this?
Это у Вас первый раз?	Is this the first time you've had this?
Вы принимаете другое лекарство?	Are you taking any other medication?
Аллергия на что-нибудь?	Are you allergic to anything?
Вам делали прививку против столбняка?	Have you been vaccinated against tetanus?
У Вас есть аппетит?	Is your appetite okay?

Examination   Осмотр

Я измерю Вам температуру/давление.	I'll take your temperature/ blood pressure.
Засучите рукав.	Roll up your sleeve, please.
Разденьтесь до пояса.	Please undress to the waist.
Ложитесь, пожалуйста.	Please lie down.
Откройте рот.	Open your mouth.
Дышите глубоко.	Breathe deeply.
Покашляйте.	Cough, please.
Где болит?	Where does it hurt?
Здесь болит?	Does it hurt here?

Diagnosis   Диагноз

Вам нужно сделать рентген.	I want you to have an X-ray.
Вам нужно сдать кровь/кал/ мочу на анализ.	I want a specimen of your blood/stools/urine.
Я Вас направлю к специалисту.	I want you to see a specialist.
Я Вас направлю в стационар.	I want you to go to hospital.
Это сломано/растянуто.	It's broken/sprained.
Это вывихнуто/порвано.	It's dislocated/torn.

У Вас ...	You have (a/an) ...
аппендицит	appendicitis
цистит	cystitis
грипп	flu
отравление	food poisoning
перелом	fracture
гастрит	gastritis
грыжа	hernia
воспаление ...	inflammation of ...
корь	measles
пневмония	pneumonia
ишиас	sciatica
ангина	tonsilitis
опухоль	tumor
венерическое заболевание	venereal disease
У Вас заражение.	It's infected.
Это инфекционное заболевание.	It's contagious.

Treatment Лечение

Я Вам дам ...	I'll give you ...
антисептическое средство	an antiseptic
болеутоляющее средство	a painkiller
Я Вам пропишу ...	I'm going to prescribe ...
курс антибиотиков	a course of antibiotics
свечи	some suppositories
У Вас есть аллергия на лекарства?	Are you allergic to any medication?
Принимайте одну таблетку ...	Take one pill ...
каждые ... часа	every ... hours
раз в день	... times a day
перед едой	before meals
Сходите к врачу, когда приедете домой.	Consult a doctor when you get home.

Parts of the body   Части тела

arm	рука *rooka*
back	спина *speena*
bladder	мочевой пузырь *machyeevoy poozir'*
bone	кость *kost'*
breast	грудь *grood'*
chest	грудная клетка *groodnaya klyetka*
ear/eye	ухо/глаз *ookha/glas*
face	лицо *leetso*
finger/thumb	палец/большой палец *paleets/bal'shoy paleets*
foot	нога *naga*
glands (tonsils)	гланды *glandi*
hand	рука *rooka*
head	голова *galava*
heart	сердце *syertse*
jaw	челюсть *chyelyoost'*
joint	сустав *soostaf*
kidney	почка *pochka*
knee	колено *kalyena*
leg	нога *naga*
lip	губа *gooba*
liver	печень *pyechyeen'*
mouth	рот *rot*
muscle	мышца *mishtsa*
neck	шея *sheya*
nose	нос *nos*
rib	ребро *reebro*
shoulder	плечо *pleechyo*
skin	кожа *kozha*
stomach	живот/желудок *zhivot/zheloodak*
thigh	бедро *beedro*
throat	горло *gorla*
toe	палец ноги *paleets nagee*
tongue	язык *eezik*
vein	вена *vyena*

Gynecologist Гинеколог

I have …	У меня … *oo meenya …*
abdominal pains	боли в животе *bolee v zhivatye*
period pains	боли при менструации *bolee pree meenstroogtsiee*
a vaginal infection	воспаление влагалища *vaspalyeneeye vlagaleeshchya*
I haven't had my period for … months.	У меня нет менструации уже … месяца. *oo menya nyet meenstroogtsiee oozhe … myeseetsa*
I'm on the Pill.	Я принимаю противозачаточные таблетки. *ya preeneemayoo prateevazachyatachniye tablyetkee*

Hospital Больница

Please notify my family.	Пожалуйста, сообщите моей семье. *pazhalsta saabshchyeetye mayey seemye*
What are the visiting hours?	Когда часы посещений? *kagda chyasi paseeshchyeneey*
I'm in pain.	У меня боли. *oo meenya bolee*
I can't eat/sleep.	Я не ем/сплю. *ya nee yem/splyoo*
When will the doctor come?	Когда придёт врач? *kagda preedyot vrach*
Which ward is … in?	В какой палате ...? *f kakoy palatye …*
I'm visiting …	Я посещаю … *ya paseeshchyayoo …*

Optician Оптика

I'm near- [short-] sighted/ far- [long-] sighted.	У меня близорукость/дальнозоркость. *oo meenya bleezarookast'/dal'nazorkast'*
I've lost …	Я потерял(а) … *ya pateeryal(a) …*
one of my contact lenses	контактную линзу *kantaktnooyoo leenzoo*
my glasses	мои очки *maee achkee*
a lens	линзу *leenzoo*
Could you give me a replacement?	Можно заменить? *mozhna zameeneet'*

Dentist Зубной врач

I have toothache.	У меня болит зуб. *oo meenya baleet zoop*
This tooth hurts.	Вот этот зуб болит. *vot etat zoop baleet*
I've lost a tooth/cap.	Я потерял(а) зуб/коронку. *ya pateeryal(a)/ slamal(a) zoop/karonkoo*
I've lost a filling.	Пломба выпала. *plomba vipala*
Can you repair this denture?	Вы можете починить этот протез? *vi mozhetye pachyeeneet' etat pratyes*
I don't want it extracted.	Можно не удалять? *mozhna nee oodalyat'*

Я Вам сделаю укол/ обезболивание.	I'm going to give you an injection/ a local anesthetic.
Вам нужно поставить пломбу/ коронку.	You need a filling/cap [crown].
Придётся удалить.	I'll have to take it out.
Это можно поправить только временно.	I can only fix it temporarily.
Приходите через ... дня (дней).	Come back in ... days.
Нельзя есть ... часа.	Don't eat anything for ... hours.

Payment and insurance Оплата и страховка

Do I pay you now?	Платить сейчас? *plateet' seechyas*
How much do I owe you?	Сколько с меня? *skol'ka s meenya*
I have insurance.	У меня есть страховка.
Can I have a receipt for my health insurance?	Дайте мне квитанцию для медицинского страхования. *daytee mnye kveetantseeyoo dlya meedeetseenkava strakhavaneeya*
Would you fill out this health insurance form, please?	Не могли бы Вы заполнить бланк для страхования, пожалуйста? *nee maglee bi vi zapolneet' blank dlya strakhavaneeya*
Can I have a medical certificate?	Можно медицинское свидетельство? *mozhna meedeetsinskaye sveedyeteel'stva*

MAKING APPOINTMENTS ➤ 161

Dictionary

English–Russian

Most terms in this dictionary are either followed by an example or cross-referenced to pages where the word appears in a phrase. Only the masculine ending (-ый, -ой, -ий) of adjectives is given in the dictionary. The feminine and neuter endings are -ая, -ое respectively.

The notes below provide some basic grammar guidelines.

Nouns

There are three genders in Russian: masculine (m), feminine (f), and neuter (n) ▸ 15. The endings of nouns vary according to their "role" in the sentence. There are six different cases in both the singular and plural. Adjectives agree in number and gender with the noun they modify.

The following notes give an overview of how the cases are used.

Nominative (N): refers to the subject of the sentence – the person or thing performing the action.

Genetive (G): is used to designate a person/object to whom/which somebody or something belongs (it can often be translated by "of" in English).

Dative (D): designates the person/object to whom/which something is given or done.

Accusative (A): usually denotes the direct object of an action.

Instrumental (I): answers the questions "by whom?", "by what means?", "how?".

Prepositional (P): is always used with a preposition. The most common are в, на, (on, in) and о (about).

Verbs (For information about the verb "to be" ▸ 17.)

The infinitive of most verbs ends in **т′** (-ть). Russian verbs conjugate (change their endings) according to the subject of the verb (I, you, he/she/it, we, you (pl.), they.)

The negative is formed by adding **nee** (не) before the verb.

Past tense

The past tense is formed by removing the -ть of the infinitive and adding:

-л (-**l**)	masculine ending	-ла (-**la**)	feminine ending
-ло (-**lo**)	neuter ending	-лы (-**li**)	plural ending

It is the gender and number of the subject that control the choice of ending, for example: I spoke (said by a man) = говорил, I spoke (said by a woman) = говорила.

"to have"

When "to have" means "possess" it is expressed by the preposition у followed by the genitive case of the word denoting the possessor + есть (in the present tense) + the thing possessed (in the nominative case). In the present tense есть may be omitted. For example, У меня (есть) машина. **(oo meenya (yest′) masheena)** = "in the possession of me is a car" = I have a car.

A

a few немного/несколько neemnoga/<u>nye</u>skal'ka 15

a little немного nee<u>mno</u>ga 15

a lot много <u>mno</u>ga 15

a.m. до полудня da pa<u>loo</u>dnya

abbey аббатство m a<u>bat</u>stva 99

abdominal pains боли в животе fpl <u>bo</u>lee v zheeva<u>tye</u> 167

about (approximately) около <u>oka</u>la 15

abroad заграницей zagra<u>nee</u>tsey

accept: do you accept ...? Вы принимаете ...? Vi preenee<u>ma</u>yetee ...? 42, 136

access (n) допуск m <u>do</u>poosk 100

accessories принадлежности fpl preenad<u>lye</u>zhnastee 144

accident несчастный случай m nesh<u>chas</u>niy <u>sloo</u>chay 152; (road) авария f a<u>va</u>reeya 92

accidentally случайно sloo<u>chay</u>na 28

accompaniments гарнир m gar<u>neer</u> 38

accompany, to провожать prava<u>zhat'</u> 65

accountant бухгалтер m boo<u>gal</u>tyer 121

acne прыщи mpl pri<u>shchee</u>

across через <u>chye</u>reez 12

acrylic акрил m a<u>kreel</u>

actor актёр m ak<u>tyor</u> 110

actress актриса f ak<u>tree</u>sa 110

adapter адаптер m a<u>dap</u>teer 26, 148

address адрес m <u>a</u>drees 84, 126

adhesive bandages пластырь m <u>plas</u>tir 141

adjoining room совмещённые комнаты/номера fpl/mpl sav<u>mesh</u>ch<u>ye</u>nyeye <u>kom</u>naty/nome<u>ra</u> 22

admission charge входная плата f fkhad<u>na</u>ya <u>pla</u>ta 114

adult взрослый <u>vzros</u>liy 81

adult (n) взрослый m <u>vzros</u>liy 81, 100

aerobic class класс аэробики m klas aye<u>ro</u>beekee 115

after (time/place) после <u>po</u>slee 13, 95

after-shave лосьон после бритья m las<u>yon</u> <u>po</u>slee bree<u>tya</u> 142

afternoon, in the днём m dnyom 221

age: what age? какой возраст? m ka<u>koy</u> <u>voz</u>rast? 113

agree: I don't agree я не согласен ya nee sa<u>gla</u>seen

air: ~ conditioning кондиционер m kandeetsee<u>o</u>nyer 22, 25; **~ pump** воздух m <u>voz</u>dookh 87; **~ sickness bag** гигиенический пакет m geegeeye<u>nee</u>cheskiy pa<u>kyet</u> 70; **~mail** авиапочта f aveea<u>po</u>chta 155

airport аэропорт m aera<u>port</u> 96

aisle seat боковое место n baka<u>vo</u>ye <u>mye</u>sta 74

alarm clock будильник m boo<u>deel'</u>neek 149

alcoholic (drink) алкогольный alka<u>gol'</u>niy

all всё vsyo

all-night ночной nach<u>noy</u> 140

allergic, to be иметь аллергию f ee<u>myet'</u> aleer<u>gee</u>yoo 164

allergy аллергия f aleer<u>gee</u>ya 165

allowance разрешение n razry<u>esh</u>ye<u>nee</u>ye 67

almost почти pach<u>tee</u>

alone только <u>tol'</u>ka

already уже oo<u>zhe</u> 28

also также <u>tag</u>zhe 19

alter, to переделывать peeree<u>dye</u>livat' 137

alumin(i)um foil фольга f fal'<u>ga</u> 148

always всегда fse<u>gda</u> 13

amazing поразительный para<u>zee</u>tyelniy 101

ambassador посол m pa<u>sol</u>

ambulance скорая помощь f <u>sko</u>raya <u>po</u>mashch 92

American *(adj)* американский ameeree**kan**skeey 150, 152

amount сумма f <u>soo</u>ma 42

amusement arcade аттракционы mpl atraktse**eo**ni 113

anaesthetic обезболивающее n abeezbolee**va**yooshcheye

and и/a ee/a 19; **and so on** и так далее ee tag <u>da</u>leeye 19

animal животное n zhee**vot**naya 106

anorak куртка f **koort**ka

another другой(-ая) m/f droo**goy**(-aya) 21; *(time)* в другой раз v droo**goy** ras 125

antacid средство от изжоги n **sryet**stva at ee**zzho**gee

antibiotics антибиотики mpl anteebee**o**teekee 165

antifreeze антифриз m antee**freez**

antique антиквар m antee**kvar** 157; **~ store** антикварный магазин m antee**kvar**niy maga**zeen** 130

antiseptic антисептическое средство n anteesep**tee**cheskoye **sryet**stva 165; **~ cream** антисептическая мазь f anteesep**tee**cheeskaya maz' 141

any какой-либо ka**koy**-**lee**ba

anyone: does anyone speak English? здесь кто-нибудь говорит по-английски? zdyes' **kto**-neebood' gava**reet** pa an**glee**yskee

anything else? что-нибудь ещё? **chto**-neebood' ee**shchyo**

apartment квартира f kvar**tee**ra 28, 123

apologize: I apologize прошу прощения pra**shoo** pra**shchye**neeya

appendicitis аппендицит m apeendee**tseet** 165

appendix аппендикс m ap**yen**deeks 166

apple яблоко n **ya**blaka 160

appointment приём m pree**yom** 161; **to make an ~** записываться za**pee**sivat'sya 147

approximately приблизительно preeblee**zee**teel'na 152

April апрель m a**pryel'** 218

architect архитектор m arkhee**tek**tar 104

area code код m kod 127

arm рука f roo**ka** 166

around *(place)* по ра 12; *(time)* около <u>o</u>kala 13

arrive, to прилетать preelye**tat'** 68, 70, 71

art gallery картинная галерея f kar**tee**naya galye**rye**ya 99

arthritic, to be иметь артрит ee**myet'** ar**treet** 163

artificial sweetener сахарин m sakha**reen** 38

artist художник m khoo**dozh**neek 104

ashtray пепельница f **pyepyel'**neetsa 39

ask: I asked for ... я просил(а) ... ya pra**seel**(a) ... 41

asking просьба f **pros'**ba 37

aspirin аспирин m aspee**reen** 141

asthmatic *(n)* астматик m ast**ma**teek 163

at last! наконец nak**an**yets 19

at *(place)* в, на v/f, na 12; *(time)* в v 13

at least по крайней мере ра **kray**ney **mye**rye 23

athletics атлетика f at**lye**teeka 114

ATM *(automated teller)* банкомат banka**mat** 139

attack нападение n napa**dye**neeye 152

attractive привлекательный preevlee**ka**teel'niy

August август m **af**goost 218

aunt тётя f **tyo**tya 120

Australia Австралия f Af**stra**leeya 119

authentic: is it authentic? это настоящее? **e**ta nastay**ash**cheey

authenticity подлинность f **pod**leenast' 157

A-Z

automatic *(car)* с автоматической трансмиссией s aftama<u>tee</u>cheeskay transmee<u>see</u>eyey 86;

~ camera автоматический фотоаппарат m aftama<u>tee</u>cheskiy <u>fo</u>taa<u>pa</u>rat 151

automobile машина f ma<u>shee</u>na 86

autumn осень f <u>o</u>seen' 219

available *(unoccupied)* свободный sva<u>bod</u>niy 77

avalanche лавина f la<u>vee</u>na

B **baby** ребёнок m ree<u>byo</u>nak 39, 113, 162; **~ food** детское питание n <u>dyet</u>skaye pee<u>ta</u>neeye 142; **~ wipe** подгузник m pad<u>gooz</u>neek 142; **~-sitter** няня f <u>nya</u>nya 113; **~-sitting** присмотр за детьми m prees<u>mo</u>tar za deet'<u>mee</u> 113

back спина f spee<u>na</u> 166; **~ache** боль в спине f bol' v spee<u>nye</u> 163

backpacking туризм m too<u>reezm</u>

bad плохой pla<u>khoy</u> 14

baggage багаж m ba<u>gazh</u> 32, 67, 71; **~ check** багажное отделение n ba<u>gazh</u>noye ade<u>lye</u>neeye 71, 73

bakery булочная f <u>boo</u>lachnaya 130, 158

balcony балкон m bal<u>kon</u> 29

ball мяч m myach 157

ballet балет m ba<u>lyet</u> 108, 111

bananas банан m ba<u>nan</u> 160

band *(musical group)* группа f <u>groo</u>pa 111, 157

bandages бинт m beent 141

bank банк m bank 130, 138

bar *(hotel, etc.)* бар m bar 26, 112

barber парикмахер m pareekh<u>ma</u>kheer

basement подвал m pad<u>val</u> 132

basket корзинка f kar<u>zeen</u>ka 158

basketball баскетбол m baskeet<u>bol</u> 114

bath towel банное полотенце n <u>ba</u>noye pala<u>tyen</u>tse 27

bathroom туалет m tooa<u>lyet</u> 26, 98

battery *(car)* аккумулятор m akamoo<u>lya</u>tar 88; *(camera, etc.)* батарейка f bata<u>rey</u>ka 137, 151

battle site место сражения n <u>mye</u>sta srazh<u>ye</u>neeya 99

be, to быть byt' 17

beach пляж m plyazh 116

beard борода f ba<u>ra</u>da

beautiful красивый kra<u>see</u>viy 14; прекрасный pree<u>kras</u>niy 101

because потому что pata<u>moo</u>chto 16; **~ of** из-за eez-za 16

bed кровать/постель f kra<u>vat'</u>/pas<u>tel'</u> 21; **~ and breakfast** с завтраком m s <u>zav</u>trakam 24

bedding постельное бельё n pas<u>tel'</u>noye byel<u>yo</u> 29

bedroom спальня f <u>spal'</u>nya 29

beer пиво n <u>pee</u>va 40, 160

before *(time)* до da 13, 221; **~ meals** перед едой <u>pye</u>reet ee<u>doy</u>

begin, to начинать nachee<u>nat'</u>

beginner новичок m navee<u>chyok</u> 117

beige бежевый <u>bye</u>zheeviy 143

Belarus Белоруссия f Beela<u>roo</u>seeya 119

belong: this belongs to me это принадлежит мне eta preenadlee<u>zheet</u> mnye

belt ремень/пояс m ree<u>myen'</u>/<u>po</u>yas 144

berth полка f <u>pol</u>ka 74, 77

best лучший <u>looch</u>shiy

better лучше <u>looch</u>she 14

bib салфетка f sal<u>fyet</u>ka

bicycle велосипед m vyelasee<u>pyet</u> 75, 83

bidet биде n bee<u>de</u>

big большой bal'<u>shoy</u> 14, 134; великий vee<u>lee</u>key 117; **bigger** больше <u>bol'</u>shye 24

bikini бикини pl bee<u>kee</u>nee 144

bill счёт m schyot 32, 35, 42

bin liner мешок для мусора m meeshok dlya moosara
binoculars бинокль m beenokal'
bird птица f pteetsa 106
birthday день рождения m dyen' razhdyeneeya 219
biscuits печенье n peechyenye 160
bite (insect) укус m ookoos
bitten: I've been bitten by a dog меня укусила сабака meenya ookooseela sabaka
bitter горький gor'kiy 41
bizarre причудливый preechoodleeviy 101
black чёрный chyorniy 143; **~ and white film** (camera) чёрно-белая chyorna-byelaya 151; **~ coffee** чёрный кофе m chyorniy kofye 40
bladder мочевой пузырь m macheevoy poozir' 166
blanket одеяло n adyeyala 27
bleach отбеливатель m atbyeleevatel' 148
bleeding кровотечение n kravateechyeneeye 92, 162
blinds (n) шторы fpl shtori 25
blister волдырь m valdir' 162
blocked, to be засорен(а) zasaryon/zasoryena 25
blood кровь f krov' 164; **~ group** группа крови f groopa krovee; **~ pressure** кровяное давление n kraveenoye davlyeneeye 164
blouse блузка f bloozka 144
blow-dry фен m fyen 147
blue синий seeniy 143
blush [rosé] wine розовое вино n rozovoye veeno 40
boarding card посадочный талон m pasadachniy talon 70
boat лодка f lotka 81; **~ trip** водная экскурсия f vodnaya ekskoorseeya 81
boil (medical) нарыв m nariv 162
boiled вареный varyoniy
boiler бойлер m boyler 29
bone кость f kost' 166
book книга f kneega 150

book, to (reserve) заказывать zakazivat'
booking заказ m zakaz
booklet of tickets талоны mpl taloni 79
bookstore книжный магазин m kneezhniy magazeen 130, 150
booted, to be надеть штрафной башмак nadyet' shtrafnoy bashmak 87
boots сапоги mpl sapagee 145; (for sport) спортивная обувь f sparteevnaya oboov' 115
boring скучный skoochniy 101
born: I was born in я родился в ... ya radeelsya v
borrow: may I borrow your ...? можно мне взять взаймы ваш ...? mozhna mnye vzyat' vzaymy vash …
botanical garden ботанический сад m bataneecheskiy sat 99
bottle бутылка f bootilka 37, 159; **~ of wine** бутылка вина f bootilka veena 40; **~-opener** открывалка f atkrivalka 148
bowel кишечник m keeshyechneek
box of chocolates коробка шоколада f karopka shakalada 156
boy мальчик m mal'cheek 120, 157
boyfriend друг m drook 120
bra бюстгальтер m byoostgal'tyer 144
bracelet браслет m braslyet 149
bread хлеб m khlyeb 38
break, to сломать slamat' 28; **~ down** (car) сломаться slamat'sya 88
break-in взлом m vzlom 153
breakdown truck буксир m bookseer 88
breakfast завтрак m zaftrak 27
breast грудь f grood' 166
breathe, to дышать dishat' 92, 164
breathtaking захватывающий zakvativayooshchiy 101
bridge мост m most 107
briefs трусики pl trooseekee 144
bring somebody, to привести preeveestee 125

Britain Великобритания f Vyeleekabreetaneeya 119
British (adj) британский breetanskeey 152
brochure брошюра f brashoora
broken сломан sloman 137; **to be ~** сломаться slamat'sya 25; (bone) сломать slamat' 164
bronchitis бронхит m brankheet
brooch брошь f brosh 149
brother брат m brat 120
brown коричневый kareechneeviy 143
browse, to смотреть smatryet' 133
bruise синяк m seenyak 162
bucket ведёрко n veedyorka 157
build, to строить stroyeet' 104
building здание n zdaneeye 104
built построенный pastroyeniy 104
bureau de change обмен валюты m abmyen valyooti 138
burger гамбургер m gamboorger 40; **~ bar** кафе-гамбургер n kafye gamboorger 35
burn ожог m azhok 162
bus автобус m aftoboos 70, 78, 98; **~ route** автобусный маршрут m aftoboosniy marshroot 96; **~ station** автобусная станция f aftoboosnaya stantseeya 78; **~ stop** автобусная остановка f aftoboosnaya astanofka 65, 96; стоянка f stayanka 78
business бизнес m beeznes 121; **~ class** бизнес-класс m beeznes-klas 68; **~ trip** командировка f kamandeerofka 123; **on ~** по делу m pa dyeloo 66
busy, to be (occupied) занят(а) zanyat 125
but но no 19
butane gas газовый баллон m gazaviy balon 30, 31
butcher мясной магазин m myasnoy magazeen 130
butter масло n masla 38, 160
button кнопка f knopka

buy, to покупать pakoopat' 67, 80, 133
by (time) к k 13; **~ car** на машине na masheenee 17, 94; **~ credit card** кредитной карточкой kredeetnoy kartochkoy 17
bye! пока! paka

C **cab** такси n taksee 84
cabaret кабаре n kabare 112
cabin каюта f kayoota 81
café кафе n kafye 35, 40
cagoule плащ m plashch 145
cake пирожное n peerozhnoye 40
calendar календарь m kaleendar' 156
call, to вызвать vizvat' 92; (phone) звонить zvaneet' 127, 128; **~ collect** звонить по коллекту zvaneet' pa kalyektoo 127; **~ for somebody** заходить за zakhadeet' 125; **call the police!** вызовете милицию vizaveetee meeleetsiyoo 92
camera фотоаппарат m fotaaparat 151; **~ case** футляр m footlyar 151; **~ store** фототовары mpl fotatavari 130, 151
campbed раскладушка f raskladooshka 31
camping кемпинг m kyempeeng 30; **~ equipment** снаряжение n snaryazhyeneeye 31
campsite кемпинг m kyempeeng 123
can банка f banka 159; **~-opener** открывалка f atkrivalka 148
can: can I? можно мне ...? mozhno mnye ...? 18; **can I have ...?** можно мне ...? mozhno mnye ...? 18; **can you help me?** помогите мне pamageetye mnye 18; **can you recommend ...?** вы можете порекомендовать ...? vi mozheetee pareekamyendavat' ...? 112
Canada Канада f Kanada 119
cancel, to (reservation) отменять atmyenyat' 68

cancer (*disease*) рак m rak

candle свеча f sveecha 148

candy конфеты, сладости fpl kanfyeti, sladastee 150

cap (*dental*) коронка f karonka 168

car машина f macheena 81, 86, 87, 88, 89, 153; **~ ferry** грузовой паром m groozavoy parom 81; **~ hire** прокат автомобилей m prakat aftamabeelyey 70, 86; **~ park** автостоянка f aftastayanka 26, 87, 96; **~ rental** прокат автомобилей m prakat aftamabeelyey 70, 86

car (*compartment of train*) вагон m vagon 77

carafe графин m grafeen 37

caravan трейлер m treylyer 30, 81

cards карты fpl karti 121

careful: be careful! будьте осторожны! bood'tee astarozhni

carpet (*rug*) ковёр m kavyor

carrier bag авоська f avos'ka

carry-cot люлька f lool'ka

cart тележка f teelyeshka 158

carton пакет m pakyet 159

cash наличные pl naleechniye 136, 138; **~ desk** касса f kasa 132; **~ machine** банкомат bankamat 139

cashier касса f kasa 132

casino казино n kazeeno 112

cassette кассета f kasyeta 157

castle замок m zamak 99

catch, to (*bus*) успеть на автобус oospyet' na aftoboos

cathedral собор m sabor 99

Catholic католический kataleechyeeskiy 105

cave пещера f peeshchyera 107

CD компакт-диск m kampakt deesk; **~-player** лазерный проигрыватель m lazeerniy praeegrivatel'

center (*of town*) центр (города) m tsentr (gorada) 21

central heating центральное отопление n tseentral'naya ataplyeneeye

ceramics керамика f keerameeka

certificate сертификат m seerteefeekat 149, 157; свидетельство n sveedyeteel'stva 168

chain цепочка f tseepochka 149

change (*coins*) сдача f sdacha 136; **keep the change** оставьте сдачу f astav'tye zdachoo 84

change, to (*buses, etc.*) делать пересадку dyelat' pyeryesatkoo 75, 79, 80; (*baby*) перепеленать pyeryepyelyonivat' 39; (*money*) обменять abmeenyat' 138; разменивать razmyeneevat' 87; (*alter*) поменять pamyenyat' 68

changing facilities (*baby*) место перепеленать ребёнка n myesta pyereepeeleenat' reebyonka 113

charcoal уголь m oogal 31

charge плата f plata 30, 115

charter flight чартерный рейс m chartyerniy reys

cheap дешёвый deeshoviy 14, 134; **cheaper** дешевле deeshyevlee 21, 24, 109, 134

check: please check the ... пожалуйста, проверьте... pazhalsta pravyertee; **~ in** регистрироваться reegeestreeravat'sya 68; **~ out** (*hotel*) выезжать vieezhat'

check-in desk регистрационная стойка f reegeestratseeoonaya stoyka 69

checkout контроль m kantrol' 158

cheers! за ваше здоровье! za vashye zdarov'ye

cheese сыр m sir 160

chemist аптека f aptyeka 130, 140

check [cheque] book чековая книжка f chyekavaya kneeshka

chess шахматы pl shakhmati 121; **~ set** шахматы pl shakhmati 157

chest (*body*) грудная клетка f groodnaya klyetka 166

chewing gum жевательная резинка f zheevateel'naya reezeenka 150

child ребёнок m reebyonak 98, 152;
children дети npl dyetee 22, 66, 74, 100, 113, 120; (adj.) детский dyetskiy 39; **child seat** (in car) детское сиденье n dyetskaye seedyenye 86; **child's seat** (high chair) детский стульчик m dyetskiy stoolcheek 39; **child's cot** детская кроватка f detskaya kravatka 22

childminder воспитатель m vaspeetateel'

Chinese (cuisine) китайская (кухня) keetayskaya (kookhnya) 35

chips (crisps) чипсы pl cheepsi 160

choc-ice шоколадное мороженое n shakaladnaye marozhenoye 110

chocolate шоколад m shakalat 160; (flavor) шоколадное shakaladnaye 40; **hot ~** горячий шоколад m garyachiy shakalat 40; **~ bar** шоколадка f shakalatka 150

Christmas Рождество n Razdeestvo 219

church церковь f tserkav' 96, 99, 105

cigarettes, packet of сигареты fpl seegaryeti 150

cigars сигары fpl seegari 150

cinema кинотеатр m keenateeatr 96, 110

claim check багажная квитанция f bagazhnaya kveetantseeya 71

clamped, to be надеть штрафной башмак nadyet' shtrafnoy bashmak 87

class (type of seat, etc.) класс m klas 68

clean чистый chyeesti 14; чистый cheestiy 39, 41

clean, to чистить cheesteet' 137

cliff обрыв m abriv 107

cling film обёрточная бумага f abyortachnaya boomaga 148

clinic поликлиника f paleekleeneeka 131

cloakroom гардероб m gardeerop 109

clock часы pl chasi 149

close, to (store, etc.) закрываться zakrivat'sya 100, 140

clothes одежда f adyezhda 144;
~ peg прищепка f preeshchyepka 148; **~ store** одежда f adyezhda 130

cloudy, to be облачно oblachna 122

clubs (golf) клюшки fpl klyooshkee 115

coach (long-distance bus) междугородный автобус m myezhdoogarodniy aftoboos 78;
~ bay стоянка f stayanka 78;
~ station автобусная станция f aftoboosnaya stantseeya 78

coach (train compartment) вагон m vagon 75

coast побережье n pabeeryezhye

coat пальто n pal'to 144

coatcheck гардероб m gardeerop 109

coathanger вешалка f vyeshalka

cockroach таракан m tarakan

code (area, dialling) код m kod

coffee кофе m kofye 40

coin монета f manyeta

cola кока-кола f koka kola 40

cold ('flu) простуда f prastooda 141, 163

cold (adj.) холодный khalodniy 14, 41, 122; **~ meats** мясные изделия npl myasniye eezdyeleeya 160

collapse: he's collapsed он потерял сознание on pateeryal saznaneeye

collect, to забирать zabeerat' 151

color цвет m tsvet 143; **~ film** цветная плёнка tsvyetnaya plyonka 151

comb расчёска f raschyoska 142

come back приходить preekhadeet' 36, 140

commission комиссионный сбор m kameeseeoniy sbor 138

compact camera компактный фотоаппарат m kamp**ak**tniy f**o**taaparat 151

compact disc компакт-диск m kamp**ak**t-deesk 157

company *(business)* предприятие n preetpree**ya**teeye

company *(companionship)* компания f kamp**a**neeya 126

compartment *(train)* купе n koop**e**

complaint жалоба f zh**a**loba 41

computer компьютер m kamp**yoo**teer

concert концерт m kants**ye**rt 108, 111; ~ **hall** концертный зал m kants**ye**rtniy zal 111

concession скидка f sk**ee**tka

concussion: he has concussion у него сотрясение мозга n oo nee**vo** satrya**sy**eneeye m**o**zga

conditioner кондиционер m kandeetseean**ye**r 142

condoms презервативы mpl preezeervat**ee**vi 141

conductor дирижёр m deereezh**yo**r 111

confirm, to *(reservation)* подтвердить pattveerd**ee**t' 68

congratulations! поздравляем! pazdravl**ya**eem

conscious: he's conscious он в сознании on f sazn**a**neeye

constipation запор m zap**o**r

Consulate консульство n kons**oo**l'stva 152

consult, to консультироваться kans**oo**l't**ee**ravat'sya 165

contact, to связаться svya**za**t'sya 28

contact lenses контактные линзы CORR fpl kant**ak**niye l**ee**nzi 167

contagious инфекционный eenfeektse**o**nniy 165

contain, to содержать sadeerzh**a**t' 39, 69, 155

contemporary dance современный танец m savree**my**eniy t**a**neets 111

contraceptive противозачаточное средство n proteeva**za**chatachnaya sry**e**tstva

cook повар m p**o**var

cook, to готовить gat**o**veet'

cooker плита f pl**ee**ta 28, 29

cookies печенье n peech**ye**nye 160

cooking *(cuisine)* кухня f k**oo**khnya

coolbox холодильник m khlad**ee**l'neek

copper медь f myed' 149

copy копия f k**o**peeya 155

corkscrew штопор m sht**o**par 148

corner угол m **oo**gal 95

correct правильно pr**a**veel'na 77

cosmetics косметика f kasm**ye**teeka

cottage дача f d**a**cha 28

cotton [cotton wool] вата f v**a**ta 141

cough кашель m k**a**sheel 141; ~ **syrup** жидкость от кашля f zh**ee**tkast' at k**a**shlya 141

cough, to кашлять k**a**shlyat' 164

could I have ...? можно мне ...? m**o**zhno mnye ...? 18

country *(nation)* страна f str**a**na

country music музыка кантри f m**oo**zika k**a**ntree 111

courier *(guide)* курьер m koor**ye**r

course *(part of meal)* блюдо n bly**oo**da

cousin кузен/кузина m/f kooz**ye**n/kooz**ee**na

craft shop магазин ремесленных изделий m maga**zee**n reem**ye**slyanikh eezd**ye**leey

cramps судороги fpl s**oo**daragee 163

creche ясли pl y**a**slee

credit card кредитная карточка f kreed**ee**tnaya k**a**rtachka 42, 136, 139; ~ **number** номер кредитной карточки m n**o**meer kreed**ee**tnay k**a**rtachkee 109

crib детская кроватка f d**e**tskaya krav**a**tka 22

crisps чипсы pl ch**ee**psi 160

crockery посуда f pasooda 29, 148

cross (*crucifix*) распятие n raspyateeye

crossroad перекрёсток m peereekryostak 95

crowded тесно tyesna 30

crown (*dental*) коронка f karonka 168

cruise (*n.*) круиз m krooeez

crutches костыли mpl kastilee

crystal хрусталь m khroostal' 149

cup чашка f chashka 39, 148

cupboard шкаф m shkaf

currency валюта f valyoota 67, 138; ~ **exchange** (*office*) обмен валюты m abmyen valyooti 70, 73, 138

curtains занавеси fpl zanaveesee

customs таможня f tamozhnya 67, 157; ~ **declaration** таможенная декларация f tamozheenaya deeklaratseeya 155

cut порез m paryez 162

cut glass резное стекло n reeznoye steeklo 149

cut and blow-dry стрижка и сушка феном f streeshka ee sooshka fyenam 147

cut and style стрижка и укладка f streeshka ee ooklatka 147

cutlery прибор m preebor 29, 148

cycle route велосипедный маршрут m veelaseepyedniy marshroot 106

cycling велоспорт m vyelasport 114

cystitis цистит m tseesteet 165

D **daily** ежедневно eezheednyevna

damaged, to повредить pavryedeet' 71; **to be ~** повреждён(а) pavryezhdyon/pavrezhdyena 28

damp (*n.*) сырость f sirast'; (*adj.*) сыро sira

dance (*performance*) танец m taneets 111

dancing, to go пойти потанцевать paytee patantseevat' 124

dangerous опасно apasna

dark тёмный tyomniy 14, 24, 134, 143

daughter дочь f doch 120, 162

dawn рассвет m rasvyet 221

day день m dyen' 97; (*ticket*) на день na dyen' 79

deaf (*adj.*) глухой glookhoy 163

December декабрь m deekabr' 218

deck chair шезлонг m shezlonk 116

declare, to предъявлять preedyavlyat' 67

deduct, to (*money*) вычитать vicheetat'

deep глубокий gloobokeey; ~ **freeze** замораживать zamarazheevat'

defrost, to размораживать razmarazheevat'

degrees (*temperature*) градусы mpl gradoosi

delay задержка f zadyerzhka 70

delicatessen магазин деликатесов m magazeen deeleekatyessaf 130, 158

delicious вкусный fkoosniy 14

deliver, to доставлять dastavlyat'

denim джинсовая ткань f dzheensovaya tkan' 146

dentist зубной врач m zoobnoy vrach 131, 161, 168

dentures протез m pratyez 168

deodorant дезодорант m deezadarant 142

depart, to (*train, bus*) отправляться atpravlyat'sya

department (*in store*) отдел m adyel 132; ~ **store** универмаг m ooneeveermag 130

departure lounge накопитель m nakapeetyel'

deposit аванс m avans 24, 83

describe, to описывать apeesivat' 152

destination место назначения n myesta naznachyeneeya

details подробности fpl padrobnastee

detergent моющее средство n <u>moyoosh</u>cheeye <u>sryet</u>stva

develop, to (photos) проявлять praeev<u>lyat'</u> 151

diabetes диабет m dee<u>a</u>byet

diabetic (n.) диабетик m dee<u>aby</u>eteek 39, 163

diagnosis диагноз m dee<u>a</u>gnas 164

dialling code код m kod 127

diamond брильянт m bree<u>lyant</u> 149

diapers пелёнка f pee<u>lyon</u>ka 142

diarrhea понос m p<u>a</u>nos 141, 163;
I have ~ у меня понос
oo me<u>nya</u> p<u>a</u>nos

dice кости fpl <u>kos</u>tee

dictionary словарь m sla<u>var'</u> 150

diesel дизельное топливо n <u>deezeel'</u>naye <u>top</u>leeva 85, 87

diet: I'm on a ~ я на диете dee<u>ye</u>ta

difficult трудный <u>trood</u>niy 14

dining: ~ car ресторан m rye<u>sta</u>ran 75; **~ room** столовая f sta<u>lo</u>vaya 26, 29

dinner: to have ~ ужинать <u>oozh</u>eenat' 124; **~ jacket** смокинг m <u>smo</u>keeng

dipped beam нижний свет m <u>neezh</u>niy svyet 86

direct (of train, etc.) прямой pry<u>amoy</u> 75

direct, to направлять napravl<u>yat'</u> 18

direction направление n napravl<u>ye</u>neeye 80; **in the ~ of** по направлению к ... pa napravl<u>ye</u>neeyoo k ... 95

directions указания npl ooka<u>za</u>neeya 94

director (of company) директор m dee<u>ryek</u>tar

directory (telephone) телефонный справочник m teele<u>fo</u>niy <u>spra</u>vachneek; **Directory Enquiries** справочная служба f <u>spra</u>vachnaya <u>sloozh</u>ba 127

dirty грязный <u>gryaz</u>niy 14, 28

disabled (n) инвалид m eenva<u>leed</u> 22

disabled (npl.) инвалиды mpl eenva<u>lee</u>di 100

disco дискотека f deeska<u>tye</u>ka 112

discount скидка f <u>skeed</u>ka 74

dish (meal) блюдо n <u>blyoo</u>da 37

dish cloth тряпка f <u>tryap</u>ka 148

dishwashing liquid средство для мытья посуды n <u>sryet</u>stva dlya mi<u>tya</u> pa<u>soo</u>di 148

dislocated, to be вывихнуть <u>vi</u>veekhnoot' 164

display cabinet/case витрина f vee<u>tree</u>na 134, 149

disposable camera одноразовый фотоаппарат m adna<u>ra</u>zaviy fota<u>a</u>parat 151

distilled water дистиллированная вода f deesteelee<u>ro</u>vanaya va<u>da</u>

disturb: don't disturb не беспокоить nee beespa<u>ko</u>yeet'

dive, to нырять nir<u>yat'</u> 116

diving equipment акваланг m akva<u>lank</u> 116

divorced, to be разведён razvee<u>dyon</u> 120

dizzy: I feel ~ у меня кружится голова oo me<u>nya</u> <u>kroo</u>zheetsya gala<u>va</u>

do: what do you do? ваша профессии? <u>va</u>sha pra<u>fye</u>seeya? 121; **do you have ...?** у Вас есть ...? oo vas yest' 37

doctor врач m vrach 131, 161, 167

doll кукла f <u>kook</u>la 157

dollar доллар m <u>do</u>lar 67, 138

don't mention it не за что <u>nye</u> za shta 10

door дверь f dvyer' 25

double двухместный dvookh<u>myes</u>niy 81; **~ bed** двуспальная кровать f dvoo<u>spal'</u>naya kra<u>vat'</u> 21; **~ room** двухместный номер m dvookh<u>myes</u>tnyi <u>no</u>mer 21

downtown area центр города m <u>tsyen</u>tar <u>go</u>rada 99

A-Z

dozen дюжина f dyoozheena 217
dress платье f plat'yee 144
drink, to пить peet' 70, 124, 126; выпить vipeet' 125
drinking water питьевая вода f peet'yevaya vada 30
drip, to: the faucet [tap] drips кран протекает kran prateekayeet
drive, to ехать yekhat' 93
driver водитель m vadeetyel'; **driver's licence [license]** водительские права npl vadeeteel'skeeye prava 93
drop off, to (children) приводить preevadeet' 113; высадить visadeet' 83
drowning: someone is drowning кто-то тонет kto-ta toneet
drugstore аптека f aptyeka 130
drunk (adj.) пьяный pyaniy
dry cleaner химчистка f kheemcheestka 131
dry cut сухая стрижка f sookhaya streeshka 147
dry clean, to отдавать в химчистку adavat' f kheemcheeskoo 131
dubbed, to be дублирован doobleeravan 110
during во время vo vryemya
dustbins мусорные баки mpl moosornye bakee 30
duty: to pay duty платить пошлину f plateet' poshleenoo 67
duvet пододеяльник m padadeeyal'neek

E   e-mail электронная почта f eleektronaya pochta 155
ear ухо n ookha 166; **~ drops** капли для ушей fpl kaplee dlya ooshey; **~ache** боль в ухе f bol' v ookhee 163
earlier раньше ran'shee 125, 147
early ранний ranneey 14, 221

earrings серьги fpl syer'gee 149
east восток m vastok 95
Easter Пасха f Paskha 219
easy лёгкий lyokhkeey 14
eat, to есть yest' 41, 167
eat: places to eat места где поесть meesta gdye payest' 123
economy class экономический класс m ekanameecheeskiy klas 68
egg яйцо n yaytso 160
either ... or или ... или eelee ... eelee 16
elastic (adj.) эластичный elasteechniy
electric: ~ outlet розетка f razyetka 30; **~ shaver** электробритва f elyektrabreetva
electricity электричество n eleektreechestva 28; **~ meter** счётчик m schyotcheek 28
electronic: ~ flash вспышка f vspishka 151; **~ game** электронная игра f eleektronaya eegra 157
elevator лифт m leeft 26, 132
else: something else что-то ещё chto-ta eeshchyo
embassy посольство n pasol'stva
emerald изумруд m eezoomroot
emergency крайний случай m krayniy sloochay 152; **~ exit** аварийный выход m avareeyniy vikhat; **it's an emergency** это срочно eta srochna 127
empty пустой poostoy 14
enamel эмаль f eemal' 149
end, to кончаться kanchat'sya 108
engaged, to be обручиться abroocheet'sya 120
engineer инженер m eenzhenyer 121
England Англия f Angleeya 119
English (adj.) английский angleeyskeey 11, 67, 110, 150, 152, 161; **~-speaking** говорящий по-английски gavaryashchcheey pa angleeyskee 98, 152
enjoy, to нравиться nraveet'sya 110, 121, 124

enlarge, to (*photos*) увеличивать ooveeleecheevat' 151

enough достаточно dastatachna 15, 42, 136

ensuite bathroom ванна в номере f <u>va</u>na v <u>no</u>meeree

entertainment guide путеводитель по местам отдыха m pooteeva<u>dee</u>teel'/pa mees<u>tam</u> <u>ot</u>dikha

entrance fee входная плата f fkhad<u>na</u>ya <u>pla</u>ta 100

entry visa въездная виза f vyezd<u>na</u>ya <u>vee</u>za

envelope конверт m kan<u>vyert</u> 150

epileptic (*n.*) эпилептик m epee<u>lyep</u>teek 163

equipment (*sports*) снаряжение n snarya<u>zhye</u>neeye 115

error ошибка f a<u>sheep</u>ka

escalator эскалатор m ees<u>ka</u>lator

essential основной asnav<u>noy</u> 89

EU Европейский союз m yevra<u>pey</u>skeey sa<u>yooz</u>

Eurocheque еврочек mpl <u>yev</u>rachyek

evening: in the ~ вечером m <u>vye</u>cheeram 109, 221; **~ dress** вечернее платье vee<u>chyer</u>neeye <u>plat</u>'ye 112

events представление n preetsta<u>vlye</u>neeye 108

every: ~ day каждый день m <u>kazh</u>diy dyen'; **~ week** каждую неделю <u>kazh</u>dooyoo ne<u>dye</u>lyoo 13; **every ... hours** каждые ... часа <u>kazh</u>diye ... cha<u>sa</u>

examination (*medical*) осмотр m as<u>mo</u>tar

example, for например na<u>pree</u>myer

except кроме <u>kro</u>mee

excess baggage перевес багажа m pyerye<u>vyes</u> baga<u>zha</u> 69

exchange, to обменивать ab<u>mye</u>neevat' 138

exchange rate курс обмена m koors ab<u>mye</u>na 138

excluding meals без питания n bez pee<u>ta</u>neeya 24

excursion экскурсия f eks<u>koor</u>seeya 97

excuse me извините/простите eezvee<u>nee</u>tye/pra<u>stee</u>tye 10, 94, 224

exhausted, to be уставать osta<u>vat</u>' 106

expected, to be обязательно abee<u>za</u>teel'na 111

expensive дорогой dara<u>goy</u> 14, 134

experienced опытный <u>o</u>pitniy 117

expiration date срок действия m srok <u>dey</u>stveeya 109

expiry date срок действия m srok <u>dey</u>stveeya 109

exposure (*photos*) фотография/фото f/n fota<u>gra</u>feeya/<u>fo</u>ta 151

express экспресс m eks<u>pryes</u> 155

extension добавочный номер m da<u>ba</u>vachniy <u>no</u>meer 128

extra (*additional*) ещё ye<u>shchyo</u> 23

extracted, to be (*tooth*) удалять ooda<u>lyat</u>' 168

extremely крайне <u>kray</u>ne 17

eye глаз m glas 166

F **fabric** (*material*) ткань f tkan' 146

face лицо n leet<u>so</u> 166

facial чистка лица f <u>cheest</u>ka leet<u>sa</u> 147

facilities удобства npl oo<u>dob</u>stva 22

factor ... номер ... m <u>no</u>myer 142

faint, to feel чувствовать слабость <u>choofstva</u>vat' <u>sla</u>bast' 163

fairground луна-парк m loona-park 113

fairly bad довольно плохо da<u>vol</u>'na <u>plo</u>kha 19

fall (*season*) осень f <u>o</u>seen' 219

family семья f seem<u>ya</u> 66, 74, 120, 167

famous знаменитый znamee<u>nee</u>tiy

fan (*air*) вентилятор m veenteel<u>ya</u>tar 25

far далеко daleeko 12;
is it ~? это далеко?
eta dalyeko 73; **far-
sighted** дальнозоркость 167 f dal'nazorkast' 167
 fare плата f plata 79
farm ферма f fyerma 107
fast быстро bistra 93; (clock)
спешат speeshat 221
father отец m atyets 120
faucet кран m kran 25
faulty: this is faulty это испорчено
eta eesporcheena
favorite любимый lyoobeemiy
fax факс m faks 22, 155
February февраль m feevral' 218
feed, to кормить karmeet' 39
feeding bottle бутылка для
кормления f bootilka dlya
karmlyeneeya
feel sick, to тошнить tashneet' 98
female женщина f zhyenshcheena 152
ferry паром m parom 81
fever жар m zhar 163
few несколько nyeskal'ka 15
field поле n polye 107
fifth пятый pyatiy 217
fight (brawl) драка f draka
fill in, to заполнять zapalnyat' 155
filling (dental) пломба f plomba 168
film (movie) фильм m feel'm 108, 110;
(camera) плёнка f plyonka 151
filter фильтр m feel'tar 151
fine (well) хорошо kharasho 118
finger палец m paleets 166
fire: ~ alarm пожарная тревога f
pazharnaya treevoga; **~ department
[brigade]** пожарная бригада f
pazharnaya breegada 92; **~ escape**
пожарная лестница f pazharnaya
lyesneetsa; **~ extinguisher**
огнетушитель m agneetoosheeteel';
there's a fire! пожар! m pazhar
firewood дрова pl drava
first первый pyerviy 68, 75, 81, 217
first class (train) мягкий вагон m
myahkiy vagon 74; (plane) первый
класс m pyerviy klas 68

fish: ~ counter рыбный отдел m
ribniy adyel 158; **~ restaurant**
рыбный ресторан m ribniy ryestaran
35; **~ store [fishmonger]** рыба m
riba 130
fit, to (clothes) подходить
patkhadeet' 146
fitting room примерочная f
preemyerachnaya 146
flashlight фонарь m fanar' 31
flat (puncture) прокол m
prakol 83, 88
flea блоха f blakha
flight рейс m reys 70; **~ number**
номер рейса m nomyer reysa 68
flip-flops шлёпанцы mpl
shlyopantsee 145
floor (level) этаж m etazh 132;
~ show варьете n var'yetye 112
florist цветы mpl tsvyeti 130
flower цветок m tsveetok 106
flu грипп m greep 165
flush: the toilet won't flush в туалете
не спускается вода v tooalyetee
nee spooskayeetsya vada
fly (insect) муха f mookha
foggy, to be туман m tooman 122
folk: ~ art народное искусство n
narodnaye eeskoostva; **~ music**
народная музыка f
narodnaya moozika 111
follow, to (pursue) преследовать
preeslyedavat' 152
food еда/пища f yeda/peeshcha;
(cuisine) кухня f kookhnya 119;
~ poisoning отравление n
atravlyeneeye 165
foot нога f naga 166
football футбол m footbol 114
footpath тропинка f trapeenka 107
for: ~ a day на день na dyen' 86;
~ a week на неделю na
nyedyelyoo 86
foreign currency иностранная валюта
f inastranaya valyoota 138
forest лес m lyes 107
forget, to забывать zabivat' 41, 42
fork вилка f veelka 39, 41, 148

form бланк/форма m/f
blank/forma 71, 153, 168

formal dress вечернее платье n
veechyerneeye plat'ye 111

fortunately к счастью
k shchyasyoo 19

fountain фонтан m fantan 99

four-door car с четырьмя дверями
s chyeetir'mya dveeryamee 86

four-wheel drive с полным приводом
s polnim preevadam 86

fourth четвёртый cheetvyortiy 217

foyer (hotel, theater) фойе n faye

fracture (of a bone) перелом m
peereelom 165

frame (glasses) оправа f aprava

free (not busy)
свободный svabodniy 124;
(available) свободный svabodniy 77

freezer морозильная камера f
marazeel'naya kameera 29

frequent: how frequent?
как часто? kak chasta 76

frequently часто chasta

fresh свежий svezheey 41

Friday пятница f pyatneetsa 218

fried жареный zharyeniy

friend друг m drook 162; **friendly**
дружеский droozheeskeey

fries жареный картофель m
zharyeniy kartofyel' 38

frightened, to be бояться bayat'sya

fringe чёлка f chyolka 147

from от/из at/eez 12; **from ... to**
(time) с ... до z ... da 13

front door key ключ от входной двери
m klyooch at fkhadnoy dvyeree 28

frosty, to be мороз m maroz 122

fruit juice сок m sok 40

frying pan сковорода f skavarada 29

fuel (gasoline/petrol)
бензин m beenzeen 86

full полный polniy 14; **~ beam**
верхний свет m vyerkhniy svyet
86; **~ board** с полным питанием n
s polneem peetaneeyem 24;
~ insurance полная страховка f
polnaya strakhofka 86

fun: to have ~
веселье: веселиться
n veesyel'ye:
veeseeleet'sya

furniture мебель f myebeel'

fuse пробка f propka 28;
~ box распределительный щит m
raspryedyeleetyel'ny shcheet 28

G **gallon** галлон m galon
game игра f eegra 157;
матч m mach 114

garage гараж m garazh 26;
станция обслуживания f
stantseeya apsloozheevanya 88

garbage bags полиэтиленовые
мешки m palee-eteelyenaviye
meeshkee 148

garden сад m sat

gas (fuel) бензин m beenzeen 88;
~ station заправочная станция f
zapravachnaya stantsiya 87

gas: I smell gas! я чувствую запах
газа! ya choostvooyoo zapakh
gaza; **~ bottle** газовый баллон m
gazovy balon 28

gastritis гастрит m gastreet 165

gate (airport) выход m vikhad 70

gauze бинт m beent 141

gay club гей-клуб m gyey-kloop 112

general delivery до востребования
do vastryebavaneeya 155

gentle лёгкий lyokhkeey 106

genuine настоящий nastayashchiy 134

Georgian (adj.) грузинский
groozeenskeey 35

get off, to (bus, etc.) выходить
vikhadeet' 79, 80

get, to (find) взять vzyat' 84; **~ to**
добираться/доехать dabeerat'sya/
dayekhat' 73, 94; **how do I get
to ...?** как мне добраться до ...?
kak mne dabrat'sya do ... 73

gift подарок m padarak 67, 156;
~ store подарки mpl padarkee 130

girl девочка f
<u>dye</u>vachka 120, 157
girlfriend подруга f
pad<u>roo</u>ga 120
give, to давать da<u>vat'</u>
glands гланды fpl <u>glan</u>di 166
glass стакан m <u>sta</u>kan 37, 39, 41, 148
glasses (optical) очки pl ach<u>kee</u> 167
glossy finish (photos) глянец m
<u>glya</u>neets
glove перчатка f peer<u>chat</u>ka
go: ~ on дальше <u>dal'</u>she 19;
~ for a walk пойти погулять
paytee pago<u>olyat'</u> 124; **~ shopping**
пойти по магазинам paytee pa
maga<u>zee</u>nam 124; **let's go!** пошли!
pash<u>lee</u>; **go away!** уходите!
ookha<u>dee</u>tye; **where does this bus
go?** идти: куда идёт этот автобус?
eetee: kooda ee<u>dyot</u> etat af<u>to</u>boos
goggles очки pl ach<u>kee</u>
gold золото n <u>zo</u>lata 149; **~-plate**
позолоченный paza<u>lo</u>cheniy 149
golf гольф m gol'f 114; **~ course**
корт для гольфа m
kort dlya gol'fa 115
good хороший kha<u>ro</u>sheey 14, 35,
42; **~ afternoon** добрый день m
<u>do</u>briy dyen' 10; **~ evening**
добрый вечер <u>do</u>briy <u>vye</u>chyeer
10; **~ morning** доброе утро
<u>do</u>braye <u>oo</u>tra 10;
~ night спокойной ночи
spa<u>koy</u>nigh <u>no</u>chyee 10
good-bye до свидания 10
gram грамм m gram 159
grandparents бабушка и дедушка
f/m <u>ba</u>booshka ee <u>dye</u>dooshka
grapes виноград m veena<u>grat</u> 160
grass трава f tra<u>va</u>
gray серый <u>sye</u>riy 143
graze ссадина f sa<u>dee</u>na 162
great блестяще blees<u>tya</u>shchye 19
green зелёный zee<u>lyo</u>niy 143
greengrocer овощи и фрукты mpl
<u>o</u>vashchee ee <u>froo</u>kti 130
grey серый <u>sye</u>riy 143
grilled жаренные на гриле
zha<u>ree</u>niye na <u>gree</u>lee

grocery store бакалея f
baka<u>lye</u>ya 131
ground (camping) кемпинг m
<u>kyem</u>peeng 30; **groundcloth
[groundsheet]** полотнище n
pa<u>lo</u>tneeshchye 31
group группа f <u>groo</u>pa 66, 100
guarantee гарантия f
ga<u>ran</u>teeya 135
guide (tour) гид m geet 98;
~book путеводитель m
pooteeva<u>dee</u>teel' 100, 150
guided tour экскурсия f
eks<u>koor</u>siya 100
guitar гитара f gee<u>ta</u>ra
gum десна f dees<u>na</u>
guy rope оттяжка f at<u>tyash</u>ka 31
gynecologist гинеколог m
geenee<u>ko</u>lak 167

H **hair** волосы mpl <u>vo</u>lasi 147;
~ brush щётка для волос f
shch<u>yot</u>ka dlya va<u>los</u> 142;
~ mousse мусс для волос m moos
dlya va<u>los</u> 142; **~ spray** лак для
волос m lak dlya va<u>los</u> 142;
~cut стрижка f <u>stree</u>shka 147;
~dresser парикмахер m
pareekh<u>ma</u>kher 147; **~stylist**
мастер m <u>mas</u>teer 147
half половина f pala<u>vee</u>na 217;
~ board с завтраком и ужином m
s <u>zav</u>trakam ee <u>oo</u>zheenam 24;
~ past пол m pol 220
hand рука f roo<u>ka</u> 166; **~ luggage**
ручная кладь f rooch<u>na</u>ya klad'
69; **~ washable** ручная стирка f
rooch<u>na</u>ya <u>steer</u>ka 146
handbag сумка f <u>soom</u>ka 144
handicap (golf)
гандикап m gandee<u>kap</u>
handicapped (n.)
инвалид m eenva<u>leed</u> 163
handicrafts ремёсла npl ree<u>myos</u>la
handkerchief платок m pla<u>tok</u>
hanger вешалка f <u>vye</u>shalka 27

hangover похмелье n pakh<u>myel</u>'ye 141

happy: I'm not happy with the service я не доволен обслуживанием ya nee dav<u>oo</u>leen apsl<u>oo</u>zheevaneeyem

harbor гавань f <u>gav</u>an' 81

hat шапка f <u>shap</u>ka 144

have to, to (must) должен/должна <u>dol</u>zhen/<u>dol</u>zhna

hayfever сенная лихорадка f seen<u>a</u>ya leekhar<u>at</u>ka 141

head голова f gal<u>a</u>va 166; **~ waiter** метрдотель m myetrdat<u>el</u>' 41; **~ache** болит голова b<u>a</u>leet gal<u>a</u>va 163

heading, to be (in a direction) ехать в y<u>e</u>khat' 83

health: ~ food store диетические продукты mpl deeyee<u>tee</u>cheeskeeye prad<u>oo</u>kti 131; **~ insurance** медицинское страхование n meedeet<u>seen</u>skaya strakhav<u>a</u>neeye 168

hear, to слышать <u>sli</u>shat'

hearing aid слуховой аппарат m slookhav<u>o</u>y ap<u>a</u>rat

heart сердце n <u>syert</u>see 166; **~ attack** сердечный приступ m seerd<u>ye</u>chniy pr<u>ee</u>stoop 163; **~ condition** заболевание сердца n zabalee<u>va</u>neeye <u>syert</u>sa

hearts (cards) черви fpl <u>chyer</u>vi

heater обогреватель m abagreev<u>a</u>teel'

heating отопление n atapl<u>ye</u>neeye 25

heavy тяжёлый teezh<u>o</u>liy 14, 134

height рост m rost 152

hello здравствуй(те) zdr<u>a</u>stvooy(tye) 10, 118

help, to помогать pama<u>gat</u>' 18, 94; **can you help me?** помогите мне pamag<u>ee</u>tye mnye 92

hemorrhoids геморрой m geema<u>ro</u>y

her её ey<u>o</u> 16

here здесь/сюда zdyes'/syoo<u>da</u> 12

hernia грыжа f <u>gri</u>zha 165

hers её ey<u>o</u> 16; **it's hers** это ее <u>e</u>ta ee<u>yo</u>

hi привет preev<u>yet</u> 10

high высокий vis<u>o</u>kiy; **~ beam** верхний свет m v<u>yer</u>khniy svyet 86; **~ blood pressure** высокое кровяное давление n v chyet<u>veert</u>'kaee krave<u>e</u>noye davl<u>ye</u>neeye 163; **~ street** главная улица f <u>glav</u>naya <u>oo</u>leetsa 96

highlight, to (hair) осветлить asveetl<u>ee</u>t' 147

highway (авто)шоссе n (afta)shass<u>e</u> 92, 94

hike (walk) поход m pakh<u>ot</u> 106

hiking поход m pakh<u>ot</u>; **~ boots** ботинки mpl bat<u>ee</u>nkee 145; **~ gear** туристское снаряжение n too<u>ree</u>skaya snareezh<u>ye</u>neeye

hill холм n kholm 107

him ему eem<u>oo</u> 16

hire (out), to давать/взять напрокат dav<u>at</u>'/vsyat' naprak<u>at</u> 29, 86, 115, 116, 117

his его ev<u>o</u> 16; **it's his** это его <u>e</u>ta ee<u>yo</u>

hitchhiking голосовать galas<u>a</u>vat' 83

HIV-positive положительная реакция на СПИД f palazh<u>ee</u>teel'naya ree<u>a</u>ktseeya na speed

hobby (pastime) хобби n kh<u>o</u>bee 121

hold on, to подождать padazh<u>dat</u>' 128

hole (in clothes) дырка f d<u>ir</u>ka

holiday: on ~ в отпуске v <u>ot</u>pooskee 66, 123; **~ resort** курорт m koor<u>ort</u>

home: to go ~ ехать домой y<u>e</u>khat' dam<u>oy</u> 123; **we're going home** мы идём домой mi eed<u>yom</u> dam<u>oy</u>

homosexual (adj.) гомосексуальный gomaseeksoo<u>al</u>'niy

honeymoon: we're on honeymoon у нас медовый месяц oo nas meed<u>o</u>viy m<u>ye</u>syats

horse лошадь f l<u>o</u>shad'; **~-racing** конные скачки fpl k<u>o</u>niye sk<u>a</u>chkee 114

hospital больница f bal'<u>nee</u>tsa 131, 161, 164, 167
hot горячий gar<u>ya</u>cheey 14, 122; *(weather)* жаркая <u>zhar</u>kaya 122; **~ dog** хот-дог m khot-dok 110; **~ spring** источник m gar<u>ya</u>cheey eest<u>o</u>chneek; **~ water** горячая вода f gar<u>ya</u>chaya vada 25
hotel гостиница f gast<u>ee</u>neetsa 21, 123; **~ room** номер m <u>no</u>myer 21
hour час m chas 97; **in an ~** через час <u>che</u>ryes chas 84; **hours** *(opening)* часы работы mpl cha<u>si</u> ra<u>bo</u>ti 161
house дом m dom
housewife домохозяйка f domakhaz<u>ya</u>yka 121
hovercraft ракета rak<u>ye</u>ta 81
how? как? kak 17; **how are you?** как дела? kak d<u>ee</u>la? 118; **how far ...?** как далеко ...? kak dal<u>ee</u>ko 94, 106; **how long?** сколько/как долго sk<u>ol</u>'ka/kak d<u>ol</u>ga 75, 76, 78, 94, 135; **how many?** сколько? sk<u>ol</u>'ka 15, 80; **how much?** сколько? sk<u>ol</u>'ka 15, 21, 69, 84, 109; **how much ...?** сколько ...? sk<u>ol</u>ka 69; **how often?** как часто kak ch<u>as</u>ta 140; **how old?** сколько лет? sk<u>ol</u>'ka lyet? 120
hundred сто sto 216
hungry голодный gal<u>od</u>niy
hurry: I'm in a ~ я спешу ya spesh<u>oo</u>
hurt, to be ушибиться oosheeb<u>ee</u>t'sya 92, 162; **it hurts** у меня болит ... oo mee<u>nya</u> ba<u>leet</u> ... 162
husband муж m moozh 120, 162

I **I'd like (some) ...** я хотел(а) бы ... ya khat<u>yel</u>(a) bi 18, 36, 40
I'll have ... я возьму ... ya vaz'<u>moo</u> 37

ice лёд m lyod 38
ice cream мороженое n mar<u>o</u>zheenaye 40, 160; **ice-cream parlor** кафе-мороженое n ka<u>fye</u> mar<u>o</u>zheenaye 35
icy гололёд m gala<u>lyot</u> 122
identification удостоверение n oodastav<u>ee</u>ryeneeye 134
ill, to be заболеть zaba<u>lyet</u>' 152
illegal: is it illegal? это незаконно? eta nee<u>za</u>kona
imitation искусственный eesk<u>oo</u>stveeniy 134
immediately немедленно neem<u>ye</u>dleenna
in *(place)* в, на v/na 12; *(time)* через ch<u>ye</u>reez 13
included, to be входить fkh<u>o</u>deet' 86, 98
incredible невероятный neeveer<u>a</u>yatniy
indicate, to указывать ook<u>a</u>zivat'
indigestion изжога f eez<u>zho</u>ga
indoor pool закрытый бассейн m zak<u>ri</u>tiy ba<u>seyn</u> 116
inexpensive недорогой needarag<u>oy</u>
infected, to be заразиться zaraz<u>eet</u>'sya 165
infection воспаление n vaspal<u>ye</u>neeye 167
inflammation воспаление n vaspal<u>ye</u>neeye 165
informal *(dress)* форма одежды свободная f <u>for</u>ma ad<u>ye</u>zhdi svab<u>od</u>naya
information: ~ desk справочное бюро n <u>spra</u>vachnoye byo<u>ro</u> 73; **~ office** справочное бюро n <u>spra</u>vachnaya byo<u>ro</u> 96; **Information** справочная служба f <u>spra</u>vachnaya sl<u>oo</u>zhba 127
injection воспаление n vaspal<u>ye</u>neeye 168
injured, to be получить травму paloo<u>cheet</u>' tr<u>a</u>vmoo 92, 162
innocent невинный nee<u>vee</u>niy
insect насекомое n nasee<u>ko</u>moye 25

insect: ~ bite укус насекомого m ookoos naseekomava 141, 162;
~ repellent средство от комаров sryetstva at kamaraf 141

inside внутри vnootree 12

insist: I insist я настаиваю ya nastayeevayoo

insomnia бессонница f beesoneetsa

instant coffee растворимый кофе m rastvareemiy kofee 160

instead of вместо vmyesta

instructions инструкция f eenstrooktsiya 135

instructor инструктор m eenstrooktar

insulin инсулин m eensooleen

insurance страховка f strakhofka 86, 89, 93; **~ claim** страховой иск m strakhavoy eesk; **~ company** страховая компания f strakhavaya kampaneeya 93

interest (hobby) интересы/хобби n eenteeryesi/khobee 121

interesting интересный eenteeryesniy 101

International Student Card студенческий билет m stoodyenchyesky beelyet 29

interpreter переводчик m peereevotcheek 153

intersection пересечение n peereeseechyeneeye 95

introduce oneself, to представляться preetstavlyat'sya 118

invitation приглашение n preeglashyeneeye 124

invite, to приглашать preeglashat' 124

iodine йод m yot

Ireland Ирландия f Eerlandeeya 119

is there ...? (➤ 17) есть ...? yest' ...? 17

it is ... (➤ 17) это eta 17

Italian итальянский eetalyanskeey 35

itemized bill счёт по пунктам m shchyot pa poonktam 32, 42

J **jacket** пиджак m peedzhak 144

jam варенье n varyenye

jammed, to be застревать zastrevat' 25

January январь m eenvar' 218

jar банка f banka 159

jaw челюсть f chyelyoost' 166

jazz джаз m dzhas 111

jeans джинсы pl dzheensi 144

jellyfish медуза f meedooza

jet-ski джет-ски pl dzhyet-skee 116

jeweler ювелирный магазин m yooveeleerniy magazeen 131, 149

job: what's your job? кем Вы работаете? f kyem vi rabotayeetee

join in, to вступать в fstoopat' v 115

joint сустав m soostaf 166;
~ passport совместный паспорт m savmyestniy paspart

joke шутка f shootka

journalist журналист m zhoornaleest

journey поездка f payezdka 76, 78

jug графин m grafeen

July июль m eeyool' 218

jump leads кабель с зажимами m kabeel' s zazheemamee

jumper джемпер m dzhyempeer 144

junction (intersection) перекрёсток m peereekryostak

June июнь m eyooon' 218

K **keep: keep the change!** оставьте себе сдачу astav'tee seebye sdachoo

kerosene керосин m keeraseen;
~ stove примус m preemoos 31

ketchup кетчуп m kyetchoop

kettle чайник m chyayneek 29

key ключ m klyooch 27, 28, 88;
~ ring брелок m breelok 156

kiddie pool детский бассейн m dyetskiy baseyn 113

kidney почка f pochka 166

kilo кило n keelo 159
kilogram килограмм m keelagram 69
kilometer километр m keelamyetar
kind (pleasant) любезный lyoobyezniy
kiss, to целовать tseelavat' 126
kitchen кухня f kookhnya 29
knapsack рюкзак m ryoogzak 31, 145
knee колено n kalyena 166
knickers трусики pl trooseekee
knife нож m nozh 39, 41, 148
kosher кошерный kashyerniy

L **label** ярлык m yarlik
lace кружево f kroozheeva
ladder стремянка f streemyanka
lake озеро n ozeera 107
lamp лампа f lampa 25, 29
land, to приземляться preezyemlyat'sya 70
language course языковые курсы mpl yazikaviye koorsi
large (adj.) большой balshoy 40, 110
last последний paslyedneey 14, 68, 75, 80, 81
last, to длиться dleet'sya
late (adj.) поздний pozneey 14; **to be ~** (delayed) задерживаться zadyerzheevat'siya 70; (adv.) позже pozhe 221
later позже pozhe 125
laugh, to смеяться smeeyat'sya 126
laundromat прачечная f pracheechnaya 131
laundry: ~ service прачечная f pracheechnaya 22; **~ soap** стиральный порошок m steeral'niy parashok 148
lawyer адвокат m advakat 152
laxative слабительное n slabeeteelnaya
lead, to (road) вести veestee 94
leader (of group) руководитель m rookavadeeteel'

leaflet брошюра f brashoora 97
leak, to (roof, pipe) течь tyech
learn, to (language) изучать eezoochat'
leather кожа f kozha 146
leave, to уезжать ooyezhat' 32; (plane) вылетать vilyetat' 68; (train, etc.) отправляться atpravlyat'sya 76, 81, 98; **~ from** (transport) отправляться atpravlyat'sya 78; **leave me alone!** оставьте меня в покое! astaftee meenya v pakoye 126
left, on the налево nalyeva 76, 95
left-luggage office багажное отделение n bagazhnoye adelyeneeye 71
leg нога f naga 166
legal: is it legal? зэто законно? eta zakona
leggings леггинги pl lyegeengee
lemon лимон m leemon 38
lemonade лимонад m leemanat 40
lend: could you lend me ...? не могли бы вы дать мне взаймы ...? nee maglee bi vi dat' mne vzaymi
length (of) длина f dleena
lens (camera) объектив m 151; (optical) стекла npl styokla 167; **~ cap** крышка объектива f krishka abyekteeva 151
lesbian club лесбийский клуб m leesbeeyskey kloop
less меньше myen'she 15
lesson урок m oorok 115
let, to: let me know! дайте мне знать! daytee mnye znat'
letter письмо n pees'mo 154; **~box** почтовый ящик m pachtoviy yashcheek
level (ground) площадка f plashchadka 30
library библиотека f beebleeatyeka 99, 131
license plate регистрационный номер m reegeestratsioniy nomeer 93

lifebelt спасательный пояс m
spa<u>sa</u>teel'niy <u>poyas</u>
lifeboat спасательная лодка f
spa<u>sa</u>teel'naya <u>lo</u>tka
lifeguard спасатель m
spa<u>sa</u>tyel' 116
lifejacket спасательный жилет m
spa<u>sa</u>teel'niy zhee<u>lyet</u>
lift лифт m leeft 26, 132; **~ pass**
пропуск на лифт m <u>pro</u>poosk na
leeft 117; (hitchhiking) подвозить
pad<u>va</u>zeet' 83
light (opp. heavy) лёгкий <u>lyokh</u>keey
14, 134; (opp. dark) светлый
<u>svet</u>liy 14, 134, 143
light (bicycle) фара f <u>fa</u>ra 83;
(electric) свет m svyet 25; **~ bulb**
лампочка f <u>lam</u>pachka 150
lighter (cigarette) зажигалка f
zazhee<u>gal</u>ka 150
like, to нравиться <u>nra</u>veet'sya 101,
124; **do you like?** вам нравится?
vam <u>nra</u>veetsya 125; **I don't like it**
мне это не нравится mnye eta nee
<u>nra</u>veetsya; **I like it** мне это
нравится mnye eta <u>nra</u>veetsya;
I'd like ... я хотел(а) бы ...
ya kha<u>tyel</u>(a) bi ... 18, 36, 40
like this (similar to) как это kak eta
limousine лимузин m leemoo<u>zeen</u>
line (metro) линия f <u>lee</u>neeya 80
line (profession) профессия f
pra<u>fe</u>seeya 121
linen лён m lyon 146
lip губа f goo<u>ba</u> 166; **~stick** губная
помада f goob<u>na</u>ya pa<u>ma</u>da
liqueur ликер m lee<u>kyor</u>
liquor store винный магазин m
<u>veen</u>niy maga<u>zeen</u> 131
liter литр m <u>lee</u>tar 87, 159
little (small) маленький <u>ma</u>leen'keey
live together, to жить вместе
zheet' <u>vmes</u>tye
liver печень f <u>pye</u>cheen' 166
living room гостиная f
gas<u>tee</u>naya 29
loaf of bread буханка хлеба f
boo<u>khan</u>ka <u>khle</u>ba 160

lobby (theater, hotel)
фойе n fa<u>ye</u>
local местный
<u>mye</u>stniy 37;
~ anesthetic
обезболивание n
abeez<u>bo</u>leevaneeye 168
lock замок m za<u>mok</u> 25; **~ oneself**
out, to захлопнуть дверь
za<u>klop</u>noot' dvyer' 27
long длинный <u>dlee</u>nniy 146;
long-distance bus
междугородный автобус m
myezhdooga<u>rod</u>niy af<u>to</u>boos 27
long-sighted дальнозоркость f
dal'na<u>zor</u>kast' 167
look: ~ for искать ees<u>kat'</u> 18, 133;
to have a ~ (check) посмотреть
pasma<u>tryet'</u> 89; **I'm just looking** я
просто смотрю ya <u>pro</u>sta smat<u>ryoo</u>
loose (clothing) свободный
sva<u>bod</u>niy 146
lorry грузовик m grooza<u>veek</u>
lose, to потерять pateer<u>yat'</u> 28, 153;
I've ~ ... я потерял(а) ... ya
pateer<u>yal</u>(a) ... 100, 153
lost-and-found office [lost property]
бюро находок n byoo<u>ro</u>
na<u>kho</u>dak 73
louder громче <u>grom</u>chee 128
love, to любить lyoo<u>beet'</u>
lovely прекрасный pree<u>kras</u>niy 125
low beam нижний свет m <u>neezh</u>niy
svyet 86
low-fat низкое содержание жира
<u>neez</u>kaye sadeer<u>zha</u>neeye <u>zhee</u>ra
lower нижний <u>neezh</u>ney 74
luggage багаж m ba<u>gash</u> 32, 71;
~ carts багажные тележки fpl
ba<u>gazh</u>niye tye<u>lyezh</u>kee 71;
~ locker камера хранения f
<u>ka</u>meera khran<u>ye</u>neeya 71, 73;
~ trolleys багажные тележки fpl
ba<u>gazh</u>niye tye<u>lyezh</u>kee 71
lump (medical) шишка f
<u>shish</u>ka 162
lunch обед m a<u>byet</u> 98
lung лёгкое n <u>lyokh</u>kaya 166

M machine washable машинная стирка f masheenaya steerka 146

madam госпожа f gaspazha

magazine журнал m zhoornal 150

magnificent великолепный veeleekalyepniy 101

maid горничная/уборщица f gorneechnaya 27, 28

mail (n.) почта f pochta 27, 155; **by ~** письмом m pis'mom 22; **~box** почтовый ящик m pachtoviy yashcheek

mail, to отправлять atpravlyat'

main главный glavniy 130; **~ course** второе n ftaroye; **~ street** главная улица f glavnaya ooleetsa 95, 96

make: ~ a complaint жаловаться zhalavat'sya 137; **~ an appointment** записаться на приём zapeesat'sya na preeyom 161

make-up грим m greem

male мужчина m moozhcheena 152

mallet деревянный молоток m deereevyanniy malatok 31

man (male) мужской mooshskoy

manager директор m deeryektar 25, 41, 137

manicure маникюр m maneekyoor 147

manual (car) с ручным переключением передач s roochnim peereeklyochyeneeyem peereeedach

many много mnoga 15

map карта f karta 94, 99, 106, 150

March март m mart 218

margarine маргарин m margareen 160

market рынок m rinak 99, 131

married, to be женат (for men)/замужем (for women) zheenat/zamoozheem 120

mascara тушь f toosh

mask (diving) маска f maska

mass месса f myesa 105

massage массаж m masazh 147

mat finish (photos) матовый matoviy

match (sport) матч m mach 114

matches спички fpl speechkee 31, 148, 150

matinée дневное представление n dnevnoye preetstavlyeneeye 109

matter: it doesn't matter это не имеет значения eta nee eemyeet znachyeneeya; **what's the matter?** в чем дело? f chyom dyela

mattress матрас m matras 31

May май m may 218

May I ...? Можно мне ...? mozhna mnye … 37

maybe может быть mozheet bit'

me (to, for) мне mnye 16

meal блюдо n blyooda 38

mean, to значить znachet' 11

measles корь f kor' 165

measure, to снять мерку snyat' myerkoo 146

measurement измерение n eezmeeryeneeye

meat мясо n myasa 41

medical certificate медицинское свидетельство n meedeetseenskaya sveedeeteel'stva

medication [medicine] лекарство n leekarstva 141, 164

medium (adj.) средний sryedneey 40, 106

meet, to встречаться fstreechat'sya 106, 125; **pleased to meet you** очень приятно ochen' preeyatna 118

member (of club) член m chlyen 112, 115

men (toilets) мужской mooshskoy

menu меню n meenyoo

message передача f pyeredacha 27

metal металл m meetal

metro station станция метро f stantseeya myetro 80

microwave (oven) микроволновая печь f meekravalnovaya pyech

midday полдень m poldeen' 221

midnight полночь f polnach 221

migraine мигрень f meegryen'

mileage километраж m keelamye<u>trash</u> 86

milk молоко n mala<u>ko</u>;
with ~ с молоком s mala<u>kom</u> 40

million миллион meelle<u>eon</u> 216

mind: do you mind? (вы) не возражаете? (vi) nee vazra<u>zha</u>yetee? 77, 126

mine мой moy 16;
it's mine! это мой! eta moy

mineral water минеральная вода f meene<u>eral'</u>naya va<u>da</u> 40

mini-bar мини-бар m <u>mee</u>nee bar 32

minimart гастроном m gastra<u>nom</u> 158

minute минута f mee<u>noo</u>ta

mirror зеркало n <u>zyer</u>kala

missing, to be
не хватать nee khva<u>tat'</u> 137;
пропасть pra<u>past'</u> 152

mistake ошибка f a<u>sheeb</u>ka 32, 41, 42

misunderstanding: there's been a ~
это недоразумение n eta needarazoo<u>mye</u>neeye

mobile home караван m kara<u>van</u>

modern современный savree<u>myen</u>niy 14

moisturizer *(cream)*
увлажняющий крем m oovlazh<u>nyay</u>ooshcheey krem

monastery монастырь m mana<u>stir'</u> 99

Monday понедельник m panee<u>dyel'</u>neek 218

money деньги pl <u>dyen'</u>gee 42;
~ order почтовый перевод m pach<u>to</u>viy peere<u>evot</u>

month месяц m <u>mye</u>syats 218;
monthly *(ticket)*
на месяц na <u>mye</u>syats 79

moped мопед m ma<u>pyed</u> 83

more больше <u>bol'</u>she 15; I'd like some more можно ещё ... <u>mozhna</u> ye<u>shchyo</u> ... 39

morning, in the
утром m <u>oo</u>tram 221

mosque мечеть f me<u>chyet'</u> 105

mosquito bite
комариный укус m kama<u>ree</u>niy oo<u>koos</u>

mother мать f mat' 120

motion sickness морская болезнь f mar<u>skaya</u> ba<u>lyezn'</u> 141

motorbike мотоцикл m matat<u>seekal</u> 83

motorboat моторка f ma<u>tor</u>ka 116

motorway (авто)шоссе n (afta)shas<u>se</u> 92, 94

mountain гора f ga<u>ra</u> 106, 107;
~ bike горный велосипед m <u>gor</u>niy veelasee<u>pyet</u>; ~ pass перевал m peere<u>eval</u> 107; ~ range хребет m khree<u>byet</u> 107

mouth рот m rot 166; ~ ulcer язвы во рту fpl <u>yaz</u>vi va rtoo

move, to переезжать pyereyezzh<u>at'</u> 25; don't move him! не двигайте его! nee <u>dvee</u>gaytee evo 92

movie фильм m feel'm 108, 110;
~ theater кинотеатр m keenatee<u>atar</u> 96

Mr. (господин) m gaspa<u>deen</u>

Mrs. (госпожа) f gaspa<u>zha</u>

much много <u>mno</u>ga 15

mug кружка f <u>kroosh</u>ka 148

mugged, to be
обокрали aba<u>kral</u>ee 153

mugging кража f <u>kra</u>zha 152

multiplex cinema
многозальный кинотеатр m mnaga<u>zal</u>niy keenatee<u>atr</u> 110

mumps корь f kor' 166

muscle мышца f <u>mish</u>tsa 166

museum музей m moo<u>zey</u> 99

music музыка f <u>moo</u>zika 111, 121

musician музыкант m moozi<u>kant</u>

must: I must я должен ya <u>dol</u>zheen

mustache усы mpl oo<u>si</u>

mustard горчица f gar<u>cheet</u>sa 38

my мой moy 16

myself: I'll do it myself я сделаю это сам ya <u>sdye</u>layoo eta sam

N name (first name)
имя n <u>ee</u>mya
118, 120; (family name)
фамилия f fam<u>ee</u>leeya
22, 36; my name is меня
зовут m<u>ee</u>nya za<u>voo</u>t 118; what's
your name? как Вас зовут? n
kak vas za<u>voo</u>t 118

napkin салфетка f sal<u>fye</u>tka 39

nappies пелёнка f peel<u>yo</u>nka 142

narrow узкий <u>oo</u>skeey 14

national национальный
natseea<u>nal'</u>niy

nationality национальность f
natseea<u>nal'nast'</u>

nature reserve заповедник m
zapa<u>vye</u>dneek 107

nausea тошнота f ta<u>sh</u>nata

near около <u>o</u>kala 12

nearby рядом <u>rya</u>dam 21, 87

nearest ближайший
blee<u>zhay</u>sheey 80, 88, 92, 130, 140

neck шея f <u>shye</u>ya 166; (clothes)
ворот m <u>vo</u>rat 144

necklace ожерелье n
azhee<u>rye</u>l'ye 149

need: I need to ... мне нужно ...
mne n<u>oo</u>zhna 18

nephew племянник m plee<u>mya</u>neek

nerve нерв m nyerf 166

nervous system нервная система f
<u>nye</u>rvnaya sees<u>tye</u>ma 166

never никогда neek<u>ag</u>da 13;
~ mind ничего neechye<u>vo</u> 10

new новый <u>no</u>viy 14; New Year
Новый год m <u>no</u>viy got 219

New Zealand Новая Зеландия f
<u>no</u>vaya zee<u>lan</u>deeya 119

newsagent's (newsdealer) газетный
киоск m ga<u>zye</u>tniy kee<u>os</u>k 150

newspaper газета f ga<u>zye</u>ta 150

next следующий <u>slye</u>dooyoosh<u>chye</u>ey
68, 75, 78, 80, 81, 87; next stop!
на следующей! na <u>slye</u>dooyoosh<u>chye</u>y
79; next to рядом с <u>rya</u>dam s 12, 95

nice хороший kha<u>ro</u>sheey 14

niece племянница f plee<u>mya</u>neetsa

night: at ~ ночью f <u>no</u>chyoo 221

nightclub ночной клуб m
nach<u>noy</u> kloop 112

no нет nyet 10

no one никому neeka<u>moo</u> 16

noisy шумный <u>shoo</u>mniy 14, 24

non-alcoholic безалкогольный
beezalka<u>gol'</u>niy

non-smoking (adj.) некурящий
nekoor<u>ya</u>shchyeey 36

nonsense ерунда eeroon<u>da</u> 19

noon полдень m <u>pol</u>deen' 220

normal нормальный nar<u>mal</u>niy 67

north север m <u>sye</u>veer 95

nose нос m nos 166

not: not bad неплохо neep<u>lo</u>kha 19;
not good не очень хорошо nee
<u>o</u>cheen' kharash<u>o</u> 19; not that one
не тот (та) nye tot (ta) 16; not yet
нет ещё nyet ee<u>shchyo</u> 13

notebook записная книжка f
zapees<u>na</u>ya <u>knee</u>shka 150

nothing ничего neechye<u>vo</u> 16;
~ else ничего больше
neechye<u>vo</u> <u>bol</u>'she 15

notice board доска объявлений f
das<u>ka</u> aby<u>av</u>lyeniy 26

notify, to сообщать saap<u>shchat'</u> 167

November ноябрь m na<u>yabr'</u> 218

now сейчас/теперь
see<u>chyas</u>/tee<u>pyer'</u> 13, 84

number (telephone) номер m <u>no</u>myer
84; ~ plate номерной знак m
namee<u>rnoy</u> znak; sorry, wrong
number извините, неправильный
номер m eezvee<u>nee</u>tee
neep<u>ra</u>veel'niy <u>no</u>meer

nurse сестра f sees<u>tra</u>

nylon нейлон n nee<u>lon</u>

O occasionally иногда eenag<u>da</u>
occupied занятый
<u>za</u>neetiy 14

October октябрь m
ak<u>tyabr'</u> 218

odds (betting) шансы mpl
<u>shan</u>si 114

of course конечно ka<u>nyesh</u>na 19
off-licence винный магазин m
veeniy maga<u>zeen</u> 131
office контора f ka<u>ntora</u>
often часто <u>chya</u>sta 13
oil нефть f nyef'
okay хорошо/о'кей
kha<u>rasho</u>/o ke 10, 19
old старый <u>stariy</u> 14; **~ town**
старый город m <u>stariy gorat</u> 96,
99; **~-fashioned** старомодный
stara<u>modniy</u> 14
olive oil оливковое масло n
a<u>leef</u>kavaya <u>masla</u>
omelet омлет m am<u>lyet</u> 40
on *(day, date)* в v 13; *(place)* на
na 12; **~ foot** пешком pesh<u>kom</u>
17; **~ my own** один a<u>deen</u> 120;
~ the left налево na<u>lyeva</u> 12; **~ the
other side** на другой стороне na
droo<u>goy</u> staro<u>nye</u> 95; **~ the right**
направо na<u>prava</u> 12; **on/off switch**
включено/выключено
vklyo<u>cheena</u>/<u>vi</u>klyocheena
once однажды/один раз
ad<u>nazhdi</u> 217
one like that как тот (та) kak tot
(ta) 16; **~-piece** костюм m
kasty<u>oom</u> 144; **~-way ticket** в один
конец v a<u>deen</u> ka<u>nyets</u> 68, 74, 79
open *(adj.)* открытый at<u>kritiy</u>
14, 100; **~-air pool** открытый
бассейн m at<u>kritiy</u> ba<u>seyn</u> 116
open, to открываться
atkri<u>vat</u>'sya 132, 140
opening hours часы работы mpl
cha<u>si</u> ra<u>boti</u> 100
opera опера f <u>opeera</u> 108, 111;
~ house оперный театр m
<u>opeerniy</u> tee<u>atar</u> 99, 111
operation операция f apee<u>ratseeya</u>
opposite напротив na<u>proteef</u> 12
optician оптик m <u>opteek</u> 131, 167
or или <u>eelee</u> 19
orange *(fruit)*
апельсин m apeel'<u>seen</u> 160;
(color) оранжевый a<u>ranzheeviy</u> 143
orchestra оркестр m ar<u>kyestar</u> 111

order, to заказывать
za<u>kazivat</u>' 32, 37, 41, 135
ordering заказ m
za<u>kaz</u> 37
organized hike/walk
турпоход m toorpa<u>khot</u>
Orthodox православный
pravas<u>lavniy</u> 105
others другие droo<u>geeye</u> 134
our наш nash 16;
ours наш nash 16
outdoor на открытом воздухе
na at<u>kritam</u> <u>vozdookhee</u>
outside на улице na <u>ooleetsye</u> 36;
снаружи sna<u>roozhee</u> 12
oval овальный a<u>val'niy</u> 134
oven духовка f doo<u>khofka</u>
over there вон там von tam 76
overcharge: I've been overcharged
меня обсчитали
mee<u>nya</u> apscheetalee
overdone *(adj.)* пережаренный
pyerye<u>zharyeniy</u> 41
overheat перегреться
peeree<u>gryet</u>'sya
overnight
одна ночь f ad<u>na</u> noch' 23;
~ service срочная <u>srochnaya</u> 151
owe: how much do I owe?
сколько я Вам должен?
<u>skol'</u>ka ya vam <u>dolzheen</u>
own: on my own я один/одна
ya a<u>deen</u>/ad<u>na</u> 65
owner владелец m vla<u>dyeleets</u>

<u>P</u> **p.m.** после полудня
<u>poslee</u> pa<u>loodnya</u>
pacifier соска f <u>soska</u>
pack, to упаковывать oopa<u>kovivat</u>' 69
package посылка f pa<u>silka</u> 155
packed lunch готовый завтрак m
<u>gatoviy</u> <u>zaftrak</u>
packet пакет m pa<u>kyet</u>;
~ of cigarettes пачка сигарет f
<u>pachka</u> seega<u>ryet</u> 150
paddling pool детский бассейн m
<u>dyetskiy</u> ba<u>seyn</u> 113

padlock замок m zamok

pail ведёрко n veedyorka 157

pain, to be in иметь боли eemyet' bolee 167

painkillers болеутоляющее (средство) n boleeootalyayooshchyeye (sretstva) 141, 165

paint, to написать napeesat' 104

painted написанный napeesaniy 104

painter художник m khoodozhneek 104

painting картина f karteena

pair of пара f para 217

palace дворец m dvaryets 99

palpitations сердцебиение n syertseebeeyeneeye

panorama панорама f panarama 107

pants (U.S.) брюки pl bryookee 144

panty hose колготки pl kalgotkee 144

paper бумага f boomaga 150; **~ napkin** бумажная салфетка f boomazhnaya salfyetka 148

paracetamol парацетамол m paratseetamol

paraffin керосин m kyeraseen 31

paralysis паралич m paraleech

pardon? извините? eezveeneetye 11

parents родители mpl radeeteelee 120

park парк m park 96, 99, 107

parking: ~ lot автостоянка f aftastayanka 26, 87, 96; **~ meter** автомат m aftamat 87

parliament building правительственное здание n praveetyel'stvyenaye zdaneeye 99

parting (hair) пробор m prabor

partner (boyfriend/girlfriend) друг/подруга m/f drook/ padrooga

party (social) вечер m vyecheer 124

pass (mountain) проход m prakhot

pass, to проезжать prayezhat' 77

passport паспорт m paspart 66, 69

pastry store кондитерская f kandeetyerskaya 131

patch, to заштопать zashtopat' 137

path тропинка f trapeenka 107

patient (n.) пациент m patseeyent

pavement тротуар m trattooar; **on the ~** на тротуаре m na tratooaree

pay phone телефон-автомат m teeleefon aftomat

pay, to платить plateet' 42, 136

payment оплата f aplata

peak пик m peek 107

pearl жемчуг m zhyemchook 149

pebbly (beach) галька f gal'ka 116

pedestrian: ~ crossing переход m peereekhot 96; **~ zone [precinct]** пешеходная зона f peesheekhodnaya zona 96

pedicure педикюр m peedeekyoor

pen ручка f roochka 150

pencil карандаш m karandash 150

pensioner пенсионер m peenseeanyer 100

people люди m lyoodee 92, 119

pepper перец m pyeryets 38

per: ~ day в/на день f/na dyen' 30, 83, 86, 87, 115; **~ hour** в/на час f/na chas 87, 115; **~ night** в сутки f sootki 21; **~ week** в/на неделю f/na nyedyelyoo 83, 86

perhaps может быть mozhet' bit' 19

period (historical) период m peereeat 105; (menstrual) менструация f meenstrooatsiya 167; **~ pains** боли при менструации fpl bolee pree meenstrooatsee 167

perm, to делать химическую завивку dyelat' kheemeecheeskooyoo zaveefkoo 147

petrol бензин m beenzeen 86, 87, 88; **~ station** заправочная станция f zapravachnaya stantsiya 87

pewter олово n olava 149

pharmacy аптека f aptyeka 130, 140, 158

phone: ~ card телефонная карточка f teeleefonaya kartachka 127; **~ call** звонок m zvanok 152

phone, to звонить zva<u>neet'</u>
photo: to take a ~
  фотографировать fatagra<u>fee</u>ravat'
photocopier ксерокс m <u>ksye</u>raks 155
photographer фотограф m fa<u>tog</u>raf
photography фотография f
  fotagra<u>fee</u>ya 151
phrase фраза f <u>fra</u>za 11; **~ book**
  разговорник razga<u>vor</u>neek 11
pick up, to *(get)* взять fzyat' 28, 109;
  (collect) забирать za<u>bee</u>rat' 113
picnic пикник m peek<u>neek</u>;
  ~ area площадка для привала f
  plash<u>chat</u>ka dlya pree<u>va</u>la 107
piece кусочек m koo<u>so</u>chyeek 40,
  159; *(of baggage)* место багажа n
  <u>mye</u>sta ba<u>ga</u>zha 69
Pill *(contraceptive):* **to be on the
  Pill** противозачаточные
  таблетки: принимать fpl
  proteevaza<u>cha</u>tachniye tab<u>lyet</u>kee:
  pree<u>nee</u>mat' 167
pill *(tablet)* таблетка f tab<u>lyet</u>ka 165
pillow подушка f pa<u>doosh</u>ka 27;
  ~ case наволочка f <u>na</u>valachka
pilot light запальник m za<u>pal</u>'neek
pink розовый <u>ro</u>zaviy 143
pipe *(smoking)* трубка f <u>troop</u>ka
pitch *(for camping)* разбивать лагерь
  razbee<u>vat</u>' <u>la</u>ger'
pizzeria пиццерия f peet<u>sere</u>eya 35
place *(space)* место n <u>mye</u>sta 29
place a bet, to поставить ставку
  pa<u>sta</u>veet' <u>staf</u>koo 114
plane самолёт m sama<u>lyot</u> 68
plans планы mpl <u>pla</u>ni 124
plant *(n.)* растение n ras<u>tye</u>neeye
plasters пластырь m <u>plas</u>tir 141
plastic bags пластиковый мешок m
  <u>plas</u>teekaviy mee<u>shok</u>
plate тарелка f
  ta<u>rel</u>ka 39, 41, 148
platform платформа f
  plat<u>for</u>ma 73, 76, 77
platinum платина f <u>pla</u>teena 149
play, to *(games, etc.)* играть ee<u>grat</u>'
  121; *(perform)* исполнять
  eespal<u>nyat</u>' 111

play group детская
  группа f <u>dyet</u>skaya
  <u>groo</u>pa 113
playground
  детская площадка f
  <u>dyet</u>skaya plash<u>chat</u>ka 113
playing: ~ cards игральные карты
  fpl ee<u>gral</u>'niye <u>kar</u>ti 150;
  ~ field спортплощадка f
  sportplash<u>chat</u>ka 96
playwright драматург m
  drama<u>toork</u> 111
pleasant приятный pree<u>yat</u>niy 14
please пожалуйста pa<u>zhal</u>sta 10
plug штепсель m <u>shtyep</u>seel' 148
pneumonia пневмония f
  pneevma<u>nee</u>ya 165
point to, to показывать paka<u>zivat</u>' 11
poison яд m yat 141
poles палки fpl <u>pal</u>kee 117
police милиция f mee<u>leet</u>seeya 92,
  152, 153; **~ station** отделение
  милиции n atdee<u>lye</u>neeye
  mee<u>leet</u>seyee 96, 131, 152
polyester полистерол m
  palee<u>ste</u>rol
pond пруд m proot 107
pop поп(-музыка) m
  pop(-<u>moo</u>zika) 111
popcorn воздушная кукуруза f
  vaz<u>doosh</u>naya kookoo<u>roo</u>za 110
popular популярный
  papoo<u>lyar</u>niy 111, 157
port *(harbor)* порт m port
porter носильщик m
  na<u>seel</u>'shcheek 71
portion порция f <u>port</u>seeya 39
possible: as soon as possible как
  можно скорей kak <u>mozh</u>na ska<u>rey</u>
post *(n.)* почта f <u>poch</u>ta; **~ office**
  почта f <u>poch</u>ta 96, 131, 154;
  ~box почтовый ящик m
  pach<u>to</u>viy <u>ya</u>shcheek 154
post, to отправлять atprav<u>lyat</u>'
postcard открытка f
  at<u>krit</u>ka 150, 154, 156
poste restante до востребования do
  vast<u>rye</u>bavaneeya 155

A-Z

~ potatoes картофель/ картошка m/f kartofyel/kartoshka 38
pottery керамика f keerameeka
pound (sterling) фунт m foont 67, 138
power: ~ cut перебой в электроснабжении m peereeboy v elyektrasnabzhyenee; **~ point** розетка f razyetka 30
pregnant: I'm pregnant я беременна ya beeryemeenna 163
premium (gas/petrol) бензин 98 m beenzeen dyevyanosta vas'moy
prescribe, to выписывать vipeesivat' 165
prescription рецепт m reetsyept 141
present (gift) подарок m padarak
press, to гладить gladeet' 137
pretty красивый kraseeviy
priest священник m svyashchyeneek
prison тюрьма f tyoor'ma
program программа f programa 108, 109
pronounce, to произносить praeeznaseet'
Protestant протестантский prateestantskeey 105
pub пивная f peevnaya
public: ~ building горсовет m garsavyet 96; **~ holiday** праздники mpl prazneekee 219
pump насос m nasos 83
puncture прокол m prakol 83, 88
puppet show кукольный театр m kookal'niy teeatat
pure (material) чистый cheestiy 146; **~ cotton** чистый хлопок m cheestiy khlopak 146
purple алый aliy 143
purpose цель f tsyel' 66
push-chair инвалидное кресло n eenvaleednaya kryesla
put, to поставить pastaveet'
put: where can I put ...? куда можно поставить ...? kooda mozhna pastaveet'

quality качество n kacheestva 134
quarter четверть f chyetveert' 217; **~ past** (after/past of time) четверть f chyetveert' 220; **~ to** (before/to of time) без четверти byez chyetveert' 220
queue, to стоять в очереди stayat' v ocheereedee 112
quick быстрый bistriy 14; **quickly** быстро bystra 17
quickest самый быстрый samiy bistriy; **what's the quickest way?** как быстрее пройти к ...? kak bistryeye praytee k ...
quiet тихий teekheey 14; **quieter** потише pateeshee 24, 126

ready готовый gatoviy 89
rabbi раввин m raveen
racetrack [racecourse] ипподром m eepadrom 114
racket (tennis) ракетка f rakyetka 115
railway железная дорога f zheelyeznaya daroga
rain, to идёт дождь eedyot dozhd 122
raincoat плащ m plashch 144
rape изнасилование n eeznaseelavaneeye 152
rapids пороги mpl parogee 107
rare (steak) с кровью s krovyoo; (unusual) редкий ryetkeey
rash сыпь f sip' 162
ravine овраг m avrak 107
razor бритва f breetva; **~ blade** лезвие n lyezveeye 142
read, to читать chyeetat' 121
ready готовый gatoviy 137, 151
real (genuine) настоящий nastayashcheey 149
receipt квитанция f kveetantseeya 89, 151; чек m chyek 32, 136, 137
reception (desk) регистрация f reegeestratseeya

receptionist регистратор m reegeestratar

reclaim tag багажная квитанция f bagazhnaya kveetantseeya 71

recommend, to рекомендовать reekameendavat' 21, 35, 141; **can you ~ ...?** Вы можете порекомендовать ...? vi mozheetye pareekameendavat' ... 97; **what do you ~?** что Вы рекомендуете? shto vi reekameendooeetye

record (L.P.) пластинка f plasteenka 157; **~ store** пластинки fpl plasteenkee 131

red красный krasniy 143; **~ wine** красное вино n krasnoye veeno 40

reduction (in price) скидка f skeedka 24, 68, 74, 100

refrigerator холодильник m khaladeel'neek 29

refund вернуть деньги veernoot' dyen'gee 137

refuse bag полиэтиленовые мешки m palee-eteelyenaviye meeshkee 148

region район m rayon 106

registered mail заказное отправление n zakaznoye atpravlyeneeye

registration: ~ form регистрационная форма f ryegeestratseeonaya forma 23; **~ number** номер m nomeer 88

regular (gas/petrol) бензин 93 m beenzeen dyevyanosta tryetiy beenzeen 87; (size) средний sryedneey 110

religion религия f reeleegeeya

remember, to помнить pomneet'; **I don't remember** я не помню ya nee pomnyoo

rent (out), to давать/взять напрокат davat'/vsyat' naprakat 29, 86, 115, 116, 117; **I'd like to ~ ...** я хотел(а) бы взять напрокат ... ya khatyel(a) bi vzyat' naprakat ... 83

repair, to (от)ремонтировать/ (по)чинить (at)reemanteeravat'/ (pa)chyeeneet' 89, 137, 168

repairs ремонт m reemont 89

repeat, to повторять paftaryat' 94, 128; **please ~ that** повторите, пожалуйста paftareetye pazhalsta 11

replacement (n.) замена f zamyena 167; **~ part** запасная часть f zapasnaya chast' 137

report, to заявить zayaveet' 152

required (necessary) обязательно abeezateel'na 112

reservation заказ m zakas 22, 36, 68, 74, 77, 112; **reservations desk** касса f kasa 109

reserve, to заказать zakazat' 22, 36

rest, to отдыхать atdikhat'

restaurant ресторан m reestaran 35, 112

retail торговля f targovlya 121

retired, to be на пенсии na pyensee 121

return, to (surrender) возвратить vazvrateet' 86

return ticket билет туда и обратно m beelyet tooda ee abratna 68, 74, 79

reverse the charges, to оплата вызываемым f aplata vizivayemim

revolting невкусный neefkoosniy 14

rheumatism ревматизм m reevmateezm

rib ребро n reebro 166

right (correct) правильный praveel'niy 14, 77, 79, 80, 94; **that's ~** правильно: это правильно praveel'na: eta praveel'na

right of way преимущество n preemooshcheestva 93

right: on the ~ направо naprava 76, 95

ring кольцо n kal'tso 149

rip-off (n.) дорого doraga 101

river река f reeka 107; **~ cruise** речной круиз m ryechnoy krooeez 81

road дорога f daroga 94, 95; **~ map** карта дорог m karta darog 150

robbed: I've been robbed меня обокрали meenya abakralee 153

robbery грабёж m
grab<u>yosh</u>

rock рок(-музыка) m
rok(-<u>moo</u>zika) 111

roll *(bread)* булочка f
<u>boo</u>lachka 160

romantic романтичный
raman<u>teech</u>niy 101

roof *(house, car)* крыша f <u>krisha;</u>
~rack багажник на крыше m
ba<u>gazh</u>neek na <u>krishee</u>

room комната f <u>kom</u>nata 29

rope верёвка f veer<u>yof</u>ka

ruble [rouble] рубль m roobl 138, 139

round круглый <u>kroog</u>liy 134; **round-
trip ticket** билет туда и обратно m
bee<u>lyet too</u>da ee ab<u>ratna</u> 68, 74, 79

round *(of golf)* раунд m <u>ra</u>oond 115

rowing boat лодка f <u>lot</u>ka 116

rubbish мусор m <u>moo</u>sar 28

rucksack рюкзак m ryook<u>zak</u>

ruins развалины fpl raz<u>va</u>leeni 99

run: ~ into *(crash)* врезаться
<u>vryez</u>at'sya 93; **~ out** *(fuel)*
кончиться <u>kon</u>cheet'sya 88

running shoes кроссовки fpl
kras<u>of</u>kee 145

rush hour час пик m chas peek

Russia Россия f ra<u>see</u>ya 119

Russian *(adj.)* русский <u>roos</u>keey 35,
126; **~ language** русский язык m
<u>roos</u>kee ya<u>zeek</u>

S **safe** *(lock up)* сейф m seyf 27
safe *(adj.)* безопасный
beeza<u>pas</u>niy 116

safety безопасность f beeza<u>pas</u>nast';
~ pin булавка f boo<u>laf</u>ka 142

sailing boat яхта f <u>yakh</u>ta 116

salad салат m sa<u>lat</u>

sales торговля f tar<u>gov</u>lya 121;
~ tax НДС m en de es 24

salt соль f sol' 38, 39

salty солёный sal<u>yo</u>niy

same тот же самый
tot zhye <u>sa</u>miy 75

sand песок m pee<u>sok</u>

sandals сандалии mpl san<u>da</u>lee 145

sandwich бутерброд m
booty<u>er</u>brot 40

sand песок m pee<u>sok</u> 116

sandy beach песчаный пляж m
pee<u>schan</u>iy plyazh

sanitary napkins [towels]
гигиеническая салфетка f
geegee<u>neech</u>eskaya sal<u>fyet</u>ka 142

satellite TV спутниковое
телевидение n <u>spoot</u>neekavaya
tyelye<u>veed</u>yeneeye 22

satin сатин m sa<u>teen</u>

satisfied: I'm not satisfied with this
я не доволен этим
ya nee da<u>vo</u>leen <u>e</u>teem

Saturday суббота f soo<u>bo</u>ta 218

sauce соус m <u>so</u>-oos 38

saucepan кастрюля f kas<u>tryoo</u>lya 29

sauna сауна f <u>sa</u>oona 22

sausage сосиска/колбаса f
sa<u>see</u>ska/kalba<u>sa</u> 160

say, to говорить gava<u>reet'</u>; **how do
you ~ ...?** как Вы говорите ...?
kak vi gava<u>ree</u>tee ...

scarf шарф m sharf 144

scenic route живописный маршрут m
zheeva<u>pees</u>niy marsh<u>root</u> 106

scheduled flight регулярный рейс m
reegoo<u>lyar</u>niy ryeys

sciatica ишиас m <u>ee</u>sheeas 165

scissors ножницы pl <u>nozh</u>neetsi 148

scooter мотороллер m mata<u>rol</u>eer

Scotland Шотландия f
shat<u>lan</u>deeya 119

screwdriver отвёртка f at<u>vyor</u>tka 148

sea море n <u>mor</u>ye 107; **~front**
берег моря m <u>byer</u>eek <u>mor</u>ya;
~sickness морская болезнь f
mar<u>skaya</u> ba<u>lyesn'</u>; **I feel ~sick**
у меня морская болезнь
oo mee<u>nya</u> mar<u>skaya</u> ba<u>lyesn'</u>

season ticket проездной билет m
praeez<u>noy</u> bee<u>lyet</u>

seasoning приправы fpl
pree<u>pra</u>vy 38

seat место n <u>mye</u>sta 68, 74, 77, 109

second второй fta<u>roy</u> 217

second: ~ **class** (train) купейный вагон m koopeyniy vagon 74; ~**hand** подержанный padyerzhaniy

secretary секретарь m seekreetar'

sedative успокаивающее n oospakayeevayooshcheeye

see, to видеть/(по)смотреть veedyet'/(pa)smatryet' 24, 93

self-employed работать на себя m rabotat' na seebya 121

self-service самообслуживание n samaapsloozheevaneeye 87

sell, to продавать pradavat' 133

send, to послать/посылать paslat'/pisilat' 88, 155

senior citizen пенсионер m pyenseeonyer 74

separated, to be не жить вместе nye zheet' vmyestee 120

separately отдельно adel'na 42

September сентябрь m seentyabr' 218

serious серьёзный seeryozniy

service (religious) служба f sloozhba 105

service (in restaurant) обслуживание n apsloozheevaneeye; **is ~ included?** счёт включает обслуживание? schyot fklyoochayet apsloozheevaneeye 42

serviette салфетка f salfyetka 39

set menu меню n myenyoo 37

sexual сексуальный seeksooal'niy

shade тон m ton 143

shady в тени f tyenee 30

shallow мелкий melkeey

shampoo шампунь f shampoon' 142; ~ **and set** вымыть и уложить vimat' ee oolazheet' 147

shape форма; покрой f forma; pakroy 134

share, to (room) делить deeleet'

shaver электробритва f elyektrabreetva 142

shaving: ~ **brush** кисточка для бритья f keestachka dlya breetya; ~ **cream** крем для бритья f krem dlya breetya

she она ana

sheath (contraceptive) презерватив m preeseervateef

sheet (bedding) простыня f prastynya 28

ship пароход m parakhod 81

shirt рубашка f roobashka 144

shock (electric) электрошок m elektrashok

shoe(s) обувь/туфли f/fpl oboof'/tooflee 145; ~ **repair** ремонт обуви m reemont oboovee; ~ **store** обувь f aboof'; ~**mender's** ремонт обуви m reemont oboovee 131

shop магазин m magazeen 130; ~ **assistant** продавец m pradavyets

shopping: ~ **basket** корзинка f karzeenka; ~ **mall [centre]** торговый центр m targoviy tsentar 99, 131; ~ **trolley** тележка f teelyeshka; **to go** ~ идти за покупками eetee za pakoopkamee

short (vs. tall) низкий neeskeey 14

short-sighted близорукость f bleezarookast' 167

shorts шорты pl shorti 144

shoulder плечо n pleecho 166

shovel совок m savok 157

show, to показывать pakazivat' 18, 94, 133; **can you ~ me ...?** покажите мне ... pakazheetee mne ... 133

shower душ m doosh 26, 30

shut (adj.) закрытый zakritiy 14

shut, to закрываться zakrivat'sya 132; **when do you shut?** когда вы закрываетесь? kagda vi zakrivayeetees'

shutters ставни mpl stavni 25

sick: I'm going to be sick меня тошнит meenya tashneet

side (of road) сторона f starana 95; ~ **order** гарнир m garneer 37, 38; ~ **street** боковая улица f bakavaya ooleetsa 95

sightseeing: ~ tour обзорная экскурсия f ab<u>zor</u>naya eks<u>koor</u>seeya 97; **to go ~** осматривать достопримечательности asmatreevat' dastapreemee<u>chat</u>eel'nastee

sign *(road)* знак m znak 93

signpost дорожный знак m da<u>rozh</u>niy znak

silk шёлк m shyolk

silver серебро n seere<u>ebro</u> 149; **~-plate** посеребрённый pase<u>ryebryaniy</u> 149

singer певец m pee<u>vyets</u> 157

single одноместный adna<u>myesniy</u> 81; **~ room** одноместный номер m adna<u>myestnyi nomyer</u> 21; **~ ticket** билет в один конец bee<u>lyet</u> v a<u>deen</u> kanyets 68, 74, 79

single *(unmarried)* холост *(man)*/ не замужем *(woman)* <u>kholast</u>/nee za<u>moozhem</u> 120

sink раковина f <u>rakoveena</u> 25

sister сестра f see<u>stra</u> 120

sit, to сесть syest' 77

size размер m raz<u>myer</u> 146

skates коньки mpl kon'<u>kee</u> 117

ski: ~ boots лыжные ботинки mpl <u>lizh</u>niye ba<u>teen</u>kee 117; **~-school** лыжная школа f <u>lizh</u>naya <u>shkola</u>

skin кожа f <u>kozha</u> 166

skirt юбка f <u>yoop</u>ka 144

skis лыжи fpl <u>lizhee</u> 117

sleep, to спать spat' 167

sleeping: ~ bag спальный мешок m <u>spal</u>'niy mee<u>shok</u> 31; **~ pill** снотворное n snat<u>vor</u>naya

sleeve рукав m roo<u>kav</u> 144

slice ломтик m <u>lom</u>teek 159

slippers тапочки fpl <u>tapach</u>kee 145

slow медленный <u>myed</u>leenniy 14; *(clock)* отстать at<u>stat'</u> 221; **slow down!** помедленнее pa<u>myed</u>leeneeye 94

slowly медленно <u>myed</u>leena 11, 17

small маленький <u>maleen</u>'keey 14, 40, 110; *(cramped)* тесно <u>tyesno</u> 24; **smaller** поменьше pa<u>myen</u>'she 134

smell запах m <u>zapakh</u>

smoke, to курить koo<u>reet'</u> 126

smoking *(adj.)* курящий koo<u>ryash</u>chiy 36

snack bar буфет m boo<u>fyet</u> 73

snacks закуски fpl za<u>koo</u>skee

sneakers кроссовки fpl kra<u>sso</u>fkee

snorkel трубка f <u>troop</u>ka

snow снег snyek 122

soap мыло n <u>mila</u> 142; **~ powder** мыльный порошок m <u>mil</u>'niy pa<u>rashok</u>

soccer футбол m foot<u>bol</u> 114

socket розетка f ra<u>zyet</u>ka

socks носки mpl nas<u>kee</u> 144

soft drink напиток m na<u>pee</u>tak 110

sole *(shoes)* подошва f pa<u>dosh</u>va

soloist солист m sa<u>leest</u> 111

soluble aspirin растворимый аспирин m rastva<u>reemiy</u> aspee<u>reen</u>

some какой-то ka<u>koy</u> ta

someone кто-то/кто-нибудь kto-to/kto-ni<u>bood'</u>

something что-то/что-нибудь chto-to/chto-ni<u>bood'</u>

sometimes иногда eena<u>gda</u> 13

son сын m sin 120, 162

soon скоро <u>skora</u> 13; **as ~ as possible** как можно скорее kak <u>mozh</u>na ska<u>ryeye</u> 161

sore throat воспаление горла n vaspa<u>lyeneeye gorla</u> 141, 163

sorry! извините/простите eezvee<u>neetye</u>/pras<u>teetye</u> 10

sour кислый <u>kees</u>liy 41

South Africa Южная Африка f <u>yoozh</u>naya <u>afreeka</u>

South African *(n.)* южноафриканец m <u>yoozhnaafree</u>ka<u>neets</u>

south юг m yook 95

souvenir сувенир m soovee<u>neer</u> 98, 156; **~ guide** путеводитель m pooteeva<u>deeteel'</u> 156; **~ store** сувениры m soovee<u>neeri</u> 131

spa минеральные воды fpl meenee<u>ral'</u>niye <u>vodi</u> 107

space место n <u>myesta</u> 30

spade совок m sa<u>vok</u> 157
spare *(extra)* лишний <u>leesh</u>neey
speak, to говорить (c) gava<u>reet</u>' (s) 11, 41, 67, 128; **do you ~ English/ Russian?** Вы говорите по-английски/по-русски? vi gava<u>ree</u>tye pa-an<u>glee</u>yskee/ pa-<u>roo</u>skee 11, 110
special: ~ delivery экспресс m eks<u>pryes</u> 155; **~ rate** особый тариф m a<u>so</u>biy ta<u>reef</u> 86
specialist специалист m speetsea<u>leest</u> 164
specimen анализ m a<u>na</u>leez 164
spectacles очки pl ach<u>kee</u>
spell, to называть по буквам naza<u>vat</u>' pa <u>book</u>vam 11
spend, to тратить <u>tra</u>teet'
spicy острый <u>os</u>triy
spine позвоночник m pazva<u>noch</u>neek 166
spoon ложка f <u>losh</u>ka 39, 41, 148
sport спорт m sport 114, 121; **sports club** спортклуб m sport<u>kloop</u> 115; **sports ground** спортплощадка f sportplash<u>chat</u>ka 96
sporting goods store спорттовары m sporta<u>va</u>ri 131
sprained, to be растянуть rastya<u>noot</u>' 164
spring *(season)* весна f vees<u>na</u> 219
square квадратный kvad<u>rat</u>niy 134
stadium стадион m sta<u>deeon</u> 96
staff персонал m peer<u>sa</u>nal
stainless steel нержавеющая сталь f neerzha<u>vyey</u>ooshchaya stal' 149
stamp марка f <u>mar</u>ka 150, 154
stand in line, to стоять в очереди sta<u>yat</u>' v o<u>chee</u>reedee 112
start, to начинаться nachee<u>nat</u>'sya 108, 112; *(car)* заводить zava<u>deet</u>' 88
starter закуска f za<u>koos</u>ka 99
stately home усадьба f oo<u>sad</u>'ba 99
station вокзал m vak<u>zal</u> 96
stationer канцелярские товары mpl kantsee<u>lyars</u>keeye ta<u>va</u>ri
statue статуя f <u>sta</u>tooya 99
stay, to остаться as<u>tat</u>'sa 23, 123

steet kiosk уличный киоск m oo<u>leech</u>niy kee<u>osk</u> 150
sterilizing solution стерилизующий раствор m steereelee<u>zoo</u>yooshcheey ras<u>tvor</u> 142
still: I'm still waiting я всё ещё жду ya vsyo ee<u>shcho</u> zhdoo
sting укус m oo<u>koos</u> 162
stockings чулки mpl chool<u>kee</u> 144
stolen, to украсть oo<u>krast</u>' 71
stomach живот/желудок m zhee<u>vot</u>/zhee<u>loo</u>dak 166; **~ache** болит живот ba<u>leet</u> zhee<u>vot</u> 163
stools *(faeces)* кал m kal 164
stop *(bus, etc.)* остановка f asta<u>nof</u>ka 79, 80
stop, to останавливаться asta<u>nav</u>leevat'sya 76, 77, 78, 98
stopcock запорный кран za<u>por</u>ny kran 28
store магазин m maga<u>zeen</u> 130; **~ guide** перечень отделов m <u>pye</u>reechen' ad<u>ye</u>laf 132
stormy гроза f gra<u>za</u> 122
stove плита f <u>plee</u>ta 28, 29
straight ahead прямо <u>prya</u>ma 95
strained muscle растянута мышца rastya<u>noo</u>ta <u>mish</u>tsa 162
strange странный <u>stra</u>niy 101
straw *(drinking)* соломинка f sa<u>lo</u>meenka
stream ручей m roo<u>chey</u> 107
strong *(potent)* сильный <u>seel</u>'niy
student студент m stoo<u>dyent</u> 74, 100
study, to учиться oo<u>cheet</u>'sya 121
stunning ошеломляющий asheelam<u>lya</u>yooshcheey 101
style стиль m steel' 104
subtitled с субтитрами s soob<u>teet</u>ramee 110
subway метро n mee<u>tro</u> 80; **~ station** станция метро f <u>stan</u>tsiya mee<u>tro</u> 80
sugar сахар m <u>sa</u>khar 38, 39
suggest, to предлагать preedla<u>gat</u>' 123

A-Z

suit костюм m kastyoom 144

suitable for годный для godniy dlya

summer лето n lyeta 219

sun-tan cream/lotion крем для загара m krem dlya zagara 142

sunbathe, to загорать zagarat'

sunburn солнечный ожог m solneechniy azhok 141

Sunday воскресенье n vaskreesyen'ye 218

sunglasses солнечные очки pl solneechniye achkee 144

sunny на солнце n na sontse 31

sunshade зонт m zont 116

sunstroke солнечный удар m solneechniy oodar 163

super (gas/petrol) бензин 98 m dyevyanosta vas'moy beenzeen 87

superb превосходный preevaskhodniy 101

supermarket универсам m ooneevyersam 131, 158

supervision присмотр m preesmotar

supplement доплата f daplata 68, 69, 74

suppositories свечи fpl svyechee 165

sure: are you sure? Вы уверены? vi oovyereni

surfboard доска f daska 116

surname фамилия f fameeleeya

suspicious подозрительный padazreeteel'niy 152

sweater пуловер m poolovеer 144

sweatshirt рубашка/фуфайка f roobashka/foofayka 144

sweet (taste) сладкий slatkey

sweets конфеты fpl kanfyeti 150

swelling опухоль f opookhal' 162

swim, to плавать plavat' 116

swimming плавание n plavaneeye 114; **~ pool** бассейн m basyeyn 22, 26, 116; **~ trunks** плавки pl plafkee 144

swimsuit купальник m koopal'neek 144

swollen, to be распухать raspookhat'

symptoms симптомы mpl seemtomi 163

synagogue синагога f seenagoga 105

synthetic синтетика f seenteteeka 146

T **T-shirt** майка f mayka 144, 156

table столик m stoleek 35, 112

take, to (carry) нести nyestee 71; (medication) принимать preeneemat' 165; (time) длиться dleet'sya 78; **I'll take it** я возьму это ya vaz'moo eta 24, 135; **~ out** [take away] брать с собой brat' s saboy 40; **~ photographs** фотографировать fatagrafeeravat' 98, 100

taken (occupied): **is this seat taken?** это место занято? eta meysta zanyata 77

talcum powder тальк m tal'k 142

talk, to разговаривать razgavareevat'

tall высокий visokeey 14

tampon тампон m tampon 142

tan загар m zagar

tap кран m kran 25

taxi такси n taksee 70, 71, 84; **~ stand** [rank] стоянка такси f stayanka taksee 84, 96

tea чай m chay 40; **~ bag** пакетик чая m pakyeteek chaya 160; **~ towel** кухонное полотенце n kookhanaye palatyentse

teacher учитель m oocheeteel'

team команда f kamanda 114

teaspoon чайная ложка f chaynaya loshka 148

teddy bear мишка m meeshka 157

telephone телефон m teeleefon 22, 70, 92, 127; **~ bill** счёт за телефон m shchyot za teeleefon 32; **~ booth** телефон-автомат m teeleefon-aftamat 127; **~ calls** телефонные звонки mpl teeleefoniye zvankee 32; **~ directory** телефонный справочник m teeleefoniy spravachneek 127; **~ number** номер телефона m nomeer teeleefona 127

telex телекс m <u>tye</u>leeks 155

tell, to рассказывать ras<u>ka</u>zyvat' 18;
  tell me скажите мне
  ska<u>zhee</u>tye mnye 79

temperature (body) температура f
  teempeera<u>too</u>ra 164

temporarily временно <u>vrye</u>meena 89

tennis теннис m <u>te</u>nees 114;
  ~ court теннисный корт m
  <u>tye</u>neesniy kort 115

tent палатка f pa<u>lat</u>ka 30, 31;
  ~ pegs колышки mpl <u>ko</u>lishkee 31;
  ~ pole шест m shest 31

terminus (bus) кольцо n kal'<u>tso</u> 78

terrible ужасный oo<u>zhas</u>niy 19, 101

tetanus столбняк m stal<u>bnyak</u> 164

thank you спасибо spa<u>see</u>ba 10

that: ~ one вон тот (та) von tot/(ta)
  16; **that's all** это всё eta vsyo 133

theater театр m tea<u>tar</u> 96, 99, 110

theft кража f <u>kra</u>zha 153

their их eekh 16

theirs их eekh 16

them (to, for) им eem 16

then (time) ·затем/потом
  za<u>tyem</u>/ <u>pa</u>tom 13

there там tam 17;
  там/туда tam/too<u>da</u> 12

thermometer термометр m
  teer<u>mo</u>meetar

thermos flask термос m <u>ter</u>mas

these эти <u>e</u>tee 134

they они a<u>nee</u>

thick толстый <u>tol</u>stiy 14

thief вор m vor

thigh бедро n beed<u>ro</u> 166

thin тонкий <u>ton</u>keey 14

think, to думать <u>doo</u>mat' 42;
  ~ about it подумать об этом
  pa<u>doo</u>mat' ab <u>e</u>tam 135; **I think**
  я думаю ya <u>doo</u>mayoo 42, 77

third третий <u>trye</u>teey 217

third, a третья часть f
  <u>trye</u>tya chast 217

thirsty: I'm thirsty я хочу пить
  ya kha<u>choo</u> peet'

this: ~ one вот этот (эта)
  von <u>e</u>tot (<u>e</u>ta) 16

those те tye 134

thousand тысяча
  <u>ti</u>seecha 216

throat горло n
  <u>gor</u>la 166

thrombosis тромбоз m
  tram<u>boz</u>

through через <u>chye</u>reez

thumb большой палец m
  bal'<u>shoy</u> <u>pa</u>leets

Thursday четверг m cheet<u>vyerk</u> 218

ticket билет m bee<u>lyet</u> 68, 75, 77, 79,
  80, 100, 114; **~ office** билетные
  кассы fpl bee<u>lyet</u>niye <u>kas</u>si 73

tie галстук m <u>gal</u>stook 144

tight (loose) тесно <u>tye</u>sna 146

tights колготки pl kal<u>got</u>kee 144

till receipt чек m chyek

time время n <u>vrye</u>mya 76; **~ of day**
  время суток n <u>vrye</u>mya <u>soo</u>tak
  220; **on ~** во время va <u>vrye</u>mya
  76; **free ~** свободное время n
  sva<u>bod</u>naya <u>vrye</u>mya 98; **... times a
  day** ... раз в день ...raz v dyen'

timetable расписание n
  raspee<u>sa</u>neeye 75

tin банка f <u>ban</u>ka 159; **~ opener**
  открывалка f atkri<u>val</u>ka 148

tint, to тонировать ta<u>nee</u>ravat' 147

tire (n.) шина f <u>shee</u>na 83, 88

tired усталый oos<u>ta</u>liy

tissue бумажная салфетка f
  boo<u>mazh</u>naya sal<u>fyet</u>ka 142

to (place) в, на v(f)/na 12

tobacco табак m ta<u>bak</u> 150

today сегодня see<u>vod</u>nee 124, 218

toe палец ноги m <u>pa</u>leets na<u>gee</u> 166

together вместе <u>vmye</u>stye 42

toilet туалет m too<u>a</u>lyet 25, 26, 29,
  96, 98, 132;
  ~ paper туалетная бумага f
  too<u>a</u>lyetnaya boo<u>ma</u>ga 25, 142

tomorrow завтра <u>zaf</u>tra 84, 124, 218

tongs щипцы pl shchy<u>eep</u>tsi 31

tongue язык m ya<u>zik</u> 166

tonight сегодня вечером see<u>vod</u>nya
  <u>vye</u>cheeram 108, 110, 124

tonsillitis тонзиллит m tanzee<u>leet</u>

tonsils миндалины fpl meen<u>da</u>leeni

too слишком <u>sleesh</u>kam 17, 93; **~ much** слишком много <u>sleesh</u>kam <u>mno</u>ga 15

tooth зуб m zoop 168; **~ache** зубная боль f zoob<u>na</u>ya bol'; **~brush** зубная щётка f zoob<u>na</u>ya <u>shchyot</u>ka 142; **~paste** зубная паста f zoob<u>na</u>ya <u>pas</u>ta 142

top крышка f <u>krish</u>ka

torch фонарь m fa<u>nar'</u> 31

torn, to be (*muscle*) разорвать razar<u>vat'</u> 164

totally полностью <u>pol</u>nostyoo 17

tough (*food*) жёсткий <u>zhyos</u>kiy 41

tour экскурсия f eks<u>koor</u>seeya 81; **~ guide** представитель тура m pryedsta<u>vee</u>tyel'<u>too</u>ra 27

tourist турист m too<u>reest;</u> **~ office** бюро туристическое n byoo<u>ro</u> tooreesteecheskaya 97

tow truck буксир m book<u>seer</u> 88

tow, to отбуксировать atbook<u>see</u>ravat' 88

towel полотенце n pala<u>tyent</u>se 142

tower башня f <u>bash</u>nya 99

town город m <u>go</u>rat 70, 94; **~ hall** горсовет m gor<u>sa</u>vyet 99

toy игрушка f ee<u>groosh</u>ka 157; **~ store** игрушки fpl ee<u>groosh</u>kee 131

traditional традиционный tradeets<u>io</u>niy 35

traffic дорожное движение n da<u>ro</u>zhnaya dvee<u>zhye</u>neeye; **~ jam** пробка f <u>prop</u>ka; **~ violation [offence]** нарушение n naroo<u>shye</u>neeye

trail просёлочная дорога f prasy<u>o</u>lachnaya da<u>ro</u>ga 106

trailer трейлер m <u>tryey</u>lyer 30

train поезд m <u>po</u>yest 75, 76, 77, 80; **~ station** вокзал m vak<u>zal</u> 73; **~ times** расписание поездов raspee<u>sa</u>neeye poyez<u>dov</u> 75

training shoes кроссовки fpl kra<u>sof</u>kee 145

tram трамвай m tran<u>vay</u> 78, 79

transfer пересаживаться peeree<u>sa</u>zheevat'sya

transit, in в пути v poo<u>tee</u>

translate, to переводить peeree<u>vo</u>deet' 11

translation перевод m peeree<u>vot</u>

translator переводчик m peeree<u>vot</u>cheek

trash мусор m <u>moo</u>sar 28; **~ cans** мусорные баки mpl <u>moo</u>sornye <u>ba</u>kee 30

travel: ~ agency бюро путешествий n byoo<u>ro</u> pootee<u>shye</u>stveey 131; **~ sickness** морская болезнь f mar<u>ska</u>ya ba<u>lyezn'</u> 141

traveler's checks [cheques] аккредитивы mpl akree<u>dee</u>teevi 136, 138

tray поднос m pad<u>nos</u>

tree дерево n <u>dye</u>reeva 106

trim (*hair*) подстричь pat<u>streech</u> 147

trip (*journey*) поездка f pa<u>yest</u>ka 76, 78, 123

trolley тележка f tee<u>lyesh</u>ka 158

trouser press гладильный пресс m gla<u>deel'</u>niy pres

trousers брюки pl <u>bryoo</u>kee 144

truck грузовик m groozo<u>veek</u>

true правда f <u>prav</u>da; **that's not ~** это неправда eta nee<u>prav</u>da

try on, to примерять preemee<u>ryat'</u> 146

Tuesday вторник m <u>ftor</u>neek 218

tumor опухоль f o<u>pookhal'</u> 165

tunnel туннель m too<u>nel'</u>

turn: ~ down (*volume, heat*) уменьшать oomeen'<u>shat'</u>; **~ off** выключать viklyoo<u>chat'</u> 25; **~ on** включать fklyoo<u>chat'</u> 25; **~ up** (*volume, heat*) увеличивать oovee<u>lee</u>cheevat'

turning поворот m pava<u>rot</u> 95

TV телевизор m tele<u>vee</u>zar 22

tweezers пинцет m peen<u>tsyet</u>

twice дважды/два раза <u>dva</u>zhdi 217

twin bed две кровати fpl
dvye kra<u>va</u>tee 21

twist: I've twisted my ankle
вывихнуть: я вывихнул лодыжку
<u>vi</u>veekhnoot': ya <u>vi</u>veekhnool
la<u>dish</u>koo

two-door car двухдверная машина
dvookh<u>dvyer</u>naya ma<u>shee</u>na 86

type тип m teep 109; **what ~?**
какой тип? ka<u>koy</u> teep 112

typical типичный tee<u>pee</u>chiy 37

tyre *(tire)* шина f <u>shee</u>na 83, 88

U **ugly** некрасивый/
безобразный neekra<u>see</u>viy/
beeza<u>braz</u>niy 14, 101

Ukraine Украина f ookra<u>ee</u>na 119

ulcer язва f <u>yaz</u>va

umbrella *(sunshade)* зонт m
<u>zont</u> 116

uncle дядя m <u>dya</u>dya 120

unconscious без сознания
byes saz<u>na</u>neeya 92, 162

under под pot

underdone *(adj.)* недожаренный
needa<u>zhar</u>yeniy 41

underground метро n my<u>etro</u>;
~ station станция метро f
<u>stan</u>tseeya my<u>etro</u>

underpants трусы pl troo<u>si</u> 144

underpass подземный переход m
pad<u>zyem</u>niy peeree<u>khot</u> 76, 96

understand, to понимать panee<u>mat'</u>
11; **do you ~?** Вы понимаете?
vi panee<u>ma</u>yetye 11;
I don't ~ я не понимаю
ya nye panee<u>ma</u>yoo 11, 67;

undress, to раздеваться
razdee<u>vat'</u>sya 164

uneven *(ground)* неровный m
ny<u>erov</u>niy 30

unfortunately к сожалению
k sazha<u>lye</u>neeyoo 19

uniform форма f <u>for</u>ma

unit *(for phonecard, etc.)* единица f
yedee<u>neet</u>sa 155

United States
Соединенные
Штаты mpl
saeedeen<u>yo</u>niye <u>sh</u>tati

unleaded *(gas/petrol)*
очищенный
a<u>chee</u>shcheniy 87

unlock, to отпирать atpee<u>rat'</u>

unpleasant неприятный
neepree<u>ya</u>tniy 14

unscrew, to отворачивать
atva<u>ra</u>cheevat'

until до do 221

upper *(berth)* верхний <u>vyerkh</u>nneey 74

upset stomach расстройство желудка
n ras<u>troy</u>stva zhee<u>loot</u>ka 141

urgent срочно <u>sroch</u>na 161

urine моча f ma<u>cha</u> 164

U.S.A. США mpl es she a

use, to пользоваться
<u>pol</u>'zavat'sya 139

V **vacancy** вакансия/свободное
место f/n va<u>kan</u>siya/
sva<u>bod</u>noye mesta

vacant свободный sva<u>bod</u>niy 14

vacate, to освободить
asvaba<u>deet'</u> 32

vacation: on ~ в отпуске
v <u>ot</u>pooskee 66, 123

vaginal infection воспаление
влагалища n vaspa<u>lye</u>neeye
vlaga<u>lee</u>shcha 167

valid действителен
dyey<u>stvee</u>tyelyen 75

valley долина f da<u>lee</u>na 107

valuable ценный <u>tsye</u>niy

value стоимость f <u>stoee</u>mast' 155

valve запорный кран m
za<u>por</u>ny kran 28

VAT НДС m en de es 24

vegetables овощи mpl <u>o</u>vashchee 38

vegetarian вегетарианец m
vyegyeta<u>ree</u>anyets 35, 39

vein вена f <u>vye</u>na 166

venereal disease венерическое
заболевание n veeneeree<u>chee</u>skoye
zabalee<u>va</u>neeye 165

ventilator вентилятор m veenteel*ya*tar

very очень ochen' 17;
~ good отлично atleechna 19

video: ~ game видеоигра f veedeeaeegra; **~ recorder** видео m veedeea

view вид m veet

viewing point смотровая площадка f smatravaya plashchatka 99, 107

village деревня f deeryevnya 107

vineyard виноградник m veenagradneek 107

visa виза f veeza

visit визит m veezeet 66, 119

visit, to посещать paseeshchat' 123

visiting hours часы посещений mpl chasi paseeshchyeneey 167

vitamin tablets витамины mpl veetameeni 141

volleyball волейбол m valeeybol 114

voltage напряжение n napryazhyeneeye

vomit, to тошнить tashneet' 163

W **wait** ждать zhdat' 36, 41, 76, 89, 126, 140; **wait!** подождите! padazhdeetye! 98

waiter! официант! m afeetseeant 37

waiting room зал ожидания m zal azheedaneeya 73

waitress! официантка! f afeetseeantka 37

wake someone, to разбудить razboodeet' 27

Wales Уэльс m ooel's 119

walk, to идти eetee 65, 106

walking route пешеходный маршрут m peesheekhodniy marshroot 106

wallet кошелёк m kashyelyok 42

want, to хотеть khateet' 18

war memorial мемориал m myemareeal 99

ward (hospital) палата f palata 167

warm тёплая tyoplaya 14, 122;
warmer теплее tyeplyeye 24

washbasin раковина f rakaveena

washing: ~ instructions инструкция к стирке f eenstrooktseeya k steerke 146; **~ machine** стиральная машина f steeral'naya masheena 29;
~ powder стиральный порошок m steeral'niy parashok 148; **~-up liquid** средство для мытья посуды n sryetstva dlya mitya pasoodi 148

wasp оса f asa

watch часы pl chasi 149

water вода f vada 87; **~ bottle** бутылка с водой f bootilka s vadoy; **~ heater** водогрей m vadagrey 28; **~ skis** водные лыжи fpl vodniye lizhee 116;
~ temperature температура воды f teempeeratoora vadi 122; **~fall** водопад m vadapat 107

waterproof водонепроницаемый vodaneepraneetsaeemiy; **~ jacket** дождевик m dazhdeeveek 145

wave волна f valna

waxing восковая ванна f voskavaya vana 147

way: I've lost my way я заблудился (лась) ya zabloodeelsya (zabllodeelas') 94; **on the way** по пути pa pootee 83

we мы mi

wear, to одевать adeevat' 152

weather погода f pagoda 122;
~ forecast прогноз погоды pragnoz pagodi 122

wedding свадьба f svad'ba;
~ ring обручальное кольцо n abroochal'naya kal'tso

Wednesday среда f sreeda 218

week неделя f nedelya 23, 97, 218

weekend: at the ~ на уикенд na veekent 218

weekly (ticket) на неделю na nyedyelyoo 79

weigh вес m vyes

welcome to ... добро пожаловать в ...
dabro pazhalavat' v

well-done (steak)
хорошо прожаренный
kharasho prazhareeniy

west запад m zapat 95

what? что? shto; **what kind of ...?**
какой ...? kakoy ... 37, 106;
what time ...? во сколько?
va skol'ka ... 68, 76, 81; **what's the
time?** который час? katoriy chas
220; **what's wrong?** что случилось?
shto sloocheelas' 89

wheelchair инвалидное кресло n
eenvaleednaya kryesla

when? когда?/во сколько?
kagda/va skol'ka 13

where? (motion) куда? kooda 12;
(position) где? gdye 12;
where are you from?
откуда Вы? atkooda vi 119

which? который katoriy;
which stop? какая остановка?
kakaya astanofka? 80

white белый byeliy 143; **~ wine**
белое вино n byeloye veeno 40

who? кто? kto 16

whose? чей? chey 16

why? почему? pacheemoo 16

wide широкий shirokey 14

wife жена f zheena 120, 162

windbreaker плащ m plashch 145

window окно n akno 25, 77;
(in store) витрина f veetreena
134, 149; **~ seat** место у окна n
myesta oo akna 74

windscreen ветровое стекло n
veetravoye steeklo

windsurfer виндсёрфер m
veendsyerfyer 116

windy ветер m vyeteer 122

wine вино n veeno 40;
~ list карта вин m karta veen 37

winter зима f
zeema 219

with с/со s/so 17

withdraw, to снимать
sneemat' 139

without без bez 17

wood лес m lyes 107

wool шерсть f shyerst' 146

work, to работать rabotat'
28, 83, 121: **it doesn't ~** (function)
это не работает eto nye
rabotayet 25

worse хуже khoozhe 14

worst худший khoodsheey

wound рана f rana 162

write down, to записать
zapeesat' 13

writing pad блокнот blaknot 150

wrong неправильный
neepraveel'niy 14, 136

X-ray рентген m
reengyen 164

yacht яхта f yakhta

year год m got 218

yellow жёлтый zhyoltiy 143

yes да da 10

yesterday вчера fcheera 218

yoghurt йогурт m yogoort

you (formal) Вы vi;
(informal) ты ti

young молодой maladoy 14

your ваш vash 16

yours ваш vash 16

youth hostel общежитие n
abshchyezheeteeye 29

zebra crossing переход m
peereekhot

zero ноль m nol'

zip(per) молния f molneeya

zoo зоопарк m zaapark 113

A-Z

X
Y Z

Glossary
Russian–English

The Russian-English glossary covers all the areas where you may need to decode written Russian: hotels, public buildings, restaurants, stores, ticket offices, airports, and stations. The Russian is written in large type to help you identify the character(s) from the signs you see around you.

General   Общие знаки

НАЛЕВО	*nalyeva*	LEFT
НАПРАВО	*naprava*	RIGHT
ВХОД	*vkhot*	ENTRANCE
ВЫХОД	*vikhat*	EXIT
ТУАЛЕТ	*tooalyet*	TOILETS
МУЖСКОЙ ТУАЛЕТ	*mooshskoy tooalyet*	MEN (TOILETS)
ЖЕНСКИЙ ТУАЛЕТ	*zhyenskeey tooalyet*	WOMEN (TOILETS)
НЕ КУРИТЬ	*nee kooreet'*	NO SMOKING
ОПАСНО	*apasna*	DANGER
ВХОД ЗАПРЕЩЕН	*vkhot zapreeshchyon*	NO ENTRY

General Общие знаки

НА СЕБЯ/ОТ СЕБЯ	*na seebya/ at seebya*	PULL/PUSH
ПОИСК БАГАЖА	*poeesk bagazha*	LOST PROPERTY
КУПАТЬСЯ ЗАПРЕЩЕНО	*koopat'sya zapreeshcheeno*	NO SWIMMING
ПИТЬЕВАЯ ВОДА	*peetyevaya vada*	DRINKING WATER
ЧАСТНАЯ СОБСТВЕННОСТЬ	*chasnaya sopstveenast'*	PRIVATE
НЕ СОРИТЬ	*nee sareet'*	NO LITTER
ПОДЗЕМНЫЙ ПЕРЕХОД	*padzyemniy peereekhot*	UNDERPASS
БУДЬТЕ ОСТОРОЖНЫ ПРИ ВЫХОДЕ	*bood'tee astarozhni pree vikhadee*	MIND THE STEP
СВЕЖАЯ КРАСКА	*svyezhaya kraska*	WET PAINT
МЯГКИЙ ВАГОН	*myakhkeey vagon*	FIRST CLASS
КУПЕЙНЫЙ ВАГОН	*koopyeyniy vagon*	SECOND CLASS

Road signs Дорожные знаки

СТОП	*stop*	STOP
ДЕРЖИТЕСЬ ПРАВОЙ СТОРОНЫ	*deerzheetees' pravay starani*	KEEP RIGHT
ДЕРЖИТЕСЬ ЛЕВОЙ СТОРОНЫ	*deerzheetees' levay starani*	KEEP LEFT
ОДНОСТО-РОННЕЕ ДВИЖЕНИЕ	*adnastaroneeye dveezhyeneeye*	ONE WAY
ОБГОН ЗАПРЕЩЕН	*abgon zapreeshchyon*	NO PASSING [OVERTAKING]
СТОЯНКА ЗАПРЕЩЕНА	*stayanka zapreeshcheena*	NO PARKING
АВТОМА-ГИСТРАЛЬ	*aftamageestral'*	HIGHWAY [MOTORWAY]
ПЛАТА ЗА ДОРОГУ	*plata za darogoo*	TOLL
СВЕТОФОР	*sveetafor*	TRAFFIC LIGHTS
РАЗВЯЗКА	*razvyaska*	INTERSECTION [JUNCTION]

Airport/Station
Аэропорт/Вокзал

СПРАВКИ	*sprafkee*	INFORMATION
ПЛАТФОРМА 1	*platforma adeen*	PLATFORM 1
НАКОПИТЕЛЬ 1	*nakopeeteel' adeen*	GATE 1
ТАМОЖНЯ	*tamozhnya*	CUSTOMS
ПАСПОРТНЫЙ КОНТРОЛЬ	*paspartniy kantrol'*	IMMIGRATION
ПРИБЫТИЕ	*preebiteeye*	ARRIVALS
ОТПРАВЛЕНИЕ	*atpravlyeneeye*	DEPARTURES
КАМЕРЫ ХРАНЕНИЯ	*kameeri khranyeneeya*	LUGGAGE LOCKERS
ВЫДАЧА БАГАЖА	*vidacha bagazha*	LUGGAGE RECLAIM
АВТОБУС/ ПОЕЗД	*aftoboos/poeezt*	BUS/TRAIN
ПРОКАТ АВТОМОБИЛЕЙ	*prakat aftamabeeleey*	CAR RENTAL
МЕТРО	*meetro*	SUBWAY [METRO]

Hotel/Restaurant
Гостиница/Ресторан

СПРАВКИ	*sprafkee*	INFORMATION
ФОЙЕ	*faye*	RECEPTION
ЗАРЕЗЕРВИ-РОВАНО	*zareezeerveeravana*	RESERVED
АВАРИЙНЫЙ/ ПОЖАРНЫЙ ВЫХОД	*avareeyniy/ pazharniy vikhat*	EMERGENCY/ FIRE EXIT
ГОРЯЧАЯ ВОДА	*garyachaya vada*	HOT (WATER)
ХОЛОДНАЯ ВОДА	*khalodnaya vada*	COLD (WATER)
ДЛЯ СЛУЖЕБНОГО ПОЛЬЗОВАНИЯ	*dlya sloozhebnava pol'zavaneeya*	STAFF ONLY
ГАРДЕРОБ	*gardeerop*	COATCHECK [CLOAKROOM]
ТЕРРАСА/САД	*teerasa/sat*	TERRACE/GARDEN
БАР	*bar*	BAR

Stores Магазины

ОТКРЫТО	*at**kri**ta*	OPEN
ЗАКРЫТО	*za**kri**ta*	CLOSED
ОБЕД	*a**byet***	LUNCH
ОТДЕЛ	*a**dyel***	DEPARTMENT
ЭТАЖ	*e**tazh***	FLOOR
ПОДВАЛЬНЫЙ ЭТАЖ	*pad**val'**niy e**tazh***	BASEMENT
ЛИФТ	*leeft*	ELEVATOR [LIFT]
ЭСКАЛАТОР	*eska**la**tar*	ESCALATOR
КАССА	*__ka__sa*	CASHIER
РАСПРОДАЖА	*raspra**dazh**a*	SALE

Sightseeing
Достопримечательности

ВХОД БЕСПЛАТНЫЙ	*vkhot bees<u>plat</u>niy*	FREE ADMISSION
ВЗРОСЛЫЕ	*vz<u>ros</u>liye*	ADULTS
ДЕТИ	*<u>dye</u>tee*	CHILDREN
ЛЬГОТЫ	*l'<u>go</u>ti*	CONCESSIONS (students/pensioners)
СУВЕНИРЫ	*soovee<u>nee</u>ri*	SOUVENIRS
БУФЕТ	*boo<u>fyet</u>*	REFRESHMENTS
НЕ ТРОГАТЬ	*nee <u>tro</u>gat'*	DO NOT TOUCH
НЕ ФОТОГРА-ФИРОВАТЬ	*nee fatagra<u>fee</u>ravat'*	NO PHOTOGRAPHY
ВХОДА НЕТ	*<u>vkho</u>da nyet*	NO ACCESS

Public Buildings
Общественные здания

БОЛЬНИЦА	*bal'neetsa*	HOSPITAL
ВРАЧ	*vrach*	DOCTOR
ЗУБНОЙ ВРАЧ	*zoobnoy vrach*	DENTIST
МИЛИЦИЯ	*meeleetseeya*	POLICE
БАНК	*bank*	BANK
ПОЧТА	*pochta*	POST OFFICE
ПЛАВАТЕЛЬНЫЙ БАССЕЙН	*plavateel'niy basyeyn*	SWIMMING POOL
ГОРСОВЕТ	*gorsavyet*	TOWN HALL
СТОЯНКА ТАКСИ	*stayanka taksee*	TAXI STAND [RANK]
МУЗЕЙ	*moozyey*	MUSEUM

Numbers   Числительные

GRAMMAR

Numbers in their basic nominative form
The number "one" and numbers ending in "one" are followed by the nominative singular and "one" agrees with the gender of the noun.

one book	**adna kneega** (f)
twenty-one books	**dvatsat' adna kneega** (f)

The numbers "two," "three," and "four," and numbers ending in them are followed by the genitive singular. The number "two" has two forms: masculine/neuter (два) and feminine (две).

two lessons	**dva ooroka** (m)
forty-two lessons	**sorak dva ooroka** (m)

Other numbers are followed by the genitive plural.

seven books	**syem' kneek** (f)
fifty lessons	**peedeesyat oorokaf** (m)

For additional information ➤ 169.

0	ноль/нуль *nol'/nool'*	13	тринадцать *treenatsat'*
1	один/одна/одно **adeen/(adna)(adno)**	14	четырнадцать *chyeetirnatsat'*
2	два/две *dva (dvye)*	15	пятнадцать *peetnatsat'*
3	три *tree*	16	шестнадцать *shestnatsat'*
4	четыре *chyeetirye*	17	семнадцать *seemnatsat'*
5	пять *pyat'*	18	восемнадцать *vaseemnatsat'*
6	шесть *shest'*	19	девятнадцать *deeveetnatsat'*
7	семь *syem'*	20	двадцать *dvatsat'*
8	восемь *voseem'*	21	двадцать один *dvatsat' adeen*
9	девять *dyeveet'*		
10	десять *dyeseet'*		
11	одиннадцать *adeenatsat'*		
12	двенадцать *dveenatsat'*		

22	двадцать два *dvatsat' dva*	35,750	тридцать пять тысяч семьсот пятьдесят *treetsat' pyat' tiseech syem'sot peedeesyat*
23	двадцать три *dvatsat' tree*		
24	двадцать четыре *dvatsat' chyeetirye*		
25	двадцать пять *dvatsat' pyat'*	1,000,000	миллион *meelleeon*
26	двадцать шесть *dvatsat' shest'*	first	первый *pyerviy*
27	двадцать семь *dvatsat' syem'*	second	второй *ftaroy*
28	двадцать восемь *dvatsat' voseem'*	third	третий *tryeteey*
29	двадцать девять *dvatsat' dyeveet'*	fourth	четвёртый *chyeetvyortiy*
30	тридцать *treetsat'*	fifth	пятый *pyatiy*
31	тридцать один *treetsat' adeen*	once	однажды/один раз *adnazhdi*
32	тридцать два *treetsat' dva*	twice	два раза *dva raza*
40	сорок *sorak*	three times	три раза *tree raza*
50	пятьдесят *peedeesyat*	a half	половина *palaveena*
60	шестьдесят *sheezdeesyat*	half an hour	полчаса *polchyasa*
70	семьдесят *syemdeeseet*	half a tank	полбака *polbaka*
80	восемьдесят *voseemdeeseet*	a quarter	четверть *chyetveert'*
90	девяносто *deeveenosta*	a third	третья часть *tryetya chyast*
100	сто *sto*	a pair of ...	пара ... *para ...*
101	сто один *sto adeen*	a dozen ...	дюжина ... *dyoozheena ...*
102	сто два *sto dva*	1998	тысяча девятьсот девяносто восьмой год *tiseechya deeveetsot deeveenosta vas'moy got*
200	двести *dvyestee*		
500	пятьсот *peetsot*		
1,000	тысяча *tiseechya*		
10,000	десять тысяч *dyeseet' tiseech*	2001	две тысячи первый год *dvye tiseechyee pyerviy got*
		the 1990s	девяностые годы *deeveenostiye godi*

217

Days Дни

Monday	понедельник	*paneedyel'neek*
Tuesday	вторник	*ftorneek*
Wednesday	среда	*sreeda*
Thursday	четверг	*chyeetvyerk*
Friday	пятница	*pyatneetsa*
Saturday	суббота	*soobota*
Sunday	воскресенье	*vaskreesyenye*

Months Месяцы

January	январь	*eenvar'*
February	февраль	*feevral'*
March	март	*mart*
April	апрель	*apryel'*
May	май	*may*
June	июнь	*eeyoon'*
July	июль	*eeyool'*
August	август	*avgoost*
September	сентябрь	*seentyabr'*
October	октябрь	*aktyabr'*
November	ноябрь	*nayabr'*
December	декабрь	*deekabr'*

Dates Даты

It's ... today.	Сегодня ... *seevodnya ...*
July 10	десятое июля *deesyataye eeyoolya*
Tuesday, March 1	вторник, первое марта *ftorneek pyervaye marta*
yesterday	вчера *fchyeera*
today/tomorrow	сегодня/завтра *seevodnya/zaftra*
this/last week	на этой/прошлой неделе *na etiy/proshliy needyelye*
this/last month/year	в этом/прошлом месяце/году *v etam/proshlam myeseetse/gadoo*
next week	на следующей неделе *na slyedooyoosheheey needyelye*
on [at] the weekend	в выходные дни *v vikhadniye dnee*

Seasons   Времена года

spring	весна *veesna*
summer	лето *lyeta*
fall [autumn]	осень *oseen'*
winter	зима *zeema*
in spring	весной *veesnoy*
during the summer	летом *lyetam*

Greetings   Поздравления

Happy birthday!	С днём рождения! *z dnyom razhdyeneeya*
Merry Christmas!	С Рождеством! *s razhdeestvom*
Happy New Year!	С Новым годом! *s novim godam*
Happy Easter!	С Пасхой! *s paskhiy*
Best wishes!	Всего самого лучшего! *fseevo samava loochsheva*
Congratulations!	Поздравляю! *pazdravlyayoo*
Good luck!/All the best!	Удачи!/Всего самого хорошего! *oodachyee fseevo samava kharosheva*
Have a good trip!	Счастливого пути! *shchyastleevava pootee*
Give my regards to …	Передай(те) привет … *peereeday(tye) preevyet …*

Public holidays   Праздничные дни

January 1	Новый год	New Year's Day
March 8	Международный Женский День	International Women's Day
May 1–2	1-е мая	May Day/Labor Day
May 9	День Победы	Victory in Europe Day
November 7–8	Праздник Октябрьской Революции	Revolution Day
December 12	День Конституции	Constitution Day

Note: Christmas (Рождество) and Easter (Пасха) were not officially observed. However, from 1999 they are public holidays.

Time Часы

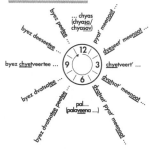

In Russian, times between the hour and the half hour are expressed as that number of minutes "of" the next hour. So, for example, "ten past two" would be "ten minutes of the third (hour)." Times between the half hour and the next hour are expressed by using the Russian word for "without" (без), the number of minutes remaining until the next hour, and the number of the next hour. So "twenty to eight" would be "without twenty eight."

Excuse me. Can you tell me the time?	Будьте добры! Который час? _bood'tye dabri katoriy chyas_
It's …	Сейчас … _seechyas …_
five past one	пять минут второго _pyat' meenoot ftarova_
ten past two	десять минут третьего _dyeseet' meenoot tryetyeeva_
a quarter past three	четверть четвёртого _chyetveert' chyeetvyortava_
twenty past four	двадцать минут пятого _dvatsat' meenoot pyatava_
twenty-five past five	двадцать пять минут шестого _dvatsat' pyat' meenoot shestova_
half past six	полседьмого _polseed'mova_
twenty-five to seven	без двадцати пяти семь _byez dvatsatee peetee syem'_
twenty to eight	без двадцати восемь _byez dvatsatee voseem'_
a quarter to nine	без четверти девять _byez chyetveertee dyeveet'_
ten to ten	без десяти десять _byez deeseetee dyeseet'_
five to eleven	без пяти одиннадцать _byes peetee adeenatsat'_
twelve o'clock	двенадцать часов _dveenatsat' chyasof_

noon/midnight	полдень/полночь _**pol**deen' **pol**nach'_
at dawn	на рассвете _na ras**svye**tye_
in the morning	утром _**oo**tram_
during the day	в течение дня _f tee**chye**neeye dnya_
before lunch	перед обедом _**pye**reed a**bye**dam_
after lunch	после обеда _poslee a**bye**da_
in the afternoon/evening	днём/вечером _dnyom/**vye**chyeeram_
at night	ночью _**noch**'oo_
I'll be ready in five minutes.	Я буду готов(а) через пять минут. _ya **boo**doo gatof (**ga**tova) **chye**rees pyat' mee**noot**_
He'll be back in a quarter of an hour.	Он вернётся через четверть часа. _on veer**nyot**sa **chye**reez **chyet**veert' chya**sa**_
She arrived half an hour ago.	Она приехала полчаса назад. _a**na** pree**ye**khala palchya**sa** na**zat**_
The train leaves at …	Поезд отправляется в … _**po**eest atprav**lya**eetsa v …_
13:04	тринадцать часов четыре минуты _tree**nat**sat chya**sof** chyee**tee**ree mee**noo**ti_
0:40	ноль часов сорок минут _nol' chya**sof sor**ak mee**noot**_
The train is 10 minutes late/early.	Поезд придёт на десять минут раньше/позже. _po**eezt** pree**dyot** na **dye**seet' mee**noot ran**'shee/**pozhee**_
It's five minutes fast/slow.	Часы на пять минут спешат/отстают. _cha**si** na pyat' mee**noot** spee**shat**/atsta**yoot**_
from 9:00 to 5:00	с девяти до пяти _z deevee**tee** da pee**tee**_
between 8:00 and 2:00	между восемью и двумя _**myezh**doo **vos**'myoo ee dvoo**mya**_
I'll be leaving by …	Я пойду часа в … _ya pay**doo** chya**sa** v …_
Will you be back before …?	Вы придёте до …? _vi pree**dyo**tye da …_
We'll be here until …	Мы здесь будем до … _mi zdyes' **boo**deem da …_

ARCTIC

NORWEGIAN
SEA

BARANTS
SEA

Murmansk

Archangel

St. Petersburg

Norilsk

Smolensk

MOSCOW

Ural Mountains

RUSSIAN

Yekaterinburg

Volgograd

Tomsk

Omsk

Krasno-
jarsk

Rostov-
na-Donu

CASPIAN SEA

C E A N

Egvekinot

B E R I N G
S E A

○ Kazachye

Petropavlovsk-
Kamchatskiy

SEA OF
OKHOTSK

○ Yakutsk

P A C I F I C   O C E A N

F E D E R A T I O N

Korsakov

Belogorsk

○ Bratsk

Ulan-Ude

Vladivostok

SEA OF
JAPAN

Quick reference Выражения

Good morning.	Доброе утро. *dobraye **oo**tra*
Good afternoon.	Добрый день. *dobriy dyen'*
Good evening.	Добрый вечер. *dobriy **vyee**cheer*
Hello.	Здравствуй(те). *zdrast**voo**ytye*
Good-bye.	До свидания. *da svee**da**neeya*
Excuse me. (getting attention. *eezvee**nee**tye/pra**stee**tye*	Извините./Простите.
Excuse me? [Pardon?]	Извините?/Простите? *eezvee**nee**tye/pra**stee**tye*
Sorry!	Извините!/Простите! *eezvee**nee**tye/pra**stee**tye*
Please.	Пожалуйста. *pa**zhal**sta*
Thank you.	Спасибо. *spa**see**ba*
Do you speak English?	Вы говорите по-английски? *vi gava**ree**tye pa an**glee**yskee*
I don't understand	Я не понимаю. *ya nee panee**ma**yoo*
Where is …?	Где ...? *gdye ...*
Where are the bathrooms [toilets]?	Где туалет? *gdye too**a**lyet*

Emergency Срочно!

Help!	Помогите! *pama**gee**tye*
Go away!	Идите отсюда! *ee**dee**tye at**syoo**da*
Leave me alone!	Оставьте меня в покое! *a**staf'**tye mee**nya** f pa**ko**ye*
Call the police!	Вызовите милицию! *vi**za**veetye mee**lee**etsiyoo*
Stop thief!	Держите вора! *deer**zhi**tye **vo**ra*
Get a doctor!	Вызовите врача! *vi**za**veetye vra**chya**
Fire!	Пожар! *pa**zhar***
I'm ill.	Я заболел(а). *ya zaba**lyel**(a)*
I'm lost.	Я заблудился(-лась). *ya zabloo**deel**sa(-las')*
Can you help me?	Помогите мне, пожалуйста. *pama**gee**tye mnye pa**zhal**sta*

Emergency ☎

Fire 01	Ambulance 03	Police 02

Embassies ☎

Australia: 095/956-6070	New Zealand: 095/956-3579
Canada: 095/956-6666	U.K.: 095/956-7200
Eire: 095/288-4101	U.S.: 095/252-2459

There are also consulates for Canada, the U.K., and the U.S. in St. Petersburg.